The Working Gal's Guide to Babyville

The Working Gal's
Guide to Babyville

Your
Must-Have Manual
for Life
with Baby

PAIGE HOBEY

with Dr. Allison Nied

Da Capo
LIFE
LONG

A Member of the Perseus Books Group

Copyright © 2006 by Paige Hobey

The e-mails, journal entries, dialogues, and third-person anecdotes in this book were created to illustrate typical new mom experiences. While fictional, they were often inspired by interviews or conversations with new mothers or the author's personal experience. When real anecdotes are included, names have been changed.

Text design by Brent Wilcox
Set in 11-point Berkeley Book by the Perseus Books Group

Library of Congress Cataloging-in-Publication Data
Hobey, Paige.
    The working gal's guide to Babyville : your must-have manual for life with baby / Paige Hobey with Allison Nied.-- 1st Da Capo Press ed.
        p.   cm.
    Includes bibliographical references and index.
    ISBN-13: 978-0-7382-1048-3 (pbk. : alk. paper)
    ISBN-10: 0-7382-1048-X (pbk. : alk. paper)
    1. Working mothers—Life skills guides.   2. Infant—Care.   3. Mother and infant.
4. Work and family.   I. Nied, Allison.   II. Title.
    HQ759.48.H62 2006
    649'.122—dc22

                                                                      2006003934

First Da Capo Press edition 2006

Published by Da Capo Press
A Member of the Perseus Books Group
http://www.dacapopress.com

Da Capo Press books are available at special discounts for bulk purchases in the U.S. by corporations, institutions, and other organizations. For more information, please contact the Special Markets Department at the Perseus Books Group, 11 Cambridge Center, Cambridge, MA 02142, or call (800) 255-1514 or (617) 252-5298, or e-mail special.markets@perseusbooks.com.

1 2 3 4 5 6 7 8 9—09 08 07 06

For my son Bailey, who inspired this book, and my husband Charlie, who never said I was crazy to try writing it.

Also for my daughter Avery Grace, who missed the writing phase but arrived just in time for this dedication.

And for my fellow new moms: Here's to raising a generation of shockingly well-adjusted, creative, enthusiastic children who make the world a better place and, more importantly, never forget Mother's Day.

—*Paige*

Contents

Babyville,
Here You Come!

Introduction

Loving Life Among the Little People

Welcome to that postpartum parallel universe we call Babyville, a land seemingly run by the little people. Think of this book as your insider's travel guide—whether you're gearing up for your newborn's grand entrance, looking for strategies to nurture a supersleeper, trying to make the most of your maternity leave, or wondering how to pump at work without feeling like an overpaid dairy cow in cute shoes.

My Adventures in Babyville

When I started this book, my son Bailey was six months old, and I was up to my ears in the new parent whirlwind you're probably experiencing now—or will be soon. I had perfected the art of appearing coherent on five hours sleep. I was trying to fit mom into my self-image somewhere between adventurous and ambitious. I was fine-tuning my potential new mom friend radar: *Pushing a stroller? Check. Has that cheerfully disoriented look of a woman thrilled to be out of the house but unsure what to do next? Check. All systems go. Approach at will and shamelessly use own baby as conversation starter.* And after being tormented for weeks, I had recently made a work decision my prebaby self would have considered crazy.

Initially I approached working momhood with a sort of naive optimism. I happily planned to have a baby and, buoyed by maternal fulfillment, transition seamlessly back to my job—combining work and family life with Zen-like grace. Or something like that. And during those all-consuming first few weeks after my son was born, the plan still felt right. I was both madly in love with him and secretly thrilled I had a job to escape to after maternity leave. I remember one night during a 3:00 A.M. feeding actually fantasizing about being back at work. The computer waiting patiently on my desk. The meetings where nobody cried, pooped, or spit up. My colleagues (such an adult word!) milling about the halls, chatting about world events and philosophy. (I said it was a fantasy.) I was nostalgic for the safety of the known career world.

But as my son grew more interactive and the every-two-hour overnight feedings gradually improved, newborn chaos was replaced by a new sense of coziness. I was getting the hang of this new mom thing, resting enough to feel actual emotions, and successfully leaving the house with baby in tow. My glorious, newfound mom–life balance began to feel threatened by an impending work schedule that would clearly disrupt our peaceful world order.

So I did what any mature career gal with hard-hitting problem-solving skills would do: I panicked. I lay awake at night mentally debating work arrangements that would allow more access to my son while still paying the bills. I considered freelancing. I thought about asking to work from home. I contemplated every variation of flextime and part-time scheduling, from half days to job sharing. I woke up at the crack of dawn and scratched out the pros and cons of all my options, devising plans for negotiating with my boss and making mini–family budgets along the edges of the paper. I was a woman obsessed.

And that's when the idea for this book was born. "You should really write this stuff down," a friend suggested as I described the myriad work options I was considering. "Maybe you could make a magazine article out of it." Or a book, I thought in a freakish moment of postpartum clarity. I sure couldn't find one to help navigate all the challenges of my new mom reality—from finding a pediatrician to finding quality child care. I had the obligatory stockpile of parenting books, but none offered what I really wanted—those nuggets of wow-that-makes-life-easier parenting wisdom without all the filler. Expert tips for helping my son sleep through the night without the three hundred pages on infant REM cycles. Practical help, like a comprehensive life-with-baby shopping list. And maybe some mom-tested advice more current than my *Girlfriend Guide*'s "real fashion secret" for pregnancy: stirrup pants.

Eventually, my company (an Internet start-up) downsized (there's a shocker) toward the end of my maternity leave, eliminating any hope for flexible work arrangements and sending full-timers' workloads into the stratosphere. So, I decided to do the freelancing mom thing with gusto, over time give this book a shot, and see where life led me. I'd been managing a team that developed pregnancy and parenting content for the Web, and after I pushed an eight pound, ten ounce person out of my body, a bigger writing project began to seem doable. Since then, my career path, like that of so many new moms, has bobbed and weaved in ways I never would have predicted. I started freelancing using my Internet development experience, then added some marketing and magazine writing. And in between other projects, I tackled this book. I didn't know if I'd ever get it published, but I wanted to try.

I set out to create the resource I needed (and answer the wide range of questions I had) when my son was born, using a concise, easy-to-execute format that is as fun to read as it is useful. I talked to new moms in every work arrangement imaginable, interviewed experts in fields from newborn sleep to child care logistics, and pulled from my own wild and wacky—and probably very typical—experiences. I also contacted Dr. Allison Nied, a great New York City pediatrician and friend, and suggested a collaborative project. She had the M.D.; I was living in the trenches of Babyville. Dr. Nied loved the idea of a year one book for working moms, and she provided detailed input on every chapter—even the career-related ones (she's a working mother herself). All infant care, feeding, sleeping, health, development, and safety content comes with her expert seal of approval, and many of Dr. Nied's quick tips are highlighted throughout the book.

And here we are. This book has been such a fun challenge to write; I really hope you find it helpful. And after you read it, I hope you feel even more supported and confident in your new role.

And Now, Your Adventures in Babyville

As you adjust to new motherhood, hang in there. This is going to be an amazing year. You'll have unforgettable memories of childbirth or adoption. You'll make great new mom friends. Your baby will—eventually—sleep through the night. And you'll develop your own strategies for integrating work and parenthood, your own support group, and your own happy routines.

It's a fascinating time to be a new mom. We have abundant opportunities and successful role models. We know more about infant cognitive development than ever before. Employers are increasingly offering flexibility and work–life supports, and even the less proactive ones are generally open to compelling proposals. And it seems the media can't get enough of us. Some say we're hyperscheduled perfectionists who apply drive sharpened at work to the nuanced role of motherhood. Others have tried to shed light on a mythical conspiracy of maternal silence. New moms are afraid to admit, the myth goes, that the "greatest job in the world" has some not so great days—and those early weeks of overnight feedings and 24/7 diaper duty can in fact be a tough adjustment. And some say we're embroiled in a "mommy war," stay-at-home moms and stay-at-work moms supposedly battling it out via passive-aggressive commentary in neighborhood parks.

My take on this topic may sound simple, but here it is: We each experience motherhood differently. Some of us get lucky. We have easy babies who sleep a lot, eat without complaint, and generally go with the flow. We receive the support we need. Our employers step up with mom-friendly accommodations or we have a handy knack for adjusting to life-altering situations without losing it. Other infants may be more challenging. Your postpartum hormones may be particularly intense, you may need more help, or you may simply require more time to settle into your new role.

We are bringing an impressive set of skills and life experiences to motherhood these days. We're waiting later to have children than previous generations did, taking more time for school and career. But whether you bring your workday urgency home is up to you. After a lifetime in fast-forward, you'll downshift to a cozy stillness during those early weeks, as your days combine hours of quiet feedings and newborn naps. But over time, you'll get some play dates on the calendar and bring your high-energy enthusiasm to your new role. And I'm guessing we can all find a happy midpoint between hyperscheduling and missing out on the fun stuff.

There will be crazy days. And nights. Just know we've all been there, the most stressful moments often make for the best stories, and in the craziness lies the wild ride of parenthood.

And while personal choices around work and family are always emotionally loaded, the new moms I know treat one another with congenial respect—like a dispersed brigade bonded through universal battles with infant spit-up and interrupted sleep. Maybe I'm missing a "mommy war" somewhere, but I like to think we're all in this thing together. In fact, the at-home versus working mom dichotomy is in itself outdated—these days we each find our own path along a spectrum of work and family life. Some of us sequence out of the workforce for a while and then return to our careers. Others start home-based businesses that can be managed as our babies nap. And some maintain the trajectory, income, and benefits of full-time career paths.

There are as many ways to combine work and motherhood these days as there are new moms out there trying it. I wish you all the best as you make your own choices—this year and over time as your family needs and career priorities shift. And trust me, they will. But that's another book . . .

Preparing for Maternity Leave

Gearing Up, Getting Prepped, and Transitioning

from Miss Independent to Mom

Maggie stopped midstride, looked up at the curly-haired toddler on the babyGap poster, and knew it was time. She crossed the street and bought new underwear. (Yes, her cotton briefs were more comfortable, but she was a woman on a mission.) She went home and finally read the instructions on her ovulation kit. Then she called Josh and gave him the good news: Time to gear up the Tivo; priorities were shifting to the bedroom. Operation Babyville was about to begin.

Four months later, standing side-by-side in the bathroom, they first saw the line. Maggie looked up at Josh in disbelief and then rechecked the test instructions. Maybe she had done it wrong, though admittedly peeing on a plastic stick wasn't rocket science. Maybe she was looking at it wrong, though assessing the presence of a line seemed pretty doable. Maybe the test was malfunctioning. Of course, two additional tests offered the same result. Ultimately, the mistake scenarios were ruled out, and the line remained. The wild ride of pregnancy had begun.

Maggie moved past morning sickness like a pro. She maintained a healthy obsession with potential baby names and surrounded herself with key prenatal literature—weekly e-mail newsletters on fetal development, eating-for-baby books, and flyers from Old Navy maternity. She knew more about pregnancy than any OB-GYN. Then she rounded into her third trimester (no pun intended), and it hit her. Her pregnancy was almost over, and by the time she could say, "Epidural, please," an actual newborn would be making full use of the painstakingly selected crib bedding in the nursery.

|•|

It's parenthood prep time—your opportunity to plan for maternity leave, gear up, learn newborn care essentials, and get a really great haircut. Yes, it'll be a while before you see that salon again. For a comprehensive guide, read on. You'll get the inside scoop on transitioning from Miss Independent to Mom, a shopping list of new baby stuff you really need (and the top 10 things you don't need even though they're cute), a final countdown to baby to-do list, and more.

Emotional Preparation:
From Miss Independent to Mom

From Jennifer's journal:

Hannah is two weeks old, and I'm still feeling like the real parents could walk in any minute, hand me $20, and offer to drive me home. After twenty-eight years of being Independent Jen, I'm suddenly a 24/7 caretaker and it feels odd—not bad, just unfamiliar, like that semester I spent in France trying to fake a decent accent and wishing I'd packed something black. And the magnitude of this parenthood commitment is slowly sinking in. Spontaneously leaving the house seems about as likely as fitting into my prepregnancy work clothes by the end of maternity leave—somewhere in the range of Never Gonna Happen.

In contrast to newborn care and postpartum recovery, my typical work challenges now seem like, well, child's play. The client needs that report by tomorrow? Calm down, people! There's no life hanging in the balance here, no physical pain to endure, no hormonal chaos to manage. What have I been stressing out about all these years? Overall, I'm completely in love with Hannah but still shaky on my new role as an actual parent. Just hoping it'll sink in by Mother's Day.

Let's put things in perspective. When we were born, the average female married and became a mother at age twenty-one, and less than 28 percent of new moms worked during year one.[1,2,3] Women went from living with family to starting a family at warp speed, often focusing on kids before or instead of careers.

Today, we're taking time for school, work, regrettable road trips, and volunteering. We're getting established in our careers, navigating the dating scene, and spending lots of time with friends. And we're kicking some serious guy butt: Women are now more likely than men to graduate from college, work as professionals, and manage teams.[4] Most of our career paths continue well past third stage labor. Over 70 percent of U.S. mothers with children under eighteen work for pay in some capacity, from full-time to freelancing, including the majority of moms year one in Babyville.[5]

We approach parenting with the diligence, planning skills, and sense of adventure we've honed during years of work and life experiences. We take classes on breast feeding and infant CPR, we consult friends about strollers, we research child care online, and we read everything ever written on infant sleep. Then our newborns arrive, and we realize we forgot one little detail: preparing for the emotional transition from independent career gal to mom.

Your New Title

Mama. Mommy. Mom. Mother. Does it feel real yet? If not, don't worry; it's going to take a little while. "Mom" happens to be a loaded word. Maternal, motherly, childbearing—these terms have lots of obvious connotations, but they don't initially bring to mind active, accomplished, or adventurous. The institution of motherhood is historically more about aprons than adventures. The Mother's Day cards you've been buying all your life suddenly become personal. That World's Greatest Mom sweatshirt in the mall is a scary but viable impending gift. You now share more than you care to admit with June Cleaver, and after years of doing your own thing, you begin to wonder if you're becoming your own mother.

Your New Role in Your Old Worlds

It was tricky enough to feel like yourself at work as your pregnant belly threatened to capsize you; now you get to balance your maternal drive and career drive. Your routines with friends may shift a bit initially as well. The book club meetings, spontaneous coffee runs, and Saturday afternoon yoga classes will be competing with newborn naptimes. And, if you have a significant other in your parenthood picture, you have to get comfortable with your new mom status in the realm of romance. Are you really expected to go straight from breast-feeding in the nursery to flaunting your (admittedly impressive) new mom cleavage in the master bedroom? To transition from maternal goddess to sex goddess faster than you can say Victoria's Secret?

Acquiring citizenship in Babyville can require some matriculation time. Your well-established self-image suddenly expands, and motherhood changes your perspective on everything else—your career, your friendships, your significant other. But as you settle into your new role, you realize the change is good. Sure, things become more complicated, but ultimately you just feel blessed to have this perfect child—plus all the rest. You find a new groove at work; you create new routines with friends; you learn to transition between maternal love and romantic love without requiring therapy. Feel better knowing you are not becoming your mother, and you are not becoming June Cleaver. You are becoming yourself, with a little buddy to accompany you on your adventures in life. And yes, the adventures are only beginning.

Becoming a Mom: Like Turning Thirty,
but with More Labor Pains and Less Party Cake

Becoming a mom is like other major milestones that fundamentally affect your sense of self—hard to imagine as you anticipate the change, but positive in the end. For example, turning thirty. Your birthday approaches. You're certain the end of your twenties will be the end of life as you know it—practical Sunday afternoons doing home repairs will replace weekend road trips, DVD rentals will replace nights out with friends, your fun new job will start to get old, and spontaneous kisses on the sidewalk will fade into memory. Then you hit the big three-o, and you wake up feeling really good. You realize you've moved beyond your twenties and you still recognize yourself in the mirror; you imagine sliding into your third decade with a graceful joie de vivre. As time passes, your fears fade. You still go out with friends (unless anything new with Jude Law has been released on DVD—one has to keep her priorities in order). You enjoy your job, and your guy still kisses you spontaneously on the sidewalk (if you stop him and suggest it). You poll your friends and they agree. One can still be independent, daring, and romantic at the age when most of our parents had three kids and a station wagon. It's a new way to think of thirty-something.

A New Way to Think of Motherhood

Similarly, many aspects of parenting have changed since we were kids— and we need a new way to think of good ol' momhood. I have a few suggestions to get things started:

- Paid maternity leave should be guaranteed for every working mom. And child care assistance. And flexible work hours. And weekly foot massages.
- The next must-have video game should feature a brilliant yet refreshingly down-to-earth mom leading her family through the Brazilian rainforest. And she should do it all using her wit and photographic memory—no violence necessary.
- All *Leave It to Beaver* and *Father Knows Best* reruns should be banned. And who's writing those mom-targeted TV commercials? A quick word to marketers: Mothers *actually aren't* emotionally devastated by laundry that doesn't smell like a field of wildflowers or dishes that don't sparkle like a new sports car. A new sports car we could get excited about. Dishes, no.
- A mom should run the United Nations. (Peacekeeping. Feeding the hungry. Calming troublemakers. Not exactly a stretch.)
- All prime-time sports programming could be replaced by heart-pumping highlights of moms juggling paperwork and pediatrician appointments with mind-boggling footwork and physical agility.

Commentators could narrate the footage, "It's Monday night, and we're bringing you the big plays! This week, Catherine Kincaid has to give her big sales pitch just minutes after dropping her six-month-old son at child care. And he's teething!"

- A mom should have to sign off on all new legislation. And federal appropriations. And did I mention the weekly foot massages?

> It wasn't that we set out to "have it all" (much too presumptuous and kind of '70s-sounding). We've simply been trying to do the things that define us most and mean the most to us. Make more than one kind of mark on the world. Raise children, and land the raise that will help pay for their education. Provide. Create a family and still create ourselves.
>
> **MARISA THALBERG,**
> *Founder and President of*
> *Executive Moms*

There are changes to be made. In the meantime, we'll redefine motherhood for ourselves. And, like turning thirty without losing touch with all things daring and romantic, we'll become the moms we want to be without losing touch with ourselves. Today's moms are hip and hilarious, savvy and strategic; we're lots of things, but none requires an apron.

Your New Baby Shopping List: The Stuff You Really Need

"I give up," Sarah's husband called from the other end of the newborn essentials aisle. "Are they kidding with all this stuff?"

Sarah looked at the dozens of infant feeding, cleaning, playing, bathing, diapering, and clothing options around them and realized they were in way over their heads. "There's no way all these things are essential," she replied. "We just have to figure out what we really need."

"Right," he responded. "Good plan. And how do we do that?"

|•|

Baby product manufacturers aren't subtle. If you're (1) pregnant, (2) a new mom, or (3) have ever set foot near a maternity ward or adoption agency, you've already experienced the direct mail equivalent of an avalanche hitting your doorstep. Plus, baby stores can overwhelm even the savviest parents with tons of unnecessary gear. How do you wade through the ads and options to pinpoint what you actually need?

Here's a quick guide. It details new parent essentials from the ideal nursery to must-haves for your diaper bag. Get the low-down here and then flip to the pullout version in the appendix. That list is designed so you can remove it and keep it in your purse while you're shopping, checking things off as you go. I hope it helps.

Nursery

Essential:

- ☑ Crib (no more than 2¼ inches between slats)
- ☐ Fitted crib sheets (2; between spit-up and leaky diapers, you'll use both)
- ☐ Waterproof crib mattress (tight enough so two fingers can't fit between the mattress and crib)
- ☑ Storage for baby clothes and gear (closet, dresser, or armoire)
- ☑ Receiving blankets (3 to 5; great for swaddling at first and then as blankies)
- ☐ Baby monitor (not needed in small apartments or homes where you can hear your baby from every room) ℞

Nice to Have:

- ☑ Changing table (money-saving alternative: change your baby on your bed)
- ☑ Changing pad and cover (for your changing table or secured on top of a dresser)
- ☐ Colorful mobile (the more engaging, the better)
- ☑ Supportive rocker or chair for feedings

Clothes for Year One

Essential:

Items needed for each stage: birth to three months, three to six months, six to nine months, and nine to twelve months

✓ ❒ Pajamas/sleepers—ideally, footed pj's during cooler seasons to minimize wrestling with baby socks that always pop off (3 to 6 per stage)

✓❒ Onesies—to wear alone or layer for extra warmth, short-sleeve or long-sleeve depending on the season (3 to 6 per stage)

❒ Soft tops and bottoms for daytime (4 to 6 per stage after the first few months—initially, pj's and/or onesies are fine all day)

❒ Cotton hats (1 to 2 for stage one—birth to three months—and during cooler seasons)

❒ Socks (3 to 6 pairs per stage)

✓❒ Sleep sack—highly recommended once your infant outgrows swaddling, a sleeveless zip-front garment that's zipped over his pajamas or onesie to keep him cozy while sleeping without putting him at risk for SIDS (only 1 needed)

For winter months, depending on your climate:

❒ Sweaters (1 to 3)

❒ Fleece bunting or snowsuit (a fleece zip-up lining for the infant carrier is also handy)

❒ Warm hat

For summer months:

❒ Bathing suit, baby sunglasses, and sun hat

Nice to have:

❒ So-cute-you-could-die baby outfits (but keep in mind, dresses get seriously tangled up in babies' knees during the squirming and crawling stage—usually between 7 and 11 months)

Diapering

Essential:

❒ Disposable diapers (45 to 60+ per week—no, I'm not kidding) or cloth diapers (24 to 36+ total, depending on your tolerance for washing them)

❏ Diaper wipes

❏ Petroleum jelly or A+D ointment (to apply during each diaper change)

❏ Diaper rash cream with zinc oxide (to use if your child gets a rash)

❏ For cloth diapering, diaper covers to prevent soaking through to clothes

Nice to have:

✔❏ Odor-preventing diaper pail and refills

Health and General Care

Essential:

❏ Thermometer

❏ Infant pain reliever (don't use before two months without consulting your pediatrician)

❏ Bulb syringe (for suctioning out stuffy noses)

✔ ❏ Brush or comb (even if you have a baby baldie, you'll use these eventually)

❏ Baby lotion (for dry skin after the first few months)

❏ Prepackaged first aid kit ⌐

Nice to have:

❏ Humidifier (to relieve congestion during colds)

Bathing

Essential:

❏ Plastic infant tub with supportive sling or baby-size sponge to prevent slipping (used until your baby can sit up)

❏ Inflatable baby tub (provides support in the real tub when your baby first sits up)

❏ Baby shampoo

❏ Washcloths (2 to 4)

Nice to have:

❏ Bath toys (from about six months on)

✔❏ Hooded towel (otherwise a regular towel will work)

☐ Soft cover for bathtub spout (once your baby is in the big tub at seven or eight months)

Baby on the Go
Essential:

☐ Car seat (secured facing backward until your child is one year and twenty pounds)

☐ Stroller (recommended options: a travel system, which works for all ages, or a universal frame stroller to use with your infant car seat and then a toddler stroller starting at about six months)

Nice to have:

☐ Front carrier, sling, or baby backpack (a front carrier can be used when your infant is eight pounds, and a backpack can be used at six months)

☐ Portable crib (great for travel, and the removable bassinet is a perfect play space or bedside sleeping option for your infant the first few months at home)

Nursing Moms
Essential:

☐ Nursing pillow (to keep your baby in position and save your back)

☐ Breast pads (to prevent leakage)

☐ Lanolin cream (to prevent chafing)

☐ Cloth diapers or burp cloths (3 to 5 for catching baby spit-up while burping after feedings)

☐ Breast pump (electric or manual; only essential if you want to continue breast-feeding after maternity leave)

☐ Pump carrying case, plastic bags for storing milk in the freezer, and supplies

☐ Bottles (2 to 3 for serving pumped milk)

Nice to have:

☐ Bottle warmer (for warming refrigerated breast milk if desired)

Bottle Feeding

Essential:

- ☐ Bottles (5 to 8)
- ☐ Nipples of different sizes as baby ages (stage 1 for infants, moving up to stage 4)
- ☐ Dishwasher caddy (to wash the plastic nipples)
- ☐ Cloth diapers or burp cloths (4 to 6)
- ☐ Formula (ask your pediatrician for a personalized recommendation)

Nice to have:

- ☐ Bottle warmer

Feeding Solids

Essential:

- ☐ High chair or booster seat with an infant-appropriate seating position
- ☐ Baby food (grains like rice cereal at four months, stage 1 food at five months, stage 2 at six months, and stage 3 at seven to nine months— or you can make your own)
- ☐ Baby spoons (3 to 5)
- ☐ Plastic baby bowls (4 to 6)
- ☐ Sippy cups (starting at about eight to ten months, 4 to 6 needed)

Childproofing

Essential:

- ☐ Safety gates (if you have stairs)
- ☐ Toilet locks
- ☐ Cabinet locks
- ☐ Electric outlet plugs
- ☐ Furniture fasteners (to secure bookshelves, dressers, and precarious items to the wall)
- ☐ Miniblind cord pulls (to wind up long cords, preventing the risk of strangulation)
- ☐ Soft pads (for coffee table edges and fireplace hearths)

Baby Playtime

No, you don't need all of these toys; pick your favorites.

Birth to Three Months
- ☐ Colorful mobile
- ☐ Bouncy seat
- ☐ Swing
- ☐ Play mat with dangling objects hanging from above

Four to Six Months
- ☐ Discovery cubes
- ☐ Teethers
- ☐ Hand and foot rattles
- ☐ Stuffed animals or soft dolls
- ☐ Exersaucer
- ☐ Board books (read daily from now on)

Seven to Nine Months
- ☐ Stacking, sorting, and nesting toys or simple interactive playthings
- ☐ Basic musical instruments like shakers or small drums
- ☐ Puppets
- ☐ Balls
- ☐ Soft blocks

Ten to Twelve Months
- ☐ Activity table
- ☐ Action-and-response toys like a jack-in-the-box
- ☐ More complex interactive toys like doll houses and toddler-size basketball hoops
- ☐ Pull-along toys
- ☐ Wooden blocks

Preserving the Memories

Nice to have:

- ☑ Digital camera (to snap tons of baby shots without worrying about film, and e-mailing family)
- ☐ Video camera (the only way to really capture baby laughs, crawling, and early steps)
- ☐ Photo albums

Diaper Bag Contents

Essential:

- ☐ Diapers (2 to 3 in your bag at all times)
- ☐ Diaper wipes (in small travel case)
- ☐ Diaper rash ointment (travel size)
- ☐ Thin, portable changing pad (just a little extra protection from the germfest in public restrooms and other on-the-run diaper changing spots)
- ☐ Cloth diaper (for burping or runny noses)
- ☐ Snacks (appropriate to age)
- ☐ Bottle or sippy cup (unless exclusively breast-feeding)

Nice to have:

- ☐ Small toys (2 to 3, appropriate to age)
- ☐ Board books
- ☐ Change of clothes (in case of spit-up or leaky diaper)

Top 10 Things You Don't Need Even Though They're Cute

As any experienced parent will admit, some of the cutest "baby must-haves" end up as why do we have this items shoved in storage. Here are ten items to avoid so you can spend your baby budget elsewhere.

GARAGE SALE TODAY!
9:00 A.M.-Noon
Tons of baby gear—never or barely used!
You benefit from our bad buys.
Everything must go!

- Never used umbrella stroller
- Never used baby quilt from crib bedding set
- Never used infant shoes, silk dresses (0–3 months size)
- Barely used crib bumper
- Barely used Kate Spade diaper bag
- Variety of barely used infant toys, four-ounce bottles
- And much more!

Miniadult Clothes for Newborns

I'd like to ask the head of babyGap what she was thinking when she stocked those (admittedly adorable) navy blue twill blazers in the birth to three months size. And the newborn denim skirt. And the corduroy pants with matching sweater vest. Here's the reality: *Newborns wear cotton sleepers. All the time.* Mostly, all they do is sleep, occasionally interrupted by eating and burping. They just need to be comfortable. And even if you're ambitious enough to bring your newborn to a formal event, the hosts won't expect your child to *follow the dress code.* ("It was sweet of you to drive seven hours for our wedding three weeks after giving birth, but we really expected your daughter to come in *formalwear.* Or at least a casually chic denim skirt.")

If it's cold outside, you'll bundle your newborn in a bunting and hat. If it's not, the cute sleeper is perfect anywhere. Yet most new parents receive or innocently buy newborn outfits that would be more appropriate for a Wall Street banker than a one-month-old. Be warned and spread the word. After the first few months, your child will gradually start wearing real clothes—although soft and comfy are great rules of thumb for baby clothes throughout year one.

Infant Shoes

Similar deal here. Why does Saucony make a newborn size, all-leather running shoe with a thick rubber sole? So you can wedge them on your five-week-old's feet and hold him up like a puppet, pretending he's about to win the Olympic two hundred meter sprint? Some family friends were suckered into buying these little newborn runners for my son, and there they sat in the nursery closet while his feet grew to twice and then three times the size of those shoes. Pediatricians recommend introducing shoes for the first time when children start walking. Prior to that, shoes only impede mobility, so skip the infant sneakers and let your baby enjoy one year of snuggly socks.

A Diaper Bag

Yes, you need a bag to transport your baby's diapers, wipes, bottles, snacks, and assorted accessories. But it doesn't have to be an actual diaper bag. Duped by the diaper bag propaganda, I ended up with two: a shoulder bag and a backpack version. A few months into parenthood, I realized my favorite bag from my premom days was easier to carry and had plenty of storage without that I'm-a-diaper-bag vibe.

Granted, the first time I packed my son's assorted paraphernalia into the nondiaper bag, it was strangely terrifying. I felt like I was violating one of the basic tenets of civilized parenthood. But once I learned diapers didn't *require* an eponymous bag, it was wildly liberating. I now use my other bag exclusively, and my real diaper bag collection is gathering dust in the closet. Bottom line, if you have a spacious tote, backpack, or messenger bag you like, you don't need to spend more money on a diaper bag.

With that said, there are some great diaper-bags-that-don't-look-like-diaper-bags in every fabric, color, price range, and style imaginable, from the ultra-hip to the ultra-affordable. The misguided baby-themed décor (think Winnie the Pooh, pastel bunnies munching on carrots) from the "I left my self-respect in the delivery room, and did you notice I'm a mom?" collection has finally been replaced. If you don't mind spending the money, a new bag could be a perfect new mom treat; search online for tons of options.

A Stroller Collection

While pregnant, I was advised we'd need three to four strollers—all "essential" for daily life. Our storage space was at a premium, so I decided to start with just one. And I bring this shocking update from the trenches of Babyville: Single-stroller success is possible! I suggest a travel system that initially carries your infant car seat and then converts to a toddler stroller. I used the same one for walks around town, in mom-and-baby jogging classes, and running errands. It's light, portable, and easy to maneuver. Granted, the real jogging strollers are easier to push if you're a major runner; otherwise one stroller can work. And if you'd prefer an option that's even lighter and more portable than the travel system, you could buy an inexpensive universal stroller base to use with your infant carrier those first few months. This works particularly well in urban areas where you may be taking taxis or wedging your stroller through crowded sidewalks and restaurants.

Four-Ounce Bottles

Here's a miniscam: four-ounce bottles. We picked up several before my son was born, assuming we were supposed to start with the smallest feeding option. I nursed him initially, and by the time we were regularly offering bottles, my son was taking about six ounces per feeding. So much for the little four-ouncers. When your baby is two months old, he'll already need four to six ounces of breast milk or formula per feeding. Bottles generally come in four-, eight-, or nine-ounce sizes, so at that point you have to use a larger option. So even if you're bottle-feeding from day one, why waste money on a size that will be useless in a few weeks? The bottle manufacturers of the world may be deeply concerned our arms will fatigue while gripping those big nine-ouncers the first few weeks of parenthood, but more likely they're just driving sales through unneeded varieties. Save a little money on the small guys and get an assortment of nine-ounce bottles you'll use until sippy cups hit the scene.

An Abundance of Beeping, Twirling, Hyperstimulating Toys

Baby toys are adorable. And very hard to resist. But your infant doesn't need many. As the first grandchild on both sides of our family, my son had no complaints in the baby toy department. Yet, despite the bright, colorful, beeping, twirling, moving, shaking toys around our house, his favorite year one playtime activities were (1) trying to wedge himself under the couch, (2) pushing buttons on the remote control when the TV wasn't even on, and (3) sticking his fingers inside the DVD player. He was also a big fan of Tupperware, wooden spoons, and bathroom items— from the gloriously fun toilet paper rolls to the bathtub (his favorite place to drop things he discovered under the couch). And every parent I know has a similar story. Get a few toys for each stage but resist the urge to pick up every new one you see, unless you just want to play with it yourself.

A Bassinet

We've all seen the pictures in the baby magazines and catalogs—the precious bassinet bathed in sunlight from a nearby window, symbolizing all things sweet. But let's get real; bassinets are expensive and babies outgrow them in weeks. They do allow your child to sleep bedside, avoiding trips down the hall for that third night feeding. But so do portable cribs, which include removable bassinets for those early weeks and can be used later as a contained play area or sleeping spot during visits away from home. And your newborn doesn't have to start in a newborn-size bed; his regular crib can work perfectly from day one.

Moses Basket

What's the deal with Moses baskets? Why would someone charge $180 for a lined basket that holds a newborn for a couple of months? Unless you're planning to reuse it as a cat bed, there are lots of more practical infant sleeping options. If your vision of motherhood involves a bundle of joy in a Moses basket (or bassinet), you could always ask around and borrow one.

A Quilt to Match Your Crib Bedding

You find the perfect crib bedding, pull out your credit card faster than you can say "dream nursery," and lug the set home in triumph. Then you run across this little tip in one of your parenting magazines: The American Academy of Pediatrics strongly recommends keeping all quilts, blankets, and pillows out of cribs due to the increased risk of suffocation and SIDS. So why are they tempting us with these coordinated sets? Unless you're looking for a wall decoration, you could skip the quilt.

A Crib Bumper

Similarly, crib bumpers serve no real purpose. The first few months, your baby can't even move around, and the bumper sits there looking cute. Eventually he starts to pull himself up, and you're supposed to remove the bumper so he doesn't use it as a springboard to the floor. And these things take up serious space in the closet. There are some adorable crib bumpers out there, and if you don't mind spending the money you can justify one for the cuteness factor alone. But to save cash, forget the bumper and focus on great crib sheets.

Final Countdown to Baby To-Do List

FROM:	Jasmine Brown
TO:	Makayla Robinson
SUBJECT:	Preparenthood panic setting in

Starting to panic. Just hit pregnancy week 32 and realized we have only TWO MONTHS LEFT to fully prepare for parenthood. When should I finalize my maternity leave? Or start interviewing baby-sitters? Where do we find a pediatrician? Or someone to help us with a will? We still need to paint the nursery, stock up on baby gear, and figure out how to install the car seat. And I thought planning our wedding was complicated. Why was I stressed about cake tastings and choosing a calligrapher? I could do that these days on my lunch break. Speaking of lunch, this baby wants a burger, and she wants it now. Gotta run!

Sometime during your third trimester, your attention shifts from heartburn-minimizing snacks and slimming maternity tops to life beyond pregnancy. If you're adopting, you'll have the same sense of urgency in the weeks before your big call. Your impending trip to Babyville comes into focus—and the view can be a little scary. Prevent panic by following this guide to your final prebaby days. It covers all the important details—from prematernity leave logistics to childbirth prep, from selecting a pediatrician to scheduling visitors (a.k.a. your newborn care support team). Get the detailed explanation for each to-do item here and then track your progress on the abbreviated pullout version of this guide provided in the appendix. And don't worry, this to-do list may seem long at first, but you'll easily cover the important stuff by the time your child arrives.

Work

Ideally two to four months before your due date or adoption:

Confirm Your Employer's Approach to Maternity Leave

The Family and Medical Leave Act of 1993 allows women and men in workplaces with fifty or more employees to take up to twelve weeks of unpaid, job-protected leave after the birth of a baby or adoption of a child, assuming they've met tenure requirements that vary by state. In smaller workplaces, which make up more than half of the private sector, maternity leave policies are basically up for grabs. Plus, no U.S. employer is required to pay new parents while out on leave. (So much for those family values politicians love to brag about.)

Parental leave pay varies significantly by employer. You could get squat or you could receive a few months fully paid—or anything in between. Dig out that employee handbook you haven't looked at since the day you were hired. Formal leave policies should be documented there. Then set up a meeting with someone in human resources who can provide the full policy scoop. Ask about:

Parental leave allocation: First, discuss the number of paid and unpaid days allowed under your employer's parental leave policy. If you're adopting a child, request adoption policy specifics.

Short-term disability (STD) coverage: I didn't consider myself disabled as a new mom (unless you count sleep deprivation as a disability), but who am

I to argue with cash coming my way? Short-term disability insurance is the official name for your new mom moneypot. Yes, I'm talking about STDs. But the good kind. The kind you want. Find out if your employer or state offers STD coverage and if so, how many weeks you should expect. Private STD benefits generally last up to eight weeks, and state STD insurance often covers a portion of your salary for four to six weeks. You can confirm state coverage by contacting your state's Department of Labor.

Additional coverage for medical complications: Your health care provider may require bed rest for a portion of your pregnancy, and cesarean sections or childbirth complications may require additional recovery time after delivery. Ask about supplemental coverage you could utilize if necessary.

Other forms of paid days at home: Discuss how many vacation, sick, and personal days you've accrued, and find out if you can borrow from future vacation days. Many new moms maximize their income at home by combining paid parental leave days and STD coverage with these other forms of paid leave. Then the unpaid days kick in.

Benefits during leave: Confirm that your health insurance benefits will continue during your time at home, and make sure your baby will be covered upon arrival. You may have to fill out some forms in advance to include him on your policy, and you definitely don't want to get stuck paying for those newborn medical bills by yourself. ("Well, we were going to get Johnny circumcised, but we decided to put that money into a nice new wet bar for the basement . . .")

Calculate How Much Unpaid Leave You Can Afford to Take

Once you've learned what paid leave to expect and how many subsequent unpaid days off you're allowed, sit down with a calculator. If your employer doesn't offer fully paid maternity leave (and few do), the duration of your time off will be defined by how many unpaid days you can afford to take. If you want more time at home than you can afford, try negotiating a gradual return to work. You could work from home at first or begin work on a part-time basis, shifting to your permanent schedule over a few weeks or months. This approach is often tolerable for employers, and it offers a great transitional period for you, your baby, and your child care provider.

Begin Exploring Your Postmaternity Leave Work Options

Hoping to shift to flextime after your baby hits the scene? Or work from home? Or job share? Discuss potential opportunities with your employer now and build your case by getting advice from employees in similar work arrangements. Hypothetically, you should give your employer your best guess at your postmaternity leave intentions before heading out. In reality, this can be challenging if you're still debating your options. If you're undecided or concerned your boss will be less than thrilled with queries about cutting back, you could address this issue during your maternity leave when you've settled on your preferred work arrangement. (But you didn't hear that from me.) To fully assess your options, check out Chapter 8, "Your Simple, Step-by-Step Guide to Making the Hardest Decision of Your Life."

Know Your Rights

Most employers will welcome news of your pregnancy and politely ignore your massive belly as you waddle into meetings. Others, however, may have a less enlightened view of your impending leave. (Response to your pregnancy announcement: "You. Are. Kidding me. You're going to be home watching *Oprah* just before year-end budgets are due?") If you're laid off, fired, or demoted once news of your pregnancy hits management, you have rights under the Pregnancy Discrimination Act. Talk to an attorney if your employer tries anything sketchy.

Start Researching Child Care Options

Day care facilities often have long waiting lists, so call as soon as possible. If you're considering a baby-sitter or nanny, you can pinpoint agencies now, but you'll schedule interviews a few weeks before heading back to work. Yes, this timing may feel like selecting your parachute two milliseconds before jumping out of an airplane, but baby-sitters available for interviews want to start work immediately. For lots of advice on the child care selection process, check out Chapter 10, "Nine Simple Steps to Great Child Care."

Ideally, two to three months before your due date or adoption:

Submit a Maternity Leave Request and Plan for Returning to Work

You probably announced your pregnancy sometime after passing that scary twelve-week mark but before your growing belly made the announcement for you. By your third trimester, your timing is obvious. Every colleague who's seen you from the neck down knows your maternity leave is around the corner. (If you're adopting, you can take the subtle route.) But many employers still require an official leave request, including a written doctor's statement indicating your due date and any related medical issues.

Confirm your maternity leave dates at least sixty to ninety days before your baby's expected arrival so your employer can hire a fill-in or delegate your responsibilities. When to start your leave? This is always tricky. By month nine you're more than ready for a break, but you don't want to waste any precious days at home with your baby. Aim to start your leave around your due date and see how you feel. If your health care provider requires bed rest, the decision is made for you, and short-term disability coverage should kick in.

Already negotiated your post–maternity leave work plan? Confirm that in writing as well. Include your return date and any adjustment to your schedule, work location, responsibilities, compensation, or benefits.

Remind Dad to Request Paternity Leave (Or At Least Vacation Time)

If there's any way you can get your significant other to exercise his paternity leave rights, give it a shot. Sadly, despite the signing of the Family and Medical Leave Act over a decade ago, many men still feel uncomfortable making a paternity leave request. Why? Often they realize no one else is doing it. And who wants to be branded "that guy who actually took paternity leave"? Lay on the guilt trip, slip ultrasound pictures in his wallet—whatever it takes to motivate him to take some time off work. At least a week or two. To make a request, he just needs to meet with human resources and go through the parental leave policy questions outlined earlier. And if nothing else, remind him to save vacation and personal days to take when your baby arrives. It's an incredible time in your life, and you'll want to experience it together. Plus, it's a heck of a lot easier to bathe a wriggling newborn when you've got a helper to run interference.

Ideally, at least one month before your due date or adoption:

Plan for Your Impending Departure

Remind your boss of your timing (she may still be in denial about your quickly approaching maternity leave), and explain your plan for the transition. Start meeting regularly with the people who will take over your responsibilities while you're at home. Begin documenting everything so you can hand projects over at any point. Leave a clear list of tasks to be covered while you're at home and set up a plan for checking in if necessary.

The remaining to-do items can be accomplished in the last month or two before your due date or adoption, except for ordering nursery furniture, which often requires three months lead time.

Baby Gear

Stock Up on Basic Baby Supplies and Nursery Furniture

Take the baby shopping list provided earlier in this chapter, grab your wallet, and hit the stores. There's nothing like buying teeny-weeny diapers and itsy-bitsy socks to get you excited about being a mom.

Wash Your Stage One Clothes and Baby Linens

Everything that's going to touch your newborn's skin should be washed in a mild, baby-friendly detergent like Dreft.

Install Your Car Seat

You won't be permitted to bring your newborn home without a properly installed car seat, so do it now to be fully prepared.

Your Prenatal Health

Channel Your Inner Quaker

The pregnancy ban on smoking, alcohol, and drugs is not a real sacrifice as you're rounding into month nine. ("I can barely fit my belly through the front door and my ankles look like an elephant's, but tonight I want to stuff myself into a black halter dress and hit the club scene! Bring on the chocolate martinis!") You've forgotten the flavor of mixed drinks at this point anyway, so maintain your party-free lifestyle and focus on the Cosmo you can toss back when your baby hits the scene—or when you've phased out breast feeding.

> **QUICK TIP FROM DR. NIED**
>
> Let the professionals help you install your car seat; most people do it improperly on their own. There's a list of certified child passenger safety technicians by state or zip code on the National Highway Traffic Safety Administration website at nhtsa.gov. You can also call their auto safety hotline at 888-327-4236.

Keep Eating the Good Stuff

You're probably having nightmares about being chased by giant spinach leaves by now, but remember you're in the home stretch. Keep up the grains, leafy greens, fresh fruits, nuts, lean meat, poultry, beans, and dairy, and continue to avoid fish with high levels of methyl mercury (swordfish, king mackerel), sushi, raw oysters, undercooked meat, pâté, unpasteurized juices, and soft cheeses. Caffeine can affect your body's ability to absorb iron, so minimize the afternoon Cokes and keep the coffee intake to a cup a day or less.

Keep Up with Your Prenatal Appointments; They're Almost Over

The last couple of months in your pregnancy, you'll meet with your health care provider almost every week. These appointments should be quick and painless unless a complication is suspected. Ignore the weight checks—you're supposed to be beautifully huge at this point—and enjoy the final countdown. If you've been experiencing bouts of depression (hopelessness, significant appetite loss), ask your health care provider for a psychiatric referral. Pregnancy and new mom hormones can wreak havoc on your mental health; seek help if needed during this challenging time.

Do Your Kegels Daily

Kegels are the weird-sounding but important pelvic exercises that strengthen the muscles used in delivery. These muscles also help you control urination and enjoy sex, so start crunching. To get the hang of Kegels, try to stop the flow while you're urinating, then mimic this clenching twenty-five to fifty times a day. (No, this is not a joke.) Here's the good news: You can do Kegels anywhere—driving to work, watching TV, even sitting in a meeting. Your colleagues will never know, and if the meeting is a waste at least you can feel good about productive multitasking.

Stay Active

Check out prenatal yoga or water aerobics classes in your area or take a walk when you can motivate after work. You want to stay strong for your delivery; these classes are an ideal place to meet soon-to-be-moms (i.e., soon-to-be-friends), and exercise is always good for the general attitude.

Then Take It Easy

Pre-pregnancy, you may have stayed up until Letterman's monologue; now you're lucky if you make it to prime time. Feel no guilt; grab your body pillow and hit the sack early. Your body is working as intensely as a marathon runner's just by supporting your growing baby, and exhaustion is natural.

Your Baby's Health

Select a Pediatrician

Although you have yet to meet your child, you have to choose his doctor. Strange but true. As you check into the hospital or birth center for delivery, you'll provide your pediatrician's name and contact information. Then, magically (okay, it's generally the result of a nurse's phone call, but it seems like magic), your baby's first doctor will find your recovery room within a day of your delivery, ready to provide the newborn exam.

Consider these key factors when choosing a pediatrician:

Hours: Obviously the doctor's hours need to work with your schedule.

Location: You'll be visiting the practice a lot that first year. Close is good.

Credentials: Is the doctor board certified in pediatrics? Is she a member of the American Academy of Pediatrics?

Doctor's philosophy and style: This is a personal feeling; select a doctor whose approach matches yours.

Availability outside of office hours: What's the policy for questions at night? For emergencies?

Insurance: Yours should be accepted, unless you recently won the lottery.

Overall vibe: Do you feel comfortable? Is everyone friendly? Is it a bright, happy environment? Go with your gut.

Make a Decision About Circumcision

If you have a boy, you'll need to tell your health care provider whether or not you want him circumcised the morning after his birth. So, think through this issue now—and expect some really funny facial expressions from dad as he weighs in on this one.

Nesting

Get Organized

The maternal nesting urge is a real phenomenon, so you may have already found yourself inexplicably cleaning out closets, reorganizing drawers, and sorting through old pictures. Go with the feeling. You'll feel better bringing your baby into a streamlined environment.

Catch Up on Home Projects

Similarly, do the big home projects now if you can. Get the leaky toilet fixed. Have the guest room painted. Make yourself a quick list and try to make headway over the next few weeks.

Childbirth Prep

Take a Childbirth Class

These classes take the fear factor out of delivery and offer a great opportunity for bonding with other pregnant moms. Ask your health care provider for references.

Write Your Birth Plan and Share It with Your Doctor or Midwife

"Birth plan" is an official-sounding term for a simple concept. You basically write out your preferences for birth and share the document with your health care provider before the big day. Is it essential? No. Doctors and midwives know what they're doing, and you can always explain your preferences during labor. Is it nice to have? You bet. It offers a sense of control and peace of mind as labor begins. And it's a heck of a lot easier to think through these issues before you're battling contractions. Some key elements, like home birth versus hospital birth, should have been decided at this point. Consider the following factors when typing out your plan:

Setting
- People you want in the room during early labor and delivery
- Dimmed lights or music (Ask if there's a CD player in your labor and delivery room.)
- Photographs or videotape

Labor Induction
- Natural methods like walking
- Herbs or castor oil
- Medical techniques such as pitocin

Pain Management Options
- Breathing techniques
- Bath or shower
- Massage, acupuncture, or hypnosis
- Narcotics or epidural

Techniques for Monitoring the Baby
- Continually using external monitors
- Occasionally using a Doppler or fetascope

Episiotomy Preferences
- Avoid one as long as possible
- Go ahead if tearing seems likely

Pushing Positions
- Squatting
- On hands and knees
- Reclining with raised knees

Birthing Tools
- Birthing tub in room
- Birthing or squatting stool
- Mirror (Useful to see which pushes are effective and view your baby's head emerging.)

- Use of forceps or vacuum

Cesareans
- View of the birth or not

Just After Birth
- Significant other's involvement (Catching the baby and cutting the cord are options.)
- Newborn testing and bathing (You can request that this occurs in the room with you.)
- Feeding preference (Tell the nurses if you want to breast-feed or will need a bottle.)
- Baby's location (Newborns can typically sleep in either parents' rooms or a nursery.)

Infant Care and Breast Feeding Prep

If You Plan to Breast-Feed, Take a Class Now

Breast feeding classes are slightly surreal but useful if you intend to nurse. In fact, it was during my breast feeding class, as I sat in a darkened room watching a woman on film express enough milk with her bare hands to put out a decent-size kitchen fire, that I realized life as a new mom may not exactly synch up with the pristine images in the parenting magazines. And that's probably a good lesson in itself. The instructor explains common breast feeding positions, answers questions, and passes out plastic dolls so you can give the recommended positions a try. (Yes, we're talking about holding a wild-haired plastic infant up to your breasts in a room full of strangers—just one more entry in your rapidly expanding things-I've-done-for-this-kid-and-he's-not-even-born-yet file.) You learn about local breast feeding hotlines, and you can check out a variety of pumps—a worthwhile exercise if you're planning to make this investment.

Take Infant Care and CPR Classes

Ask your health care provider for references.

Lose the Pregnancy Books; Prepare for Parenting

Read ahead in this book, sign up for new baby e-mail newsletters, or check out additional resources in your local bookstore or library. Like any foreign land, Babyville is easier (and more fun) to explore when you know where you're heading.

Finances, Will, and Guardianship

Start to Think About a Life-with-Baby Budget
and College Savings Plan

Average year one baby expenses are $6,300,[6] and we can anticipate private university costs in the range of $75,000 or more *a year.*[7] (Let's just hope our kids stick to the four-year plan.) Take a look at your family finances now. Even setting aside $50 to $75 a month towards college costs can significantly help offset future sticker shock. For lots of guidance on money matters, check out Chapter 7, "Living for Less and Loving It."

Create a Will and Choose a Guardian

Here's a scary fact: If you and your baby's father die without leaving a will that specifies a legal guardian, the state will appoint someone to raise your child and manage your assets. Protect your family. Contact a lawyer now or, if attorney costs are prohibitive for you, check out a credible do-it-yourself book or website.

Friends and Family

Plan Now for Visitors

The best strategy for feeling confident with a newborn is creating your own in-house baby team. If you have a significant other who can take off work for a couple of weeks, great. Start there. Then, make plans with your parents, the in-laws, siblings, out-of-town friends—anyone with two hands who can hold the baby or change a diaper. If you're really lucky, you'll have help throughout your maternity leave.

Catch Up with Friends

Make a list of friends you haven't talked to in a while and try to call a few before your baby arrives. You'll feel fully in touch as you head into the time warp of new momhood.

What's in a Name?

Pick a Name

Name selection, like so many elements of parenting, can be surprisingly challenging. How to choose a name that's spunky yet dignified, unique but not weird, meaningful but not old-fashioned, cool but not too popular? Plus, scary nickname possibilities must be considered (forget Tucker and Richard) and bad initial combinations avoided (so much for Ashley Sarah Smith). It's a tough choice. Just make it before your little one arrives; you'll need to give your baby's name to the birth certificate folks before you head home.

Pick Out Baby Announcements

You've selected the perfect name. Once your baby makes his grand entrance, it's time to spread the word. Ideally, baby announcements should be sent out two to six weeks after your child's arrival. (That would be two weeks for the psychotically organized and six weeks for the rest of us.) Select boy and girl options now so you're ready to order them or print them yourselves.

Premom Pampering
(Yes, This Is an Essential To-Do Item)

Get a Haircut

You won't be anywhere near a salon in the next couple of months, so get a good cut now. Ideally, colleagues will be so distracted by your cute hair they won't even notice the bulge of your belly button against your maternity pants as you hit month nine.

Get a Pedicure

You may not be able to see your toes while standing up, but as you're lying on the delivery table, bright painted toenails offer a perfect focal point. Plus, in the midst of childbirth chaos, it's comforting to know at least your toenails look great. If you don't feel like paying the pros, play that "I'd do it myself but I can't bend over that far" trump card, and hand a bottle of your favorite nail polish to your significant other or a (really nice) friend.

Your Newborn Is Home;
Now What?

Your Newborn Care Survival Guide

From Deciphering Baby's Tears to Swaddling

Without Fear, Sleep Secrets, and More

From Lexi's journal:

Still in shock doctors let us bring Morgan home. We have no idea what we're doing—isn't it obvious? Shouldn't there be more prep time? More training? Maybe a required new parent PowerPoint presentation on surviving the first few weeks?

Nagging pregnancy concern about lack of recent exposure to infants now a full-blown reality. Increasingly certain I'll drop wriggly newborn when descending stairs. Or inadvertently leave a blanket in the crib. Or stab her in the eye when attempting to breast-feed. Vaguely aware fears are irrational but unable to channel competent prebaby self. Last night wept for twenty minutes at unbelievable sweetness of infant socks. Morgan's toes alone could kill me. Overwhelmed with love and yet secretly repulsed by icky umbilical cord stump.

Breast feeding bordering on fiasco. In hospital, nurses unfazed by ludicrous attempts to maneuver engorged boob into wee newborn mouth. Kept offering encouragement. Now home without expert help and certain something major was missed at breast feeding class last month. Probably during multiple bathroom runs. Already know entire staff of twenty-four-hour nursing hotline by first names.

You never enter Babyville alone. Initially you're assisted by a dream team of Babyville's best and brightest—from doctors to doulas. Then, just a few days later, you're sent on your way. By yourselves. With no less than a brand-new person in tow.

Think of this chapter as your comprehensive guide to newborn care—the next best thing to an in-home dream team so you can master the fundamentals now and approach this early stage with confidence. You'll learn how newborns experience the world and get tips for facilitating sleep, minimizing meltdowns, and controlling colic. And you'll get essential infant care guidance—from successful sponge baths to baby massage. There may not be an official new parent training manual for surviving those wacky first few weeks, but this is pretty darn close.

Help! My Newborn Looks Like an Alien

"So, are you going to admit it, or should I?" Jeremy asked his wife, looking at their newborn daughter in her arms.

"Admit what?"

"Well, she's adorable, don't get me wrong. But honestly, I haven't seen a conehead like that since Dan Akroyd was on *Saturday Night Live*."

|•|

Don't be misled by the hospital brochures showing round-faced, wide-eyed "newborns" resting peacefully in their mothers' arms. It'll be a few days until your child recovers from delivery and morphs into her supercute baby self. Until then, don't worry—despite any craziness in your gene pool, her pointy head isn't permanent.

Head Shape

Your newborn's head may look a bit angular at first. Of course, you know

> **QUICK TIP FROM DR. NIED**
>
> If you feel the top and back of your infant's head, you'll notice soft spots called fontanels. Don't worry about touching them or brushing the baby's hair in those areas. They allow your child's skull to squeeze through the birth canal and then provide expansion room for brain growth.

where she's just been, and it's mind-boggling that her little noggin made it out at all. Fortunately the entire newborn body is designed for birth, and the noggin is no exception. Your baby's head changes shape as it squeezes through the birth canal—a process called molding—and it will return to nonalien proportions within a few days.

Skin

Newborn skin offers a partial preview of puberty. Think the unfortunate whiteheads without the boy band posters and marathon phone calls. At birth, your baby may have small white bumps called milia on her chin or nose. She may also have bluish patches called Mongolian spots, pale pink birth marks affectionately called stork bites, or bruises from delivery. And if white bumps and blotches aren't enough, she may even have fine hairs called lanugo on her back or shoulders. If so, don't assume your child missed a step in the evolutionary chain. These are normal newborn skin conditions, and they'll disappear within a few weeks. (Real whiteheads, neonatal acne, may arise during the first month.)

QUICK TIP FROM DR. NIED

Newborn jaundice is very common and causes yellow skin discoloration. The result of extra red blood cells breaking down, it usually begins after the first twenty-four hours of life and clears up within a week. If your newborn's skin has a yellow hue, her doctor will most likely test her bilirubin level. If the level is elevated, she may need to remain in the hospital for treatment. Jaundice can also occur once you get home, so always let your pediatrician know if you notice a yellow tint to your baby's skin.

Swelling and Flattening

So, we've got a pointy head, bad skin, and back hair. Why not top things off with swollen eyes and a flattened nose that makes your bundle of joy look like she just went a round in the ring with a professional boxer? Don't sweat these newborn issues; within days you'll have the Gerber baby you always imagined.

How Newborns Experience the World

Alexandra and her best friend stood side-by-side, watching her two-week-old twins in their crib. The boys were staring at the mobile above them with complete fascination, their eyes never leaving the rotating animals and shapes. "Life before PlayStation," Alexandra murmured. "Same entertainment fix, easier on the parental budget."

|•|

After nine months of snuggly warmth and familiar sounds, your baby will need a few days to adjust to the bright, cold, crazy world.

Vision

No, your newborn isn't ignoring you. It's just really, really bright from her perspective and she'd rather keep her eyes closed, thank-you very much. When she does occasionally take a peek, she can't see far. Newborn sight extends to about twelve inches, which is, in case you ever wondered if Mother Nature knows what she's doing, the distance from your child's face to yours when you're holding her in your arms. Newborns prefer looking at faces and bright contrasting patterns, so entertain your little one with enthusiastic expressions and hook up the mobile. Forget matching the nursery colors; get the brightest rotating variety you can find. Position it about a foot above her in the crib and watch her reach newborn nirvana.

Hearing

You probably felt a little silly chatting to your baby in utero these past nine months, but you did it anyway, and now it pays off. Your child is born, and the doctor holds her up for all to see. The assembled medical staff looks from her to you, waiting for something profound to emerge from your mouth. You stare at her in quiet awe, overcome with gratitude and a slight postchildbirth buzz, and you finally hear yourself say, "Well, hi." Timidly. Like you're greeting a new neighbor who just moved in next door. But that's enough. She turns her head directly toward you, and the rest of the room falls silent. "It's your voice," the doctor explains. "She already knows your voice."

Keep the lovefest going by talking and singing to your child until your significant other makes a helpful comment like, "Sooooo, has baby talk become the new *official language* around here? Because I'd like to prepare myself if that falsetto vocal range you're using is going to be permanent." What he doesn't know: The sing-songy voice that mysteriously emerged after childbirth like vocal milk coming in is called "motherease," and research has shown it's the perfect tone to capture babies' attention.

Touch

We all know hugs feel good, but loving touch actually makes your baby healthier. Cuddling and infant massage promote neurological development, mother–baby bonding, and a strong immune system in newborns. So go with that snugglin' feeling from day one, and show your baby how to love the skin she's in. During her (admittedly brief) awake periods, sit in a reclining position on the couch or bed with your back propped up and your knees raised, and lean her back against your thighs so she's facing you. This is the perfect position for engaging her even before she can support her head. Talk, sing, stroke her arms and legs—she'll benefit from any interaction.

> **QUICK TIP FROM DR. NIED**
>
> You can't hold your infant too much; consistent cuddling gives her a sense of security and familiarity with her parents and caregivers. Premature babies given regular massage have demonstrated significantly higher weight gain and greater motor control than preemies who weren't massaged.

Reflexes

Infants are born with a variety of survival instincts. For some newborn fun, test a few on your little one.

Rooting reflex: Your baby is literally born to eat. When you touch her cheek with a nipple, bottle, or even a finger, she'll turn and open her mouth. And when something goes in, she'll start to suck. Evolution does have its advantages. The rooting reflex lasts for three to four months and is less prominent after the first month.

Grasp reflex: I'm sure you've tried this one before. Your colleague brought her newborn son to the office for a little maternity leave field trip, and the women gathered around him like he was a nine-pound rock star. You gently pushed your finger into his clenched hand, and he gripped it like he'd known you for years. The other women slowly returned to their work, and you realized the kid still wasn't letting go—and you could be attached until he hits puberty. Well, now you've got your own finger gripper. Enjoy it; this reflex lasts about five months.

Step reflex: Despite her clearly impressive athletic prowess, your six-day-old can't actually walk. It just looks like she can. Hold your newborn in a standing position with her feet on a flat surface, and she may move them as if ready to take steps. Amaze your friends soon; this reflex only lasts for a couple of months.

Fencing reflex: If newborn steps aren't exciting enough, pull this one out of your bag of baby tricks. Gently turn your newborn's head to one side; that arm will bend while the opposite arm extends like your very own twenty-inch Olympic fencer. This reflex lasts four to five months.

Moro reflex: I'm guessing there was once a Dr. Moro with a really loud voice and a big ego. He'd walk in to examine newborns and scare the bejeesus out of them, eventually naming their flailing responses after himself. Who knows; I'm just throwing out theories. Anyway, when a newborn is startled by a noise or sudden shift in position, she'll fling her arms out and arch her back. If your child exhibits this response, soothe her by holding her close. The Moro reflex will fade by two to four months.

Smiling

While your newborn is an impressive bundle of reflexes, she isn't setting the bar too high in the attitude department. You may get a few gas-induced grins during those early weeks, but expect her first real social smiles between weeks four and eight. And even then, be patient—they may not happen often at first. (You: "Come on, sweetie! Show mommy's friends how you can smile! I'm gonna tickle your tummy! Here I come! Show me that big smile!" Her: *That nice lady's nose is really close. I wonder if it would taste good. Hmm.*)

Newborns and Sleep

It's 1:00 A.M., and four-week-old Ella has just wrestled out of her swaddling for the third time since eating half an hour ago. She does this while sleeping, like some kind of newborn Houdini escape trick, but the results are never good. She wakes up. Instantly. And lets everybody know about it. Her parents, Krista and John, look at each other in disbelief as the screams begin again.

"Wait a minute. I have an idea," John says, dragging himself out of bed and walking down the hall. When he returns, he's holding something triumphantly above his head like a marathon runner crossing the finish line. "Duct tape!" he calls out with more energy than he's had in days. Krista stares at him, convinced the sleep deprivation has finally pushed him over the edge. Then it hits her—what he's planning.

"Honey," she responds. "I don't think you're supposed to use duct tape when swaddling newborns. It would probably keep the blanket in place, but it seems a little intense."

"Oh," he drops his hands and starts to nod. "Right. I guess not."

"But it was a creative idea," she adds, getting out of bed and heading into the nursery.

|•|

You'll learn how to create positive long-term sleep habits in Chapter 14, "Nurturing a Supersleeper." But at this point, long-term sleep habits are months away. You're dealing with a newborn. It's survival time.

What to Expect

Here's what you *can* do even in those first few weeks: Create an environment to promote sleep and pray that it works. Sometimes it will; sometimes it won't. Newborns sleep most of the time anyway, from sixteen to eighteen hours a day. This sleep generally occurs in two- to three-hour segments (that's right, 24/7), requiring feeding and diaper changing in between. Sleeping improves dramatically after the early weeks, but many babies wake up at least once a night for the first several months. So, don't listen to your sister's claim that her child slept through the night by day five; she's either fantasizing or experiencing selective parenthood memory loss.

Promoting Newborn Sleep

Facilitating newborn sleep is like attempting to squeeze into your prepregnancy jeans—you can try your best, but all attempts in those early weeks may be futile. That said, there are some general tips for newborn snoozing. For example, some babies are born with their biological clocks out of whack. Not that surprising—it's all the same in the womb, right? If your child was active at night while in utero, don't be surprised if she's active at night now as well. To help transition your night owl to an appropriate schedule, create a clear sense of day and night during her awake periods. While she's awake during the day, keep the lights bright, open the shades, play music, and speak to her in an animated voice. Over time, try to extend these periods. During night feedings, keep the lights low and minimize your interactions. Try to shorten these periods over time. Within a few weeks your newborn should adjust to a typical day and night schedule.

And I can't say enough about the magic of swaddling to promote newborn sleep. By surrounding your child in a warm, snug receiving blanket, you're re-creating the security of the womb and preventing her arms from flailing around and waking her up. Swaddling works best the first four weeks of life and can be effective several weeks longer with a looser approach. Here's how you swaddle:

Step 1:   Lay a standard-size receiving blanket on a flat surface, horizontally. Fold the upper-right corner down about eight inches.

Step 2:   Lay your baby on the blanket with her head resting on the folded corner. Pull the left side of the blanket across her, tucking it snugly under her right arm and behind her back.

Step 3:   Pull the bottom of the blanket up and hold it on her chest.

Step 4:   Pull the right side of the blanket over and tuck it under her left side. Your baby's weight and the tucked-in edges should keep the blanket in place while she sleeps.

Minimizing the Risk of SIDS

Sudden infant death syndrome (SIDS) is the death of an otherwise healthy infant, typically during sleep, and pediatricians diagnose it only after ruling out all other potential causes. Bottom line, doctors can't explain why SIDS occurs. It is rare, occurring in one out of approximately 1,500 live births. However, SIDS is the leading cause of death among children one to twelve months old, most likely to strike infants between one and six months of age. Take steps to protect your child:

- Put your baby down to sleep on her back for at least a year. You may have heard of the American Academy of Pediatrics Back to Sleep campaign which promotes this approach.
- Don't put thick blankets, pillows, toys, or fluffy bedding in the crib or bassinet with your child, and never cover her face.
- Use a crib that meets current safety standards and a firm mattress that fits the crib well.
- Adjust your home thermometer so the nursery isn't too warm and don't overdress your child. If it feels comfortable for you, it's perfect for your baby.
- Don't smoke during pregnancy or around your newborn. If you're letting anyone smoke around your child, stop now.
- Breast-feed. Studies indicate breast-fed babies are at slightly lower risk for SIDS.
- Avoid cosleeping (bringing your baby into bed to sleep with you), particularly if you've been drinking alcohol, smoking (never a good thing around babies anyway), taking medications that can cause drowsiness, or if you're significantly overweight.
- Give your baby a pacifier when you put her down to sleep. A recent American Academy of Pediatrics (AAP) study demonstrated a de-

creased risk of SIDS for babies who were put to bed with pacifiers. Doctors aren't sure why a pacifier is protective. It may lead to lighter sleeping, so a baby is better able to respond to potential hazards like accidentally wedging her face against a pillow. It may help keep airways open or prevent the baby's tongue from relaxing back into her throat. Or a pacifier may help keep an infant safely on her back. If you're breast feeding, you should wait about four weeks to introduce the pacifier to avoid nipple confusion as your newborn establishes a nursing routine. And the AAP recommends phasing out the pacifier at one year, when the risk of ear infection from pacifier use increases and the risk of SIDS is much lower.

> **QUICK TIP FROM DR. NIED**
>
> While pacifiers before sleep are now recommended for babies until twelve months of age, never force an infant to use one. Some children simply don't take to pacifiers. And if your baby's pacifier falls out, don't reintroduce it while she's sleeping.

You can contact the SIDS Alliance at 800-221-7437 or visit its website at sidsalliance.org.

Should I Ever Wake My Baby for a Feeding?

Every parent eventually has this question. What if your newborn unexpectedly takes a four-hour nap? Or snoozes for six straight hours her first night at home? While these could be glorious hours of rest for new parents, we typically spend the time paralyzed with anxiety. We peer into the nursery every ten minutes. We pace the floor. We call friends with kids. We try not to call the pediatrician (no need to establish oneself as completely hysterical). We make silent vows, "If my baby survives—if she ever wakes from this infinite slumber—I'll never again complain about night feedings. I'll cherish every dirty diaper. I'll stop cussing when I hear her perfect little cries at 2:00 A.M." Then she wakes up ready for action. Your panic disappears, and you kick yourself for wasting an opportunity to sleep.

But back to the question: When, if ever, should you wake your baby to eat? This depends on two things: her age and weight.

Newborns birth to eight weeks: During your newborn's first few weeks, you're trying to establish appropriate daytime and nighttime sleep patterns and make sure she gains about an ounce a day. To that end, you could wake her from daytime naps after about three hours. This timing helps set the precedent for shorter naps and longer exploration periods during the day, which ideally will lead to the reverse at night. For the first two weeks, you could wake your newborn for overnight feedings after four to five hours. If she's feeding like a champ and putting on the pounds (okay, ounces), don't worry about extended night sleep after her first few weeks. In fact, count yourself among the lucky ones. As a rule of thumb, most babies don't sleep through the night until they're about ten to twelve pounds. Talk to your pediatrician for specific advice.

Babies two months and older: By two months, your baby should have day and night nailed. At this point, you're simply concerned about weight gain. If your child is flourishing weight-wise, there's no need to wake her from an extended sleep. If she's underweight, discuss all aspects of her diet and sleep patterns with your pediatrician.

Deciphering Tears and Controlling Colic

"Your turn," Tamika announced as the infant crying kicked in again. Her husband looked over at her and nodded, resigned to his fate. "And I just tried feeding, burping, diaper changing, and adding another layer of clothing. No luck with any of the usual culprits. You're going to have to get creative."

"It sounds like this meltdown requires my specialty," he replied. "The impossible-to-resist, incredibly soothing, repeated stair climb and descent. He's got no hope. I haven't hit the gym this week anyway; see you in twenty minutes."

|•|

Effective meltdown management is one of the great mysteries of early parenthood. Here's the scoop, from tear-stopping tips to colic busters.

Why Babies Cry

No, your newborn doesn't get cheap thrills from tormenting you. Crying is simply her only way to communicate. The messages she's sending are fairly basic—I'm famished, I'm bored, I'm lonely, I don't like this bath, I miss that cozy womb. She knows what she means, but you don't. At least not at first.

Deciphering Your Baby's Tears

I wish we could give you a newborn crying-to-English dictionary, but it's not that simple. Every baby has her own version of tears-as-talking, like a dialect of one. It's up to you to learn your child's communication style— the meanings behind her high-pitched screeching versus low-pitched wailing, the quiet whimper versus the rumbling baby groan. Pay attention; within a few weeks her different messages will be coming through loud and clear.

Minimizing the Meltdowns

Newborns cry to communicate and eventually you'll understand your baby's tears. But in the meantime, how to minimize the meltdowns? During her first few weeks, be prepared to hold your child much of the time. You can't spoil her at this age. Pull on a comfy baby sling or front pack and take her on walks around the house. The rhythmic motion of ascending and descending stairs can work like a charm. Let her snuggle against your chest while you hang out

QUICK TIP FROM DR. NIED

Many new parents mistakenly assume all crying means hunger, and they try to feed their babies each time they're fussy. Don't go down this path; it leads to exhausted moms and overfed infants. Instead, check the time. If your little one has eaten recently, consider other sources before jumping into feeding. Common causes of tears include overstimulation, a desire to change positions, discomfort, a dirty diaper, heat, cold, boredom, or gas. If you sense one of these may be the cause of your baby's complaint, try our recommended tear tamers.

on the couch. She'll likely be comforted by your familiar smell and heart-beat. And be patient. Within a few months, she'll naturally relax.

Tear Tamers

Some baby tears are inevitable, and we all know the million dollar question: How can you effectively comfort your newborn once the water-works begin? Try these parent-tested, expert-recommended strategies:

Stimulation adjustment: Check your baby's surroundings. Is the TV playing? Colorful toy dangling in her face? People talking around her? Dog barking down the hall? When some relatives came to visit us during my son's first few months, they burst through the front door belting out children's songs. They were just excited, but my son needed a slower, gentler transition to their arrival. Watch for well-intentioned enthusiasm or activity that may be overwhelming your little one, and bring her into a quiet room to relax if you suspect overstimulation.

Movement: Infants often resist being in the same position for too long. Try a tummy time break from the bouncy seat, a field trip around the house, or the famous stair climb and descent.

Temperature adjustment: Could your baby be too hot or too cold? Even if there's a blizzard outside, your newborn doesn't need the fleece outfit while lounging in the living room. Adjust her clothing or blankets as necessary.

Diaper change: Some babies don't mind a wet diaper; others can't stand one. In any case, you want to change it as soon as it's soiled to prevent diaper rash.

Burping: Your baby may have swallowed air while eating or crying, and a good burp could instantly improve her little attitude.

Food: Has she eaten recently? Try to feed your baby immediately after she wakes up so she's energized and ready to explore.

Rocking: The rhythmic motion of the rocking chair can lull your little one into a quieter state.

Swaddling: Try swaddling your newborn and holding her close. There's nothing like replicating the safety of the womb to help her relax.

Pacifier: For newborns, sucking is a natural sedative, diffusing tears and paving the way for rest. Some suck on their fingers from the beginning; others prefer a pacifier. If you're breast-feeding, wait a few weeks before introducing the pacie to prevent nipple confusion. Get the binky low-down below.

The Real Deal on Pacifiers

The pacifier is a brilliant invention, the closest thing you'll find to an off switch on your newborn tears sound system. It simply satisfies babies' innate urge to suck. No bells and whistles, but great effectiveness. In fact, a pacifier offers two benefits for your child: It can soothe her during fussy awake periods and it reduces the risk of SIDS when given to her just before sleep.

When my son was a few weeks old and working himself into a little newborn frenzy, we tried the pacifier for the first time. In an instant, his body relaxed, his crying stopped, and he gazed at us with a sort of divine gratitude as his jaw pulsed rhythmically. I pictured one of those comic strip bubbles over his head with the words, "Oh, yes. This is the good stuff."

Avoid the temptation to overuse the pacifier as a soothing tool during your child's fussy awake periods, and trust me, you will be tempted at times. (I remember pulling my son out of his fleece bunting at his eight-week pediatric visit. He already had a pacie in his mouth and three others fell out of the sleeves. "He really loves those pacifiers!" I announced, impressively trying to deflect blame to my unwitting newborn as the doctor helped me locate our binky collection scattered on the floor.) When fussiness hits, do a quick diaper, movement, stimulation, boredom, temperature, hunger check first. If nothing else does the trick, let the pacifier work its magic. You might need to try a few varieties to find one your baby prefers, and some infants never take to them at all.

When the Tears Just Won't Stop

There will be times when nothing works. Many newborns have inexplicable, inconsolable crying fits at some point. They may happen randomly, or they may follow a somewhat predictable schedule. Between four and six weeks, my son had a shrieking fit from about 8:00 P.M. to 9:30 P.M. almost every night. Generally he was an easygoing baby, and this new hysteria threw us for a loop. We tried everything to calm him, but nothing worked. Our pediatrician told us this was common; apparently newborns are often exhausted at the end of the day and become freakishly agitated (my words, not hers) before they can drop off to sleep. My husband volunteered to be the martyr and simply held our son in the rocking chair during this period each night. I think he sensed I would completely lose it if he didn't take the lead on that one. Unexplained crying ties your stomach in knots, gives you headaches, and makes you nostalgic for morning sickness and early labor contractions. Just know crying is a newborn thing, and it will pass. One night, my son stopped the insanity, and the shrieking fits never returned.

Colic

Pediatricians define colic as inconsolable crying at least three hours a day, three or more days a week. Babies don't emerge from the womb with colic; it generally begins within the first few weeks of life, peaks at six weeks, and tapers off sometime between months two and four.

> **QUICK TIP FROM DR. NIED**
>
> During crying spells, colicky babies tend to draw their arms and legs into their bodies as if they're in pain. However, there's no evidence to confirm that pain causes colic.

If your baby exhibits signs of colic, meet with your pediatrician. She can give you suggestions for managing the craziness, but it's typically a crap shoot. Try the basic tear tamers or give these colic busters a shot:

Massage: Gently massage your newborn's tummy to help relieve gas.

Car ride: A new mom friend gave me this tip. Her daughter was colicky, and the only way she could calm her was to go for a drive. Every evening when her husband got home from work, they'd drive around for a couple of hours, and their daughter would sleep peacefully in the car seat.

Consistency: Babies are comforted by consistency. When your infant's crying begins, try to provide your soothing techniques in a similar order: first rocking, second swaddling, third the stair climb—or whatever works for you.

Breast feeding assessment: If your baby isn't getting enough milk, chronic hunger can lead to extreme fussiness. Talk to your doctor or a lactation consultant about potential feeding-related issues. As a first step, she'll likely recommend minimizing your intake of caffeine, dairy, spicy foods, and vegetables like broccoli that are difficult to digest and more likely to cause gastrointestinal discomfort for both mom and baby.

Umbilical Cord, Circumcision, and Nail Care

"You know, I don't think I've ever seen an umbilical cord stump before," Sondra murmured, examining her daughter's belly. "It's obviously not something they showcase in those infant photo montages."

"No," her sister replied. "And now that we've seen one, we can understand why."

|•|

As new parents, you mentally prepare for the baby care biggies—feeding, promoting sleep, and minimizing tears. Don't forget some of the less glamorous but equally important parts of the job—from cleaning your newborn's umbilical cord stump to keeping those little nails short enough to prevent accidental scratching.

Umbilical Cord Care

Your significant other has been secretly fearing this moment since the day you conceived, but he'd never admit it. How could he? You just pushed an eight-pound person out of your body; he *cannot* wimp out when the doctor asks him to cut the cord. His hands are shaky, but he ruefully steps forward, willing himself to focus on the task at hand. And he succeeds! The cord is cut! Your baby is free! And that stump is really, really gross.

The doctor clamps your newborn's umbilical cord stump to stop the bleeding and removes the clamp before you head home a couple of days later. The stump will fall off on its own, usually in about two to three weeks. In the meantime, try to ignore its resemblance to beef jerky, keep the area clean by applying rubbing alcohol during each diaper change, and keep it dry by sticking to sponge baths. Use newborn diapers, which have a semicircular cutout at the waist to prevent the stump from being rubbed, and call your pediatrician if you notice signs of infection such as redness in the surrounding skin, a strong odor, a yellowish fluid, or fever.

Circumcision Care

You have a little boy. He's perfect. And content. And snuggled into your arms, enjoying a peaceful snooze, as you lay in the hospital recovery room. Then an OB-GYN wanders in and offers to hack off the skin around his penis with a butcher knife. (Well, she probably won't use those actual words, but that's what you'll hear.) Your significant other visibly winces, grabs his progeny from your arms, and runs screaming out of the room. (Well, he probably won't actually do that, but he'll want to.)

The circumcision decision is a toughie, and the experts aren't making it any easier. The American Academy of Pediatrics is currently neutral on this topic, so the call is yours to make. If you decide to have your son cir-

QUICK TIP FROM DR. NIED

After your son's circumcision, the doctor will apply petroleum jelly and wrap gauze around his penis. During every diaper change for the next three days, you should check the area and apply fresh petroleum jelly either with gauze directly on the penis or onto the front of the diaper. Talk to your pediatrician if you notice bleeding or signs of infection such as strong-smelling discharge, swelling, or ongoing redness. The area is usually quite red the first couple of days and may even look yellow as new skin forms. Also check for wet diapers within eight hours of the procedure.

cumsized in the hospital, as we did, you'll feel like ripping your new mom heart out as the doctor wheels your unsuspecting son away. And it won't get any better when they return with him in tears. But he'll doze off as soon as he hits your arms, and you'll cope by silently begging the gods of long-term memory to omit this little event from your son's personal files.

Nail Care

Your newborn lays her head on your chest, gazing contently at your shoulder, just as five tiny daggers rake across your skin. You bolt upright and realize her nails could really use a trim. Check your baby's nails from day one and keep them short to prevent scratches on your chest or her face. The nurses should assist you at first, but once you arrive home you're on your own. And between her squirming and itsy-bitsy nail size, the trimming process isn't easy. After my first aborted attempt, where I was devastated by drawing blood on the tip of my four-day-old son's index finger, I swore off baby nail care forever. But things did improve. After watching my husband do it for a few months, I eventually tried again and got the hang of it. You will too. Try clippers, scissors, or a baby nail file and see which works best for you.

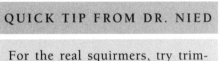

QUICK TIP FROM DR. NIED

For the real squirmers, try trimming their nails when they're taking a bottle or sleeping.

Diaper Changing

FROM:	**Elena Miguela**
TO:	**Carrie Russell**
SUBJECT:	**The Baby Poop's About to Hit the Fan**

I swear Andres is faking incompetence so I'll let him off the hook. He must be. We're talking about diapers, for Pete's sake. First, he put one on Nina backward while he was watching the news. Then he attached one so loosely it fell off during her nap (and resulted in the now infamous crib sheet surprise).

Today, he put on one of the newborn diapers she outgrew weeks ago. The poor girl looked like she was wearing a baby G-string,

---

Haven't changed a diaper since baby-sitting back in high school? Never fear. Here's the lowdown, from the great disposable versus cloth debate to the surprisingly simple but effective changing table. Plus, for the diaper-changing-challenged among us, there are step-by-step instructions that make crib sheet surprises a thing of the past.

The Great Diaper Debate: Disposable Versus Cloth

Okay, I admit it. Disposable diapers have to be one of the least environmentally friendly products on the planet. With that said, they sure make life easier for a new mom. They're a snap to put on your infant, they keep everything where it should be, and you just throw them out when you're ready for a new one. That would be about eight to ten times a day in the early weeks.

Cloth diapers are your other option. These are the old-school solution, the diapers our parents wore when they were babies, so we know it can be done. And you can feel good about adding a little less crap (literally) to the earth's landfills. A cloth diaper is attached with a safety pin (yep—that's what those are intended for) and worn under a diaper cover. When dirty, you can either wash them yourself or use a diaper service, depending on your budget. Just keep in mind, washing them yourself means an extra half hour of dirty diaper duty every couple of days (because we're talking about eight to ten changes a day, remember) in those bleary-eyed weeks of early momhood.

I greatly admire moms who go the cloth diaper route. I think of them as the same women who gracefully decline all pain medication during childbirth and make their own organic baby food. I have friends and family who fall in this category, and they are my heroes. Best of luck with your diaper decision.

For the Disposable-Diaper-Changing-Challenged Among Us

Follow these simple steps and you'll be diapering like a pro. (Sorry dads, no more excuses to shirk diaper duty.)

Step 1: Undo the little sticky tabs and pull down the front of the diaper so you can assess the damage. If the diaper is only wet, you can whip it away willy-nilly. If your baby has filled her pants (that's number two, people), keep your wits about you and take it slowly. While it's still under the baby, use the diaper to collect most of the poop. Then stealthily pull the diaper out from under your baby, closing it into a ball and securing it tightly on itself using the sticky tabs to minimize leakage and save space in the diaper pail.

Step 2: Wipe the diaper area (love that euphemism) with a wet wipe or dampened cloth, holding your baby up gently with one hand around both ankles. For boys, be sure to clean under and around the scrotum. Sure, it's funny at first, but soon you'll be oblivious. For girls, wipe from front to back to avoid infections in the vaginal area.

Step 3: Grab your clean diaper and locate the back—the side with the tabs. Lift your baby up and slide the back of the diaper beneath her. Then lay her gently on it, adjusting the positioning until you're ready to fold up the front half.

> **QUICK TIP FROM DR. NIED**
>
> For an older or particularly squirmy baby, keep an engaging toy on your changing table and let her play with it only during diaper changes. Rotate the toy often to keep her interested.

Step 4: Fold up the front of the diaper and adjust the positioning so the front and back are even at the waistline and the sides are even at the hips. Apply the sticky tabs to the front of the diaper so it's secure enough to hold without cutting into your baby's skin anywhere. Make sure the ruffled edges around the legs are pulled out.

That's it! You're ready for the trenches.

The Real Reason Safety Pins Exist: Conquering Cloth Diapers

There are a few different approaches to cloth diapering, but the most common is the triangle shape. Here's how it works:

Step 1:   Fold the cloth diaper in half to create a triangle. Lay your baby on it, with the tip of the triangle pointing down between her legs.

Step 2:   Fold the tip of the triangle up and lay it on her belly.

Step 3:   Fold in the two sides of the triangle so they cover the tip on your baby's belly.

Step 4:   Stick your safety pin through the layers to secure the diaper. Be careful not to go completely through the inner layer so you don't stick your baby or yourself.

QUICK TIP FROM DR. NIED

To avoid diaper rash, apply petroleum jelly or A+D ointment during each diaper change. If the area begins to appear irritated, use a diaper rash cream containing zinc oxide to create a better barrier. If you change your infant's diaper frequently, baby powder is not necessary.

Step 5:   To avoid seepage, always put on a diaper cover.

Diaper Rash

Once a rash appears, treat it by giving your baby some air time. That's right, we're talking about a diaper-free situation. Even ten to fifteen minutes before each diaper change will help, but the longer the better. This, of course, poses some risks, but you can minimize them by laying towels under your child. Once your baby's free-willy period is over, apply diaper rash cream and put on a new diaper. If the rash lasts longer than a couple of days, call your pediatrician.

The Surprisingly Simple but Entirely Effective Changing Table

Don't be fooled by those overstuffed changing tables in the baby furniture catalogs. Just a few items need to be within reach during diaper changes. Everything else can be stowed in nearby drawers or a closet. Changing table essentials:

- Diapers (disposable or cloth)

- Wipes
- Petroleum jelly or A+D ointment
- Diaper rash cream with zinc oxide
- A toy to keep your child distracted
- A change of clothes, if necessary (Don't leave your baby on the changing table unattended even for a nanosecond to grab clean pajamas. Get organized first, then bring her to the table. You never know when that first rollover will occur.)

Bathing and Infant Massage

From Alicia's journal:

After Luke's bath tonight, I casually pulled him out of the infant tub. No big deal. Then he squirmed. And wriggled. And slowly but surely, slipped. Brad, seeing my struggle, bounded over and dove toward us with his arms outstretched like a wide receiver making a desperate attempt at an overthrown pass. And just as his hands reached us, Luke flopped down into them. And smiled.

Can you get an ulcer in one night? I think I have one. And I'm officially going back to sponge bathing until Luke can step into a bathtub by himself.

Learn bathtime basics and infant massage techniques to keep your child clean, calm, and content.

Supersuccessful Sponge Baths

Give your baby daily sponge baths until her umbilical cord falls off, typically between two and three weeks after birth.

Essential supplies:

- Bowl or small bucket of warm water
- Soft washcloth and baby towel
- Rubbing alcohol for the cord area and mild baby soap
- Baby brush

Step 1: Face time.   First, dip your washcloth in warm water and clean your baby's face without soap. Gently wipe from the inside to the outside of each eye, then wipe the rest of her face and the outside of her ears. Don't forget to wipe behind her ears as well, and don't try to clean inside her ears or nose.

Step 2: Body beautiful.   Add the baby soap to your washcloth and clean the rest of her body, avoiding the cord area. Make sure you clean in the folds of her skin, around the genital area, and between her toes and fingers.

Step 3: Soapy baby mohawk, here we come.   Shampoo your baby's head, even if she has very little hair. This helps prevent cradle cap—a common newborn skin condition that resembles dandruff.

Step 4: Buffing and brushing.   Towel-dry her, making sure skin creases like the neck and underarms are moisture-free, clean the cord area, and put on a fresh diaper and clean clothes. Brush her hair if you're one of those lucky parents whose child has hair to brush at this stage in the game.

Infant Tub Baths

Once the cord stump has fallen off and healed, your child is ready for the baby tub. Plan to bathe her in the tub every day or two. You'll basically follow the steps outlined above, with these exceptions:

The tub: The baby tub should be filled about halfway with warm water and placed in a secure spot. Many parents place the tub in their kitchen sink so it won't move.

The posttub chaos: Before the bath, lay your towel next to the tub. There's nothing trickier than transporting a wet, squirming newborn from the bath to the towel. During this short journey she'll scream maniacally, her arms will flail wildly, you'll be convinced you're going to drop her, and just as you're about to lose it, she'll settle gently into the towel. Granted, this chaos lasts about three seconds. But somehow it seems like at least ten. Brace yourself and keep that towel close.

Baby Massage for Beginners

A cuddly massage is a perfect way to bond with your newborn, stimulate growth, and even aid digestion. And don't be intimidated by the dozens of infant massage videos on the market; no masseuse training is required. If you're gently stroking your child's arms, legs, feet, hands, or shoulders, you're giving her a massage. For more direction, try this approach:

Step 1:   Place your infant on a blanket or soft towel laid out on your bed or the floor. If you're inspired, put on some quiet music and rub a few drops of baby oil or non-perfumed massage oil on your hands.

Step 2:   Start at your baby's stomach. Place your hands flat on her tummy toward the left side of her rib cage. Gently pull them across her belly to the right side and then back to the left. Repeat this a few times.

Step 3:   Next, move to her shoulders. Put one hand on each shoulder and gently stroke down her body following along her legs to her feet. Gently rub each foot and toe.

Step 4:   Go back to her shoulders and stroke down each arm. Gently rub each hand and finger.

Step 5:   Lay your baby on her front. Rub her back, pulling slowly from her shoulders down her body to the backs of her legs. Finish by stroking her back side-to-side.

Step 6:   End by wrapping her in a towel and holding her closely. Newborn snugglin' fun.

If your child seems overstimulated, uncomfortable, or annoyed by your first attempts at massage, don't give up. She may need time to get used to the new sensations or you may just need to catch her in a better mood. Try again another day; she should eventually become receptive.

When to Call the Pediatrician

"Is it me, or is Madison making a weird sound?"

"What sound is that? Her breathing?"

"No, seriously, her breathing sounds weird. Do you think she's hyperventilating? Or could she have asthma?"

"If you want to bring her to the pediatrician again, I'm happy to drive over with you. They're probably wondering why they haven't seen us in two days anyway."

"Very funny. Okay, let's go."

|•|

Your baby probably won't have to battle anything crazier than a runny nose during her first few months, but if you have any questions or concerns about her health, call your pediatrician. Contact your doctor immediately if your newborn exhibits any of the following conditions:

- Fever (rectal temperature of 100.4 degrees or higher)
- A rash that develops on your baby's body beyond your typical diaper rash
- Rapid breathing or difficult breathing
- Vomiting
- Diarrhea
- Unusual, inconsolable crying

Breast Feeding and Bottle Feeding

Everything You Need to Know for Feeding Success

"I'm off to the day care center, and I'm not feeling very subtle." Talia carefully maneuvered past her husband with a bag on each shoulder and the infant carrier hooked over her right arm. "I know this breast pump carrier is supposed to look like a briefcase, but I don't think it's fooling anyone. And I can't wait until the security guys in our lobby try to search it."

|•|

Sometime during pregnancy it hits you—your body isn't just yours anymore. Sure, it still transports you around town, holds its own on the treadmill, and appreciates a little lovin'. But now it has become something completely different—a carrier of new human life, a walking incubator, a mom. Well, if you thought pregnancy was wacky, just get ready for breast feeding. Check your personal space and modesty at the door, tell your significant other he's got some sharing to do, and open your mind to the real reason you've got breasts. (Hint: It's not just to look cute in a tank top.) Oh right, these things actually do something useful. Wild but true.

This chapter helps you decide whether breast feeding is right for you, and if you choose to breast-feed, it walks you through every step—from getting started to secrets of success and common traps to avoid. You'll

65

also get the lowdown on pumping, weaning, and offering bottles so you're prepped and ready for feeding success.

Breast Feeding: To Do It or Not to Do It

FROM:	**Iris Kaplan**
TO:	**Danielle Mitchard**
SUBJECT:	**Nine months pregnant and feeling booby**

Just got back from my breast feeding class, and haven't been this boob aware since I tried on my first bra in eighth grade. Matt came along to "offer moral support to his pregnant wife," but I know he was secretly just hoping for some juicy cleavage footage in the instructional video.

Actually, still debating the whole nursing thing. (Why is it called nursing anyway? I'm picturing myself decked out like Florence Nightingale—starched hat, white comfort shoes—attempting to wedge my baby's head inside the unbuttoned top of an RN uniform circa 1950.) Anyway, we'll see how it goes when the little guy makes his grand entrance next month. At least after the class today, I know the football hold has nothing to do with the NFL.

There are lots of benefits to breast feeding, for both baby and mom. And the American Academy of Pediatrics recommends it for the first year. However, it's important to make the decision that's right for you. Every mom I know has approached this issue thoughtfully and with care. You will too, and you should feel great about the decision you make.

Many women take to nursing easily and with no looking back. Others have challenges. Some women have problems with postdelivery complications or milk production. Others experience baby-specific obstacles such as ineffective latching on, newborn medical concerns, or refusal to feed by the breast. And some women simply choose to bottle feed from the beginning for personal reasons.

When you decide to forgo nursing, whether it's day one or month twelve, don't let this choice affect your confidence as a mom. Women often report feelings of guilt when they move to bottles, and this doesn't help anyone. Whatever you decide to do about breast feeding, you will care for your baby beautifully, feed him nutritiously, offer him excellent health care, and he will thrive. Disclaimers and pep talk aside, here's an unbiased, no-pressure comparison of breast feeding versus formula feeding:

Breast Feeding

Benefits for baby
- Boosts the immune system
- Reduces the risk of SIDS, ear infections, pneumonia, allergies, asthma, juvenile diabetes, diarrhea, and other ailments
- Has been correlated with slightly higher IQ scores
- Is digested more easily than formula, potentially reducing the risks of gas, upset tummies, spit-up, and constipation

Benefits for mom
- Burns about 500 calories a day, so you can fit into the old jeans faster
- Helps the uterus contract and regain its original size sooner
- May help reduce the risk of breast cancer, ovarian cancer, and osteoporosis
- Stimulates the production of prolactin and oxytocin—hormones that assist in bonding and help manage stress
- Saves cash (formula generally costs $15 to $40 a week)
- Can offer a special dynamic between mom and baby as you share feeding times

Formula Feeding

Benefits for baby
- Given recent improvements, formula almost replicates mother's milk (Most pediatricians believe it's a good if not perfect alternative.)
- Takes more time to digest so your baby feels full for longer periods between feedings
- Provides close bonding moments with dad and other relatives who can now feed the baby

Benefits for mom
- Allows others to help with feeding, so you can sleep longer or leave the house without pumping or nursing first
- Can be a convenient alternative when you return to work
- Is easy to do in public places (Some women are masters of public breast feeding, casually nursing their infants while chatting with friends over coffee. Others find nursing on the run a bit awkward. Assess your own comfort level on this one.)
- Allows you to eat and drink anything
- Can offer similar moments of bonding (You don't have to be physically attached to enjoy the snuggly fun of feeding times.)

QUICK TIP FROM DR. NIED

If you're undecided, I recommend giving breast feeding a try. Even if you only nurse a short time, you and your baby will reap the health benefits during that period.

Breast Feeding Step-by-Step

From Julie's journal:

Women have been doing this forever. My body is literally designed to make it happen. Cooper was born instinctively knowing how to suck. It's like Mother Nature made everything so obvious that even a completely exhausted brand-new mom couldn't screw it up. And yet somehow I'm not getting it. My positioning feels like unintentional postnatal yoga, and the latch-on process is bordering on comical. Must locate miracle worker lactation consultant pronto before Cooper starts requesting a wet nurse.

There are five steps to effective breast feeding: get in position, establish latch-on, feed until your infant is full, break the suction, and burp your baby. (If only it was as easy as it sounds.) Here's what you need to know to master each part of the process.

Get in Position

First, get comfortable. Sit in a supportive chair, prop up your feet, put your nursing pillow in place, and remember not to lean toward your baby. He should be pulled up against you to minimize back and arm strain. There are three common breast feeding positions; pick your favorite:

Cradle position: This is the classic hold, the one you've seen in photos since the first time you wistfully flipped open a parenting magazine. Hold your newborn belly to belly with you in a horizontal position, so he faces your breast without having to turn his neck. His little butt can rest in the crook of your arm with your hand supporting the back of his head. Use a nursing pillow to keep him in the right position without straining your arm or back, and use your other hand to cup your breast as he latches on.

Football hold: You have to think a male pediatrician came up with this one, but it can work very well. Picture a running back cradling a football under his arm as he sprints down the field. Now substitute yourself for the football player and your hungry infant for the pigskin. And no, sprinting is not required—although that would be impressive. In this position, your baby reclines along your side, face up. His mouth is just under your breast and his feet are behind you. He should rest on a pillow at your waist level with his left side pressed against your right side or vice versa. Your arm circles under him, supporting his back, and the back of his head rests in your hand. This position works well if you have large breasts, if you're recovering from a C-section, or if your baby is small. It can also be helpful if your baby isn't latching on well because you can see his mouth and reposition him as necessary.

Side-lying position: Think of this as the lazy-mom position, or more accurately the sleep-deprived-and-justifiably-exhausted-mom position. You don't even have to get out of bed. You lie on one side with your baby pressed flat against you, belly to belly. Wedge a pillow behind him to keep him in place, and rest his head in the crook of your arm. Your other hand will cup your breast to help with latching on. This can be a great way to feed while in a nearly asleep daze, but correct positioning is often challenging. Some women love this hold; others never take to it.

Establish Latch-On

Once you and your infant are settled into a comfortable position and he's facing your breast, you're ready for takeoff—I mean, latch-on. Make a C shape with one hand and use it to cup your breast so the nipple juts out a bit. With your other hand, pull your baby's head toward your breast and gently push your nipple against his lips. At this point, thanks to the handy rooting reflex innate in newborns, he should open his mouth.

Timing is key here; wait until your baby's mouth is open really, really wide and then pull it quickly around your nipple. If his mouth is only partway open when it hits your nipple, the latch-on will be painful for you and he won't get much milk. Not a good scenario. Wait for the right moment, and then make it happen. When you hit this just right and your baby's wide open mouth surrounds your nipple, you've got latch-on! And this is big. Some new moms require multiple lactation consultants, a mountain of precariously wedged pillows, and a dozen failed attempts before this moment arrives. You know it's a good latch-on if your entire nipple and most or all of your areola (the pigmented circle surrounding your nipple) are inside the baby's mouth and he's sucking with a consistent, strong pull. You may notice his ear or jaw moving rhythmically—another sign of effective sucking.

> **QUICK TIP FROM DR. NIED**
>
> If your baby simply isn't in the mood to latch on, take a break for several minutes, relax, change positions, and then give it another try.

Will this hurt? Do you really want to know? Okay, honestly—it depends. Some moms report pain-free breast feeding from the beginning. But don't be surprised if latching on and initial sucking are somewhat painful the first couple of weeks until your nipples toughen up. It shouldn't be excruciating, and it shouldn't hurt after about thirty seconds. If the pain persists, your baby likely needs to latch on to a larger portion of your areola. And while tough nipples probably weren't on your New Year's resolution list, you'll be happy when you get them. If you have continuing problems, don't take it personally, don't think you ended up with one of those faulty noneating babies, and don't let the frustration get to you. The lactation ladies can usually put you on the right track.

Feed Until Your Infant Is Full

You're in the perfect position, and your baby's latching on like a champ. Now what? You can't see how much milk he's consuming, and there's no bell that rings when he's had enough. How long should you let him breast-feed on each side? Like so many fun parenting questions, there's no right answer for this one. Some babies suck harder and get their fill in ten to fifteen minutes a side. Others seem content to suck quietly forever. Ideally, your newborn will pull his head back when he's done on one side. Watch for this signal and then switch. If he never offers a signal, you should be safe to change sides after about twenty minutes. Over time, you'll learn how long your baby needs to be satisfied.

Break the Suction

If your baby latches on incorrectly or you're ready to switch sides and he seems permanently affixed, you'll need to remove him from your breast. Whatever you do, don't just start pulling him away. The suction created by his mouth is stronger than you think, and I don't need to tell you ripping a suction cup off your nipple won't feel good. Nudge a finger between your baby's lips and your breast until your feel the suction release. Then pull him away pain-free.

> **QUICK TIP FROM DR. NIED**
>
> Nurse on both sides during each feeding to maximize your baby's caloric intake. The early milk, called foremilk, is thinner and satisfies thirst. The later milk, called hind milk, offers higher caloric and nutritional value. Your nipples may feel tingly or your breast milk may spurt a bit when your hind milk is let down. Your baby needs the hind milk from both breasts, so try to make the switch before he poops out.

Burp Your Baby

After nursing on each side, pat your baby on the back until he burps. This might accompany a little spit-up, but you'd see big-time spit-up later if you didn't burp him. There are three burping options:

The shoulder lean: Hold your baby upright with his head lying against your shoulder. Your burp cloth should be under his head to avoid that carefree spit-up-on-the-shirt look.

The little sitter: Support your infant in a sitting position facing sideways on your lap, allowing him to lean slightly forward onto one of your hands while you pat him on the back. Again, keep the burp cloth handy.

The tummy down: Lay your child tummy down on your lap so his head and legs drape over slightly, then pat him on the back.

Secrets of Success

From Shanna's journal:

Ellie is breast-feeding well and gaining weight like Renee Zellweger plumping up for the next Bridget Jones sequel. No problems there. But I'm not so thrilled with the process. I keep hearing nursing is not supposed to hurt, but that's either one of those new mom urban myths or proof I'm doing something seriously wrong. As far as I can tell, it's about as pain-free as a bikini wax. And there's a reason I don't wear bikinis anymore.

While the likelihood of a perfect latch-on is often as much luck as strategy, there are some things you can do to smooth the way to breast feeding success. And by breast feeding success, I mean (1) your child is eating enough to thrive, (2) your back and arms aren't killing you, and (3) your nipples don't feel like they've been exfoliated with sandpaper.

Boppy to the Rescue

If you're even thinking about breast feeding, get a nursing pillow. It'll be the best $30 you ever spent. While nursing in the hospital, I spent half my time wedging pillows under my son and repositioning myself. The pillows inevitably slipped, I got very little support, and my arms ended up shaking from the strain. When I got home and pulled out my Boppy, breast feeding became much easier. I slipped it in place before every feeding and bada boom, bada bing—no back or arm pain: happy baby, happy mom.

Nipple Savers

You've probably heard the same breast feeding horror stories I was told while pregnant—the bleeding, chapped nipples, the crazy pain. The whole thing sounded about as appealing as giving birth several times a day just for kicks. There are, however, several proven strategies to avoid nipple abuse:

- Never let your baby feed unless he's latched on correctly. Your full nipple and all or most of your areola should be in his mouth and you should not feel pinched. Otherwise, you'll be in pain during and after the feeding.
- After each feeding, air dry your nipples for a few minutes and apply lanolin or a few drops of breast milk to protect them from chafing.
- Wear nursing pads inside your bra. They'll absorb leakage (always a good thing, unless you don't mind wandering around the grocery store with two large wet spots on your chest) and prevent rubbing against the bra fabric.
- Don't soap your chest during showers.
- Vary your feeding positions regularly, and breast-feed on the side that feels less sore first so it receives the hardest sucking. (In a perfect world you would alternate the side you start with each feeding to minimize soreness and avoid that lopsided chest look.)

Eating to Feed

You made it through pregnancy. It's time to break out the champagne, right? If you're breast-feeding—not yet. Limit the alcohol, caffeine, and herbal products, avoid smoking, and consult your doctor before taking any over-the-counter medication. And

QUICK TIP FROM DR. NIED

Don't cut back on food to drop those pregnancy pounds yet; you've got another mouth to feed out of your body. You should consume about 500 extra calories a day while nursing.

keep eating the heart-healthy food you've probably grown to despise but secretly realize is making you healthier than you've ever been. You know the drill—the wheat bread and cereals, fresh fruits and veggies, milk, cheese, and yogurt, lean beef, chicken, eggs, and nuts. Maintain your intake of iron, calcium, and folic acid, plus vitamins D and A.

Keeping Up Your Supply

In one of the many miraculous aspects of childbirth, your body will most likely produce the exact amount of breast milk your newborn needs. (If only the U.S. economy were so efficient.) However, in some cases mom's milk supply doesn't match need. This can happen because of a rare condition called primary lactation failure, because you're not eating or drinking enough, or because your body is being tricked into thinking it needs to produce less milk than it actually should. Sounds strange, but look at it this way: If you offer formula for one feeding without pumping, mistakenly stop feeding before your baby's really full, or try to artificially extend time between feedings, your body will be required to produce less milk than your baby actually wants. To keep up your supply, eat well, drink several glasses of water every day, pump if you need to skip a feeding, and try to maintain a consistent feeding schedule. When you head back to work, determine your plan of attack. You could pump during your working hours or phase those feedings out in advance. (More advice on pumping to come.)

Waking Sleepyhead

While the thought of drifting off to sleep in the middle of a great meal is hard for me to understand, many newborns do just that. They latch on well, seem to be feeding contently, and the next thing you know they're dozing in your arms. You might be tempted to leave your little sleeper in peace, but it's important to wake him long enough to eat. To keep your child awake during feedings, tickle his feet, take off extra layers of clothing so he's not snuggly warm, change his diaper, poke him gently—whatever it takes.

Success Assessment: Is It Working?

"So, do you think she's had enough?" Kate looked from her feeding newborn to her husband, who was reading beside her on the couch.

"Sure. She looks good to me," he replied, glancing up from his book. "I'd say she's full, happy, and ready for action."

Kate looked at him suspiciously. "You have no idea either."

"No idea whatsoever. But I figured if I sounded confident, you might feel better. At least give me points for good intentions."

|•|

Breast feeding is tricky because you never really know how much your baby has eaten. You may be able to feel your breast emptying, like a water balloon with a slow leak, but how can you be sure your infant is getting the food he needs to thrive? Look for these signs of breast feeding success.

Weight Gain

Your newborn will lose several ounces right after birth, but he should regain his birth weight within about two weeks. From that point until about six months of age, look for five to seven ounces a week of growth. Your pediatrician will weigh him during well-baby visits so you can track his progress.

Proof in the Pants

After week one, look for at least six wet diapers each day, and think of the first week as building up to this pace. Typically, day one your baby will have one wet diaper, day two he'll have two wet diapers, and so on until he plateaus at six wet diapers. Dirty diapers are much more variable.

Feeding Frequency

For the first few weeks, your newborn should eat about eight to twelve times every twenty-four hours, or every two to three hours.

Message left on answering machine

Hi Kelly, it's me again—phoning in for my daily report from maternity leave central. As always, I'm in the rocking chair feeding Evan. I guess I should be happy he's such a good eater, but I think my butt may have permanently merged with this chair. I'm going on six hours of feeding today alone. Does that sound crazy to you? Am I doing something wrong? Will my chest ever recover? I sense a lifetime of underwire bras in my future. Call me back!

Traps to Avoid

Breast feeding is part art, part science, part luck. It may go smoothly from the beginning; it may be a series of challenges. Minimize your risk of complications by learning to avoid a few common traps.

Mom As Pacifier

Some babies take to breast feeding beautifully—too beautifully. They love being at the breast so much they want to stay there all the time. This enthusiasm may be flattering, but it's not good for your baby, and it's really not good for you. If your child fusses unless he's at the breast for extended periods every day, talk to your pediatrician.

The Breast Feeding Martyr Syndrome

Some moms have such a hard time achieving proper latch on, they endure excruciating pain while feeding their babies. I completely understand how this happens. We love our newborns madly. We survived pregnancy and childbirth and now, to further prove our love, we suffer though nipple torture to provide that magical breast milk. Don't go down this path. There's no need to be a martyr; a good lactation consultant can put you and your baby on the road to relatively pain-free feeding.

Nipple Confusion

Nipple confusion is a weird name for a common breast feeding trap. It's much easier for babies to guzzle from artificial nipples than to suck effectively at the breast. So, if bottles or pacifiers are introduced before breast feeding is well established, problems can occur. Your baby may try his lazy man's version of sucking while on the breast, and it won't work. The subsequent frustration could lead him to reject nursing altogether.

> **QUICK TIP FROM DR. NIED**
>
> To avoid nipple confusion, wait two to four weeks to introduce bottles or pacifiers. Once breast feeding is rolling along, you should be fine.

The Slippery Slope of Supplementing

If your baby isn't gaining as much weight as expected, your doctor may suggest supplementing with formula after breast feeding. Make sure you've considered all your options before starting down this slippery slope. Supplementing may seem like an easy short-term solution, but it can make feeding complicated long-term.

I speak from experience on this one. At my son's four-week check-up, he had lost a few ounces in two weeks rather than gaining the eight ounces we expected. This was a shocker; I thought the breast feeding had been going well (although in retrospect, he was pretty darn skinny). The pediatrician recommended I start supplementing with two ounces of formula after each nursing session. This quickly beefed him up, but within a few weeks my milk supply took a nosedive. I met with a different pediatrician who told me I could pump eight times a day to get my supply back up. That's right: *pump eight times a day*. You'll be shocked to learn this pediatrician was a man—someone who'd never had motorized suction cups strapped to his nipples.

If you have yet to experience the joy of pumping, you won't fully appreciate the absurdity of this request. There's probably a perfect mother out there somewhere who would have happily succumbed to this torture, but fresh off recovery from childbirth I didn't have it in me. I pumped a few times a day plus regular breast feeding. This process lasted about three more months, and then I finally stopped the madness—a bit bewildered by how my breast feeding experience ended up so different from what I had hoped. To prevent this cycle of diminishing supply, talk to your doctor about all your options before starting to supplement. And some women don't mind pumping as much as I did, so keep an open mind until you give it a try for yourself.

Going Solo

Yes, you'll be the only one *actually nursing* your child, but you should still request assistance with overnight feedings. Particularly as your maternity leave draws to a close, you need your energy back and your head clear. If there's a significant other in your parenthood picture, enlist his help. You can pump in advance (never fun, but definitely worth a full night's sleep), and leave bottles of expressed milk in the refrigerator. He could use the bottles to offer overnight feedings on the weekends even during your maternity leave, and you can create a rotating schedule once you're back at work. At minimum, recruit him to provide the late evening feeding so you can head to bed early.

The Fun Stuff: Engorgement, Leakage, and Mastitis

"They look good, but this is ridiculous." Charlotte examined her inflated cleavage in the bathroom mirror, wincing as she adjusted her bursting-at-the-seams nursing bra. "I can't decide if I feel more like a maternal feeding machine or a porn star."

|•|

If you thought breast feeding seemed a little wacky at first, brace yourself for the fun-filled side effects and potential complications.

Engorgement

When your milk first comes in, your breasts may feel tender, swollen, and uncomfortable. Don't worry, these are simply signs you're ready to nurse. (Sure, a nice little "Go for it!" voice in your ear would have been fine, but who are we to question Mother Nature?) The engorgement should diminish within a few days. In the meantime, try these engorgement pain busters:

- Breast-feed every two to three hours.
- Pump as necessary to relieve extra pressure, potentially even pumping a few minutes before breast feeding to soften the breast and make latch-on easier.
- Feed first from the less tender breast, but empty the tender breast completely.
- Use a warm compress to improve circulation before feedings and an ice pack to relieve discomfort after feedings.

- Wear a good nursing bra day and night.
- Massage the tender area to loosen plugged ducts.
- Talk to your doctor about taking a mild pain reliever.

Leakage

If it wasn't hard enough to maintain your dignity as you maneuvered your pregnant belly into work like a barge captain steering into dock, get ready for nipple leakage. Life just doesn't get any weirder than this. Bottom line, while nursing your breasts will leak. There's no stopping leakage, only strategies for minimizing it and hiding it from the world. To minimize leakage, feed or pump regularly. To hide it from the world, I've got three words for you: Stockpile nursing pads. You'll need a lot. Use them after every feeding or pumping session and change them when they get wet to prevent infection.

And the leaking doesn't stop when you hit the sack; you'll most likely need to wear nursing pads under a comfortable bra even while sleeping. Yes, your significant other, who's already bitter about the baby's front row seating to your ample new mom chest, even gets the double-layer block in bed. Parenthood does involve sacrifices. Then again, he'll never have to push a several-pound person out of his body. Overall, not a bad deal.

Mastitis

Your little one has mastered the perfect latch-on, and he's gaining weight like a star. All appears to be perfect in your breast feeding world. Then you notice inflammation on one or both breasts, possibly involving swelling, redness, tenderness, or pain. You may also have an infection, which can be associated with fever, chills, and muscle aches. These symptoms are signs of mastitis, and you should consult your physician immediately

QUICK TIP FROM DR. NIED

You're most likely to get mastitis during the first month of nursing, and it's more likely to occur if you have cracked or bleeding nipples, if there are long intervals between your breast feeding sessions, if you miss a feeding, if you're feeling stressed, or you're overly run down.

because you may need antibiotics. If so, be sure to complete the full course prescribed by your doctor.

To avoid mastitis, apply lanolin to your nipples after feedings to prevent cracking, breast-feed regularly, try to minimize stress, and rest as much as possible. I know, rest with a newborn at home—who am I kidding? Just rest when you can and hope for the best. If possible, recruit a family member, friend, or baby-sitter to assist with newborn care. Try not to sleep on your stomach to avoid compressing your breast tissue.

The Wild World of Pumping

"A rhythmic motorized sound? No, I don't hear it," Celia frantically flipped off her breast pump and continued with the conference call. "Let's get back to those sales projections."

"Well, I tried," she thought to herself. "So much for multitasking."

|•|

If you're coming to the end of your maternity leave, want to empty engorged breasts, or hope to build up your milk supply, your love–hate relationship with the breast pump is about to begin. It's a great tool, allowing breast feeding moms to express milk that can be given to their infants by anyone, anytime. Your baby receives the nutritional benefits of your breast milk while you're away at work, running errands, or getting some needed zzz's. On the flip side, pumping is not the most fun you'll ever have. Here's the lowdown, from choosing a pump to expressing, storing, warming, and feeding breast milk.

Choosing a Pump

Pumps come in two varieties: electric and manual. Electric pumps use a motorized suction to mimic baby's sucking. You hold the plastic breast shields over your nipples and let the motor do the work. They take about ten to twenty minutes for each pumping session depending on the amount you need, and they cost between $125 and $350. Manual pumps are cheaper but can require between thirty and forty-five minutes of squeezing by hand. If you're going to be pumping regularly, they're less effective.

Once you've selected the type of pump you want, ask your doctor for specific brand recommendations. You can then purchase, borrow, or rent a pump. Many hospitals offer pumps for rent or sale.

Expressing Milk

You have your pump; it's go time. If you're away from your baby, try to pump when you would normally breast-feed. Put the breast shields in place and get to work. To facilitate letdown (initial milk flow) during pumping:

QUICK TIP FROM DR. NIED
Before buying a pump, consider how you'll use it. Will you be pumping at work every day? If so, it's probably worth the higher cost to make your pumping as efficient as possible. Just planning to pump occasionally during maternity leave? A manual pump may be fine for your needs.

- Pump at about the same times each day
- Massage your breasts gently before you start
- Drink a glass of water
- Look at a picture of your baby
- Visualize flowing water or milk (Funny, perhaps, but helpful.)

No, pumping is not a Kodak moment. And it's not what you imagined when you dreamed of having a child. Pumping may be uncomfortable, and it may seem mind-numbingly slow. You may suddenly empathize with dairy cows everywhere. But the process is worth it in the end. Try to distract yourself and the time will pass.

A friend of mine, who works at a women's nonprofit, locks her office door, straps on her phone headset, and makes business calls while pumping twice a day. She holds the breast shield on with one hand and takes notes with the other. If she doesn't have calls to make, she uses the pumping time to review paperwork or catch up on e-mail—anything that can be accomplished with one hand. This is the kind of multitasking working moms everywhere have mastered. To save time, pump both sides at once.

Storing the Milk

Store your expressed breast milk in plastic milk storage bags or bottles with tight caps. You should refrigerate the milk as soon as possible, but it can be kept at room temperature for four to six hours, so don't worry if you have to stick your newly pumped storage bag of milk in your office drawer during a quick meeting. After the meeting, move the milk to a refrigerator or an insulated container with ice packs until you're ready to head home.

You can refrigerate expressed milk for up to forty-eight hours or freeze it up to three months, and your freezer should be set at or below zero degrees Fahrenheit. Label and date each container and try to use the oldest first. Store small amounts, like two or three ounces per container, for easy thawing and minimal waste. The stuff is like liquid gold once you've gone through the effort of pumping, and you won't want to waste a drop. Once you've thawed a container of frozen breast milk, use it within twenty-four hours.

Warming and Feeding

Breast milk can be served in a bottle once it's warmed to room temperature. Don't warm it in a microwave, which can create scalding hot areas, and don't use a stovetop, which denatures the proteins. Instead, thaw frozen breast milk by leaving it in the refrigerator for twenty-four hours, submerging the container in a bowl of warm tap water, or using a bottle warmer.

Weaning

FROM:	Robin King
TO:	Angela Martin
SUBJECT:	Just call me the wean machine

All is well on the baby front. It's hard to believe, but the school year begins in a few weeks. Working motherhood here I come! Which reminds me, I better start weaning Brayden soon, or my mom will have to smuggle him into our teacher's lounge every day for emergency feedings. I would love to see Stan the uptight assistant principal try to nonchalantly eat his turkey sandwich with a nursing session underway at the next table. I guess I could also pump, but that seems equally crazy given my schedule, so weaning starts today! Wish me luck—

When to wean? Your choice. The American Academy of Pediatrics recommends breast feeding for a year. Some working moms set this as their goal, some aim for six months, and others phase out breast feeding during maternity leave. Consider your work environment and schedule. Some jobs allow for relatively easy pumping; in others it's nearly impossible. You could also breast-feed mornings and evenings and let your child care provider give your baby formula during the day. Your supply may diminish over time, but this approach can offer a happy balance for a while. When you're ready for weaning, approach the process gradually to make the transition easier for your baby and reduce your risk of engorgement. Brace yourself for some temporary mood swings; the hormonal shifts that occur during weaning can have a real impact on your emotions.

> **QUICK TIP FROM DR. NIED**
>
> When you start weaning, cut one daily feeding per week, substituting a bottle or sippy cup for the breast. So, if you're nursing five times a day, plan to reduce these feedings over five weeks. If your baby is fighting the change, you can extend this period, perhaps cutting one feeding every two weeks. Make sure the rest of your child's routine remains consistent to create a sense of security. Be patient and keep trying.

Bottle Feeding 101

"All right, I'm going to make you an offer," Holly announced to her three-month-old daughter who was clearly opposed to the plastic nipple pressed against her locked lips. "Take this bottle now, and I'll never dress you in that scary ruffled outfit from Aunt Ruth. You've got to admit, that's a decent trade-off."

|•|

You may bottle-feed exclusively from day one, offer an occasional bottle while breast feeding, or introduce bottles for the first time when you're ready to wean. Here's a quick overview so you can bottle-feed with confidence.

Selecting Bottles

You'll need about five to eight bottles, depending on your tolerance for washing them daily. I recommend buying only the nine-ounce sizes, and all major brands typically work well. Start with the stage one nipple size designed for newborns and work your way up to stage four nipples over the next few months. As a new mom, I didn't realize there were larger nipple sizes, and I continued using the stage ones for months. When a friend finally clued me in, we were ready for the stage fours, which allow a greater flow of liquid. Miraculously, our bottle feeding times were cut in half.

Selecting Formula

The formula companies have seemingly figured out how to locate every pregnant woman on the planet within moments of conception and moms planning to adopt soon after, so you've no doubt already been hounded by dozens of samples and direct mail pieces. Despite this desperate attempt at brand building, the major brands are FDA regulated and similar in nutritional and caloric value. You should typically start with a cow's milk–based formula with iron, which most closely approximates breast

QUICK TIP FROM DR. NIED

You've possibly heard of the recently released formulas with DHA and ARA, the long-chain polyunsaturated fatty acids found in breast milk that may help promote visual and brain development. These formula options have received a lot of press, but the studies to date have been inconclusive and the American Academy of Pediatrics has not yet provided an endorsement. Ask your pediatrician for more information if you're curious.

milk. If your baby has a sensitive stomach or you want to avoid dairy, there are soy-based options as well, but you should consult your pediatrician before switching to a soy-based formula.

You'll need to choose between premixed, concentrate, and powder. Premixed is the most convenient but most expensive. Powder is the cheapest but takes more time to prepare. (Granted, mixing powder with water isn't rocket science, but as a new mom you have every right to cut out even this step to make your life easier.) Concentrate falls in between. Any of these options is fine, but if your baby has trouble tolerating one you can try another.

Preparing the Bottle

Premixed formula is easy—open, pour, and serve. The concentrate and powdered varieties are also a snap, even for the culinarily challenged:

Step 1:   Brand-new bottles and nipples should be sterilized in boiling water for six to eight minutes. After regular feedings, a cycle in the dishwasher or cleaning with soap and hot water are fine unless you're using well water. If so, boil the water each time.

Step 2:   Add tap water and the recommended amount of powdered formula or concentrate. Serving portions are always provided. Shake the bottle to mix.

QUICK TIP FROM DR. NIED

Don't be misled by the various infant water offerings at the grocery store; tap water in any U.S. urban area is fine for infants, and it doesn't need to be boiled before use. If you're using well water, talk to your pediatrician.

Step 3:   Serve the prepared formula within forty-eight hours.

Introducing the Bottle

I remember the first time I tried to give my son a bottle. I prepared the formula, carried him to the couch, and quickly realized I had no idea what I was doing. Yes, I know bottle feeding seems like a no-brainer—stick the nipple in the baby's mouth and wait for him to guzzle. I tried this, and he

QUICK TIP FROM DR. NIED

Even if your positioning is perfect, your baby may refuse the bottle because he prefers the comfort and coziness of breast feeding. This challenge is overcome with patience and a little creativity. Keep trying and, if necessary, ask your significant other or a friend to help. Infants are often more receptive to bottle feeding initially from a non–breast feeding source. After some transition time, you should be happily bottle bound.

wasn't the least bit interested. I attempted different angles. I wiggled the bottle around. I held it perfectly still. No dice. Feeling like a complete idiot (bottles don't come with instructions because they assume any moron can figure them out), I called an experienced mom friend who gave me the bottle feeding lowdown.

Turns out, those artificial nipples are not the choking hazards they initially appear to be. Yes, they look huge next to your baby's mouth. And, unless you have bionic nipples, they dwarf their human counterparts. But they can be inserted more deeply than you might suspect—until the outer, rounded area rests on your child's lips. Petrified by the choking potential of the huge plastic nipple I was wielding, I wasn't putting it in my son's mouth deeply enough.

Feeding Guidelines

Wondering how much to feed, when? Use these guidelines for direction, but always listen to your child's cues. Infant hunger can vary significantly each day, and some babies simply eat more or less than these averages.

Age	Feedings Per Day	Typical Ounces Per Feeding	Total Ounces Per Day
Birth–4 weeks	8–12	2–3	14–20
1 month old	5–8	3–4	15–26
2 month old	5–8	4–6	20–32
3 month old	4–6	4–6	20–32
4 month old	4–6	4–6	22–32
5 month old	4–6	5–8	22–32
6 month old	4–5	6–8	20–32*
7 month old– 1st birthday	4–5	6–8	20–30*

*Liquid intake may actually decrease at this stage as your baby eats more solid food.

How do you know if your infant is getting the right amount of formula? Signs of too little formula intake include decreased urine output, poor weight gain, and loose, wrinkly skin. Signs of overfeeding include excessive weight gain (there's a shocker), colicky pain with feedings, and spitting up after feedings. Consult your pediatrician if you notice any of these symptoms.

QUICK TIP FROM DR. NIED

- If you're planning to return to work within a year, I recommend introducing a bottle at two to three weeks and offering at least one every few days. Don't stop for a few weeks, and don't wait until month two to start.
- To minimize the risk of choking, don't prop a bottle in your baby's mouth.
- To minimize the risk of tooth decay, don't let your baby fall asleep with the bottle.
- To minimize the risk of ear infection, don't let your baby lie flat while taking a bottle.

Your Postchildbirth Recovery Guide

From Postpartum Blues to Really Big Boobs:

The Real Deal

Meredith was not unhappy. She was fairly clear on that. But her position on the happiness meter had no obvious correlation to the tears that flowed freely down her cheeks every few hours per their own will. After one out-of-the-blue crying jag, she tried to rationally take stock of her mental and emotional state:

1. She was completely obsessed with staring at her five-day-old daughter.
2. Her cute chest had seemingly doubled in size.
3. She was more tired than she'd been since that bad case of mono in the ninth grade.
4. Her mother-in-law, with whom she'd never spent any one-on-one time, was now sitting across the kitchen table from her, waiting expectantly "to help" in some as yet undetermined way.

Okay, she thought to herself. *I'm still getting used to this new mom thing. But I have a perfect child. On balance, this is the best week of my life.* She smiled, just as the tears began again.

|•|

You did it. You survived first trimester nausea, less-than-thrilling maternity wear, labor, and delivery—or the emotional roller coaster of adoption. You have a one-of-a-kind story to tell the grandkids, and after all the waiting—your child is here. You're a mom. It's utterly miraculous. It's completely overwhelming. You're giggling like a mad woman one second and tearing up the next. You're in awe of the perfect little person in your arms, and then convinced you have the only baby on earth who can't latch on to save her life. There are myriad emotions you know you'd be feeling right now, if not for the sleep deprivation–induced fog that has taken over your world.

During those wacky first few weeks of motherhood, just hang in there. Your body will recover before you know it, your head will clear, and even your emotions will return to normal. (That obsession with staring at your child may be permanent—but don't worry, we can all relate.) Learn what to expect and, if you have a significant other, get tips for thriving as a new parent team from the beginning.

Your Emotions

From Rachel's journal:

> I never considered myself a drama queen. Even during pregnancy, I was impressively easygoing. I can say that now, because things have changed. I see a baby food commercial on TV and feel completely overcome by new mom joy. I walk outside, note the nice weather, and start to cry. Roger fails to comment when I finally wash my hair, and I consider leaving him. Two hours later, I run over and hug him because he looks so sweet giving Cole a bath. I'm just hoping this is all hormonal because the drama is exhausting. Which reminds me, I could really use a nap . . .

Here's the full scoop on those infamous postpartum emotions.

Baby Blues

We've all seen the buttoned-up, middle-aged newscasters somberly discussing postpartum blues. In their recent revelations, we've learned new moms are not always blissfully radiant as they leap out of bed for the third feeding of the night but, in fact, can be emotionally strung out during those early weeks. Thank you, intrepid truth tellers, for this shocking update.

From my perspective, any woman who gives birth *without* becoming slightly overwhelmed should make the evening news. You're beyond pooped, your breasts have morphed into flesh-colored water balloons, and you're suddenly juggling 24/7 newborn care with your own physical recovery. And those early days after adoption can similarly wreak havoc on your emotions. The sleep deprivation alone would send any sane person into tears, so new moms deserve a grace period when occasional outbursts should be encouraged by all. Don't be surprised by some irrational crying, some apathetic moments, or an occasional urge to run wildly from the house and never look back. And at those times, just repeat these words to yourself like a mantra, "This is a postpartum thing. It's totally normal, and it soon will pass."

If you continue to feel depressed, have a loss in appetite, are unable to care for your baby, or can't sleep, you should ask for assistance from the people you trust—your doctor, your significant other, a relative, or a friend. These are signs of more serious postpartum depression, and those close to you will be more than happy to help.

Baby Joy

While the baby blues have gotten lots of press lately, baby joy is the other, less publicized side of new mom emotions. Yes, you may be teary those first few days or weeks. But you'll also have moments of complete happiness, of overwhelming gratitude. It's being in love—the distracting giddiness, the physical longing—without the bickering over the remote control. Inevitably something small will trigger your emotions: noticing the squiggly perfection of your newborn's ear or the tactile pleasure of her body slowly breathing, fully asleep on your chest. Then your love for this tiny person grips you like an obsession, like a hunger. It is joy, but more—also gratefulness, reverence. You clutch your infant to your body and yet miss her; you are nostalgic for small moments even as they pass. And you completely understand why this parenthood thing, despite the occasional craziness, is so darn popular.

New Mom Paranoia

Here's another one for the no-you're-not-psychotic, many-of-us-feel-this-way category: new mom paranoia. While I had never actually cared for an infant before my son was born, I assumed if the rest of the world could do it, so could I. Then he was born. Good-bye, naive confidence. Hello, new mom paranoia. Suddenly it seemed the risks were everywhere I looked. I could easily trip while carrying my son down the stairs, inadvertently allow him to wriggle off the changing table, drop his wet little postbath body, secure his car seat straps incorrectly, or let him fall asleep on his stomach. There were so many possible baby calamities; it seemed highly unlikely I could avoid them all.

I didn't mention this to anyone at first because I realized my fears were irrational. But finally, after three straight nights of baby catastrophe nightmares, I had to talk to someone. I explained my fears to my husband, a very rational man, who offered the perfect support. ("You've been so successful at descending stairs up to this point in your life, I don't think you're going to start tripping just because you're carrying a newborn." Or something like that. And all of this with a straight face.) The good news is we all survived. And you and your baby will too. Countless infant care warnings come at you as a new mom; heed them but don't be overwhelmed.

Baby Bonding

Some women feel attached to their infants from the moment they meet. It's like their maternal instincts kick into autopilot, and the baby bond forms automatically. For many others, bonding is a gradual experience, a slow-but-sure-getting-to-know-you period. Don't worry if your personal bonding process is on the slow track. It doesn't mean you're a bad mother or emotionally stunted; just give yourself time.

Gradual baby bonding makes perfect sense when you think about it. At birth, babies can't give you a hug, they can't slap you high five, they can't even smile. They offer no visible sign of emotional connection, aside from sleeping better (occasionally) when you hold them. They're lovable, kinda like really cute stuffed animals are lovable, but stuffed animals don't scream bloody murder several times a day and require hourly diaper changes. So keep the faith; bonding will occur eventually. One day you'll pick up your child and realize infant attachment has taken over your mind and body. And at that point, there's no turning back.

The Emotional Adjustment to Time at Home

As a working woman, you're used to structured weeks, built-in socialization, and a certain sense of predictability. You get up Monday mornings, you watch Katie Couric flirt with Matt Lauer, you briefly imagine it's you flirting with Matt Lauer, you down a cup of coffee and a bagel, you head out the door—you know the drill. We have our routines at home and in the workplace. And while routines often get a bad rap, they are, if nothing else, comfortably familiar. You put in your time at the office; you leave with a sense of accomplishment; you enjoy your time off; and the cycle continues. There's something soothing about the consistency of working life.

Your child's arrival throws that sense of predictability and structure out the nursery window. Newborns (if they could laugh, which they can't) laugh in the face of schedules and consistency. They sleep when they're tired, they wake when they're inspired, they eat in random and seemingly endless cycles. Their care is a true 24/7 experience; no client lunches out, no vacation time accrued.

This is not to say newborn care isn't fun. Caring for your infant will be, in many ways, more fulfilling than any deal you've closed, any promotion you've earned. It's primal fulfillment, a full mind-body-and-emotions kind of satisfaction. Just don't be surprised if your new mom schedule requires some matriculation time. The first few weeks at home, in particular, give yourself a break as you adjust to life completely outside your known routines.

Your Body

FROM:	**Sibby Klein**
TO:	**Hilary McFarlane**
SUBJECT:	**Back at home with little Miss Avalicious**

Came home from the hospital yesterday with Ava, and I'm surprisingly pain-free. Of course, the doctor has me taking so many painkillers I probably wouldn't notice if my arm caught on fire. I'm slightly terrified to phase out the pills—there's probably some serious soreness lurking below this comfortably numb feeling.

And have I mentioned my to-die-for new mom cleavage? Why do women spend money on implants? Just have kids, ladies! You get the big boobs for free! I'd be frolicking around the house in a bikini right now if I didn't still look five months pregnant.

One day you have a several-pound person hanging out in your belly—content in her warm, swishy mama world. The next day, she's swaddled and snuggling in your arms, a bit jostled by the joyride she's just experienced, but overall ready for action. In between, your body gets to do its thing. And it is an incredible thing. A beautiful thing. A miraculous thing. And a thing that's going to make you worship the day Tylenol was invented.

Your Muscles

I've never run a marathon, and I can assure you I never will. But from what I hear about those races, childbirth has a similar effect on your body. And it's not just the body parts that come in direct contact with your baby. Don't even try to figure out how your hamstrings, shoulders, neck, and arms became sore from childbirth; it all happened during the blur of pushing. Just feel better knowing, like an athlete recovering from a major race, you've got to give yourself time to recoup.

Take all the pain relievers the nurses will give you, request daily massages from your significant other or a sympathetic friend, and remember to answer this when asked if you need anything: "Hot bath. Now, please." Steaming hot baths, in the days after childbirth, can't be described in words. They feel incredible on sore muscles, but it's more than that. It's the complete silence you experience after letting your ears fall below the water line. Silence to a brand-new mom is like a drug in itself. You'll emerge thirty minutes later a completely different person.

> **QUICK TIP FROM DR. NIED**
>
> Years ago, there was concern postpartum bathing could increase risk of infection, and some new moms are still told to avoid baths for six weeks. Don't be misled by this outdated advice; we now know postpartum bathing is fine. Talk to your OB-GYN for specifics.

Your Chest

Look out Pamela Anderson! In a fun bit of irony from Mother Nature, your chest is fuller, rounder, and bouncier than ever before during the days you are least likely to welcome any sexual advances. You notice the change the first day you're home from the hospital or birth center. You step out of the shower, nonchalantly look in the mirror, and do a slow-motion double take, staring in shock at your newfound cleavage. It's like someone snuck in overnight and switched your chest with Angelina Jolie's—like you've been duped by a teenage boy's digital photography editing, only this is the real thing. You call in your significant other and enthusiastically gesture toward yourself like a *Price Is Right* model pointing out a shiny new car. He spots your cleavage and replies with a simple, "Oh. Wow."

If you choose to breast-feed, your full breasts will continue, though they won't remain as over the top as they are when your milk comes in initially. Invest in a few good nursing bras and pads for support and leakage prevention. Wearing a bra at night will help minimize soreness and prevent milk overflow in bed. (And there's nothing like a big ol' nursing bra under a big ol' nursing nightie to make those bodacious breasts feel a tad less sexy.) If you choose to bottle-feed, wear a supportive bra with nursing pads the first couple of days while your milk flow diminishes and take a pain reliever if necessary.

Your Postbaby Belly

Your baby's born, so you can pull out your favorite jeans and torso-baring T-shirts. Right? Well, not exactly. In the days just after childbirth, your stomach will be smaller. That's the good news. But by smaller, we're talking about second trimester smaller. All things being relative, this still feels like a major improvement, so pack early stage maternity clothes when you head to the hospital, and you'll feel great when they're loose. You should catch sight of your pre-pregnancy belly in the next few months, and even earlier if you're genetically gifted. Be patient and keep those jeans handy.

Your Crotch—I Mean Vaginal and Perineal Areas

Before going through childbirth, my biggest fear (besides the pain itself) was the potential damage left in the baby's wake as his head and eight pound, ten ounce body emerged from between my legs. I'm no biology expert, but it just didn't seem likely that any part of my body could withstand that kind of pressure without some permanent repercussions. Urination seemed like it would be painful, sex out of the question, spin class a sick joke.

But here's what I learned: Initially you're sore. The first few days you wear ice-filled maxipads that have to be one of the more awkward things ever invented. And for about a week you sit on a plastic, air-filled doughnut that's only slightly less ridiculous. I remember trying to subtly shove my doughnut under a blanket on the couch when friends came by to visit. I gently sat on it, casually making conversation so nobody would notice my hands frantically maneuvering the lumpy blanket beneath me. It wasn't my smoothest moment. But after that first week, you rediscover the joy of sitting doughnut-free. Several weeks later you rediscover your sex life. I used childbirth as my permanent excuse to skip spin class, but I hear that's fine too. Bottom line: Your body is truly miraculous, and it can recover even from something as crazy as birth. (And if you have a C-section, you don't even have to deal with the plastic doughnut phase.)

Your Seemingly Infinite Period

Yes, we are talking about *that kind* of period—the kind maxipads were invented for. Postpartum, you'll experience a menstruation-like phase called lochia that generally lasts between four and six weeks. It's not fun, but feel better knowing you just had a carefree nine-month break from tampons. While steady bleeding is normal, contact your health care provider immediately if you suspect hemorrhaging. Signs include a noticeable odor, extremely heavy blood flow, or blood clots.

Your Uterus

After your child's birth, you'll feel postlabor contractions as your uterus returns to its prebaby size. Until this contraction process is complete, your larger-than-usual uterus is one of the major culprits behind your inflated belly. The afterpains may be minor, or they may take your breath away. They should fade within a couple of days, and in the meantime they're a great excuse to keep the pain reliever going.

Keeping Your Body (and Brain) on Autopilot with Little to No Sleep

The early weeks with a newborn can be a sleeping free-for-all, but they pass quickly. You will get some shut-eye, usually in bursts of about two or three hours. And you should try to take naps when your baby naps, although you may not get much quality rest from these little reprieves. Your body will be in constant baby-alert mode, tensing at the sound of any whimper from the nursery. By my son's fourth week, I remember saying to my husband, "Okay, I give up. If this sleep deprivation is going to last until he's a toddler, I just won't make it. Somebody find the receipt because this kid's going back."

But here's what I didn't know then: Multiple nightly wake-ups generally phase out by the time babies are two to three months old. At that point, your infant should be stringing at least six hours together, and while 10:00 P.M. to 4:00 A.M. or 8:00 P.M. to 2:00 A.M. isn't exactly a dream night's sleep, it is tolerable. Once you get those crucial six consecutive hours, your energy returns, your head clears, and your desire for living magically reappears. So, hang in there and know your life without sleep is temporary.

When to Call Your Doctor

"Well, this is a weird one," Nadia announced to her sister. "Now the big toe on my left foot is tingly. Do you think that's a postpartum thing?"

Her sister stared at her and tried not to laugh out loud. "You never know. Let's give the doctor another call. It's been almost two hours since that urgent earlobe cramp."

"Very funny," Nadia continued. "Seriously, can you hand me the phone?"

|•|

Typically, you leave the hospital or birth center on the road to a healthy recovery, with no need to see your doctor or midwife until your postnatal checkup weeks later. If you have any health concerns, however, don't hesitate to call. And if you experience any of the following symptoms during your first few weeks at home, contact your health care provider immediately:

- A temperature higher than 100.4F or any fever accompanied by chills
- Significant swelling in your feet or hands (Some swelling postpartum is normal.)
- Blurry vision
- Severe headaches
- Consistent pain in your stomach or legs
- A sharp, burning sensation during urination
- Extremely heavy or strong-smelling vaginal bleeding
- Consistent tenderness or red splotches on your breasts
- Stitches from an episiotomy that come undone, smell bad, or swell

Recovering from Childbirth Without
Killing the Love of Your Life

"Honey, that washcloth is getting way too close to her umbilical cord stump," Mark said nonchalantly as he walked by. "Who knows what that thing would do if it got wet?"

Jessica slowly lifted the washcloth, pulled a strand of unwashed hair from her stinging, dead tired eyes, and turned to him. "First, I had the car seat straps too loose. Then I wasn't supporting her head correctly. This morning, I wasn't patient enough as she repeatedly refused to breast-feed. Now the washcloth is too close to her umbilical cord stump? One more piece of constructive criticism on my parenting techniques, and I swear I'm going to hand this child to you and take a hot bath that lasts until my maternity leave is over."

|*|

If you have a significant other, the first few weeks of parenthood can create some fun-filled relationship challenges. You're both tired, you're operating in unknown territory, and you're still adjusting to your new roles.

Parents Who Sail Through the First Few Weeks

Everyone reacts differently to new parenthood. Some couples pull together, maintain complete patience with each other even at 4:00 A.M., and display a surreal calm during infant meltdowns. When asked how things are going, they cheerfully describe this beautiful new phase in their relationship and the glory of each day shared as a family. These people are to be avoided at all costs and officially considered ex-friends. (Kidding. Just don't feel badly if you have a few less-than-glorious moments yourself.)

The Rest of Us

The rest of us muddle through the first few weeks, doing our best and knowing that we, like soldiers who survive an intense battle, will feel closer in the end. As your body recovers from childbirth and your hormones make a mockery of your previously stable emotions, just advise your significant other to steer clear when necessary and provide bihourly body massage as requested. And don't be surprised if your loving partner has inexplicably strong opinions about mundane decisions like how tight to pull those little sticky tabs on diapers. My husband and I had healthy debates on several such issues weekly, despite the fact that neither of us knew what the heck we were talking about.

On the other end of the spectrum, your significant other may start out in the distant dad category. Think of new parenthood as the ultimate road trip, and we all know how guys hate to ask directions. While most men these days recognize they should share the infant care load, some seem to be mired in uncertainty. I'm guessing some are afraid of making a mistake, some don't want to look stupid, and some are probably faking fear to avoid diaper duty.

The Really Good Parts

Of course, there will be moments when you feel closer than ever before. Your child's birth or adoption is unforgettable. Snuggling in bed after a crazy day of infant care can be as much fun as your first date. Laughing together as your impossible-to-surprise significant other gets a face full of baby pee is precious. Standing next to each other, watching your newborn sleep peacefully in her crib, is a perfect moment.

Thriving As a New Parent Team

Just be prepared for some wackiness as you both adjust to your new roles. Develop a plan for sharing the infant care load from day one. Ask for help when you need it. Let him do the hefty lifting as your postpartum body returns to normal. Talk things out if tension builds. And try to be patient with each other. You will figure out how tightly to fasten the diapers, and then you've got the rest of your lives to hold hands and share your child's extraordinary development.

You Have Three Months (or So) Off Work: Enjoy It!

Making the Most of
Your Days at Home

Networking with New Moms,
Creating Structure for Yourself, and More

Ashley was convinced her five-week-old son Max was the most perfect male on earth, with the possible exception of Denzel Washington. Despite her complete baby love, she was feeling restless at home, and she assessed the potential causes of her maternity leave blahs:

1. No exercise since second trimester when chest still fit into sports bra.
2. Winter weather makes requisite layers of baby fleece overwhelming barrier to leaving the house.
3. Friends at work all day (i.e., no social interaction except for Max, who's not exactly a conversational dynamo).
4. Breast feeding, spit-up, and dirty diapers make daily life akin to high school biology class on bodily functions.
5. Three words: No sleep. Whatsoever.

Then, channeling her prebaby problem-solving skills, she developed a sanity-saving plan of attack:

1. Force self to leave house despite frigid weather. First errand: Find megasports bra big enough for hormonally enhanced chest.

2. Find new moms somewhere. Establish friendships. Immediately. (How? Ask sister-in-law in Seattle, seeming queen of neighborhood moms. Questions: What do moms talk about? Where can I find them? Will recipe exchanges be required?)
3. Consider signing up for cooking class in desperate attempt to finally move beyond frozen Healthy Choice dinners and acquire recipes to share with new mom friends.
4. Build fun at-home activities into daily schedule. Maybe mom-and-baby yoga tape? Max is the little Zen master—so incredibly *in the now*. And given his flexibility, he'll put my Lotus pose to shame.

|•|

Your baby's arrival brings a challenge you probably haven't faced since eighth grade summer vacation: unstructured time to fill. During maternity leave, don't let diaper changes and feedings take over your life. Connect with new parents, create a sense of structure that feels right, and take full advantage of your boss-free reality. Build in activities that will keep you energized, excited, and mentally stimulated. And, if all goes really well, plan some baby-free nights out with your significant other or a friend.

Become a New Mom Magnet

"How old is your baby?" Amanda asked the woman behind her in the grocery store line. "He seems like a great sleeper."

"He's six weeks old, and he does love to sleep. How about yours?"

"She's three weeks old today," Amanda replied, adjusting her daughter's blanket in the infant carrier. "So, you're on maternity leave?"

"I am. The free time has been great, but I'm definitely missing adult conversation."

"Me too. Would you like to meet for a walk sometime?"

"Sure, how about Friday morning in the park?"

|•|

Being a new mom is strangely like freshman year in college, new student week. You're thrilled the long-awaited experience has arrived; you're scared of feeling completely lost, and you're in awe of the nonchalant seniors who know exactly what to do. Of course, that was years ago. Since then, you've successfully made your way in the working world and learned to socialize without beer bongs. Now you're ready to apply your impressive set of life skills to motherhood.

For those of you who mastered corporate networking, you'll breeze through making new mom friends. Some of us were a little less impressive at industry events. ("Do we have to *actually talk* to all these people we don't know?" "I don't think so. Let's just hang out here and look for the best haircut in the room. I'm getting a trim tomorrow, and I need some new ideas." "Sounds good.") And we have to revert back to the new student approach without the keg handy to facilitate mingling. As my loving husband put it one day when I was bustling out to my new mom fitness class, "Don't forget your opening, 'Hi, I'm Paige. Will you be my friend?'"

> Amidst the tumultuous sea of colleagues and kiddies, it can be isolating. That old, "I have no time for me" may be a trade-off worth making again and again, but the little hidden truth no one talks about is this: You still want women friends to talk to. But really good, smart ones, who understand your life, and know important stuff . . . and who generally make you feel sure that you're doing all of this just fine.
>
> **MARISA THALBERG,**
> *Founder and President of*
> *Executive Moms*

Any new moms in your current friend file? Give them a call. Haven't called them in months, maybe years? No problem, you've now entered a secret society that renders all past actions meaningless. You know each other. You have kids. You have everything in common. First among your friends to head into parenthood? Finding new moms is easier than you think.

Ask Friends for New Mom References

To use a little business lingo, friends of friends are great prequalified leads. You're likely to get along, and you can trust each other. Ask around, get some numbers, make a few lunch plans, and go from there.

Sign Up for a Mom-and-Baby Activity

Call your local gym, library, music schools, or park district; they should offer activities for new moms with infants in tow that range from postpartum yoga to baby music and bubbles. When the infants are really young, these classes are thinly veiled excuses for new moms to hang out together, which is exactly what you want. When the children are a few months older, they actually get something out of the activity as well. Try to get involved during your maternity leave when you really need the socialization, and many classes are scheduled evenings and weekends to accommodate working parents as well.

Make Some New Mom Dates

Meet a new mom in the bookstore? Invite her over for a play date. Chat with a new mom at your gym? Suggest meeting for a walk. Fresh from the prebaby world, you may feel like a stalker. At first. Just keep in mind the golden rule of motherhood: We all need each other, and none of us has time to fart around being shy while perfectly good friend opportunities drift away. Try it once, and you'll quickly realize new moms are always happy to make plans. Stranger danger is for the kids.

Start or Join a Play Group

Yes, working moms do play groups. If fact, you really should. Although your life may feel like a whirlwind of activity, the crazy schedule can make those all-important mom friendships a challenge. Commit to regular gatherings with the kids so you don't miss out. Maternity leave is the perfect opportunity to make connections and get a play group going. You're meeting new moms through friends, in classes, and around town (a newborn is an instant conversation starter even while waiting in line for your decaf latte), and you have actual downtime to fill. If you're going back to work part-time, look for moms with compatible days off so you can continue to meet every week or two. If you're returning full-time, connect with other full-timers and make a weekend afternoon plan that fits your schedules without feeling over-booked—even if it's just once a month.

Organizing a play group is as easy as it sounds. Recruit a few moms, ideally with infants around the same age so you can share advice and experiences each step of the way. A bigger group is often better if you can find enough people; inevitably one or two women will miss each get-together, and you don't want to sacrifice your bonding time because a couple of kids have the sniffles. And no, your babies don't need to be old enough to *actually play*; these groups are primarily support systems for the moms at first. Over time, the kids will become mobile and enjoy the social interaction as well. New play groups looking for members often post notices in pediatrician offices, parks, community centers, or even local publications, so keep your eyes open and ask around.

My first play group evolved from a conversation after a postpartum fitness class at our gym. I was chatting with a mom about something deep and meaningful like the weird way baby pee often ends up all over your child's back as if the diaper were nothing more than a funnel designed to maximize urine distribution. And as we wandered out, toting our infants, she asked if I wanted to get together sometime for coffee. (Have I mentioned the beginning of new mom friendships feels a lot like blind dating?) In a shocking moment of postpartum foresight, I suggested a weekly get-together—maybe with some other moms from the class. She loved the idea, and over the next couple of classes we recruited five other moms with compatible schedules. Initially the babies dozed in their infant carriers during the "play groups," but eventually they crawled, cruised, and ran around together. And just as importantly, we moms became very close and supported each other through everything from introducing solids to feeling calm and confident in our new roles. The lesson? Be proactive during those early weeks at home, and you'll benefit from a long-term support system.

Attend a Breast Feeding Support Group

If you're nursing even a short time, these groups—often sponsored by local health care centers or lactation consultants—can be a perfect opportunity to get out of the house and meet new moms during maternity leave. And breast feeding challenges are not required. You'll still benefit from questions asked by others and free new mom networking.

Double-Date with Other New Parents

Hesitant to suggest solo plans with a woman you barely know? Start with a group activity like an early dinner or brunch and get the dads involved.

Bond Online

When all else fails, there are message boards. Many have been created for parents of babies born the same month as yours so you can share questions and advice. There are dozens of websites that offer virtual mom communities, but you could start with babycenter.com, parenting.ivillage.com, urbanbaby.com, or executivemoms.com. There may even be a site for moms in your area; do a quick search online for local offerings.

Create Your Own Sense of Structure

**Tuesday Messages Left on
New Dad's Office Voice Mail**

11:00 A.M.: Hi honey, it's me. I know we just talked an hour ago, but I wanted to touch base. How did your meeting go? I'm still waiting for Ethan to wake up. Just relaxing here, enjoying the downtime. Call me!

12:30 P.M.: Hey babe, it's me again. Ethan had a good feeding, and now he's taking another nap. So, I'm back to relaxing. Just taking it easy. Appreciating the time off work. That's about it. Call me!

1:40 P.M.: Yes, it's me again. Ethan is still asleep, and I have to be honest. All this downtime is driving me insane. Everyone keeps telling me to relax, but if I get any more relaxed my brain will turn to Play-Doh. Am I addicted to work? I used to live for the weekends; why can't I function without a 9:00 A.M. to 5:00 P.M. schedule? And with all this downtime, why can't I get anything accomplished? Wait, there's Ethan waking up. Call me!

You're a new parent, and your long-awaited maternity leave has arrived. The freedom is exhilarating, and then it hits you. You've got a non-speaking (albeit adorable) person as your newfound companion and a heck of a lot of time to fill.

Work, if nothing else, brings structure to your life, and maternity leave can stretch ahead with no daily schedule and no lunch breaks. While this flexibility can be fun, basic infant care can take over your days if you don't create some structure for yourself. You know how energized you are during busy days at work. Time flies by and you run on adrenaline. You're juggling several things and suddenly you're in the zone.

After your baby is born, you *should* take it easy. Spend relaxed afternoons in your pj's snuggling with your child. Sleep when you can and enjoy the downtime. When you're feeling well and ready for action, try these strategies to get back in the zone while at home.

Get Committed

Make a few commitments and record them in your date book or PDA. Your goal: knowing you have *some* plans as you flip through your calendar. Sign up for a mom-and-baby activity. Set up a regular play date with friends. Plan to visit the in-laws Thursday afternoons. Whatever works for you. If you have commitments, your time starts to take shape, and that's always reassuring.

Make an At-Home Plan

At work, you probably used some kind of plan to organize your time—a weekly list of things to do. Bring this approach home for inspiration during your maternity leave. When your baby is napping or you're leaving the house, whip out your list. You'll accomplish more and enjoy the cheap thrill of checking things off each week. And don't have unrealistic expectations; feel great if you take a shower *and* complete something off your list in one day. Include:

On-the-run stuff: Organize your outstanding errands, from picking up birthday gifts to stocking up on diapers. Lots and lots of diapers.

The fun stuff: Include personal goals like following your mom-and-baby yoga DVD a couple of times a week. If you don't get in the habit of doing this stuff now, you never will.

Keeping in touch: Make a list of thank you notes to send (always a major accomplishment after baby's arrival), friends and family to call, or work colleagues to e-mail. Newborn naptimes can be perfect opportunities to catch up.

Home projects you've never had time for before: You always wondered who had time to try those do-it-yourself ideas on the home decorating shows. Now you know.

At-home essentials: At work, your performance is always appraised. For good or bad, you get feedback even on the little things; your contributions are at least *acknowledged.* At home, your efforts are often way under the radar. (Something you'll never hear: "Wow, these plates are really clean! And look at the way they're stacked in the cabinet, perfectly aligned and conveniently located next to the clean bowls. Genius! Honey, you've exceeded annual dish management expectations by over 15%. Keep this up and by next year you could be Senior Dishwashing Executive!") We all know our contributions at home are labors of love, or at least survival, and they may never earn us any glamour or obvious gratitude. Give yourself some credit by including household essentials in your weekly plan.

Don't Let the Cast of *Passions* Become Your New Best Friends

At first, it is secretly thrilling to have access to the bad daytime TV you haven't seen since you were home from work with the stomach flu last winter. Then the novelty wears off, and you realize nothing makes you feel like more of a shlep than knowing the plot twists on all the soaps. When you're home, it's easy to flip on the TV as a distraction, another voice in the room. Just try not to let weeks vegging on the couch replace leaving the house.

Avoid Inertia

FROM:	**Carolyn Fleming**
TO:	**Amelia Cohen**
SUBJECT:	**Just call me spud. I'm not leaving this couch anytime soon.**

I adore Henry, but this maternity leave thing is such a tease. Three months off sounded amazing. I pictured long walks with the stroller, gorgeous fall weather, and meeting friends for coffee. I counted down the days until my freedom would begin. Then my leave did begin. And weeks passed. And I never left the house. It was way too complicated—getting Henry fed and dressed, watching in horror as he spit up all over his clean clothes, getting him dressed again, packing up the diaper bag, pulling on his bunting, and dragging him and the stroller down three flights of stairs to the street. (Clearly, we forgot about the kid angle when we bought this third floor condo.)

Now the fall weather has turned cold, my friends have stopped calling, and I'm resolved to spending my remaining days off hanging out on the living room couch. Wish me luck getting Henry out the door when we have to start day care.

The Maternity Leave Challenge

I'm convinced inertia is the most powerful force on earth. And when you're caring for a newborn, the path of least resistance exists inside the walls of your home. I know new moms who stayed home throughout their maternity leaves to avoid the hassle of packing their babies up for a walk or an afternoon with a friend. And I understand this reaction. It is a production to put on the baby fleece, pack up the diaper bag, shlep the infant carrier, wrestle with the stroller, and get yourself and your baby out the door. But still—you really, really should. If you don't get in the habit of making plans, inertia will win out.

The Don't-Let-Inertia-Hold-You-Back Pep Talk

Staying home all the time, while easy, can also lead to feelings of isolation, lethargy, and boredom. You miss out on opportunities to meet new moms, show your baby the world, and get some exercise. (Shlepping the infant carrier, if nothing else, is great for the upper arms.) Occasional days at home can be rejuvenating. Consecutive weeks never leaving the house are usually depressing. If you're sensing the drag of inertia, make a plan and try to motivate. You'll be amazed by how energized you feel after something as simple as a thirty-minute walk or lunch with a friend.

Take Advantage of Your Boss-Free Reality

"Guess what I'm doing today," Alyssa said to her husband as he got dressed for work.

"I don't know. Spending a heck of a lot of time feeding Olivia in the rocking chair?"

"Well, yes. That too. But last night I had an idea. You know that 35 millimeter camera we bought last summer? The one that's been taking up space in the hall closet for months? I'm going to use it for a black-and-white baby photo shoot. Olivia can't even roll over yet; how hard can it be?"

"Worse case scenario, you have to photograph her crying. And she's really cute even then."

Get Creative During Newborn Naps

Soon after my son was born, I met a new mom who was dying for her maternity leave to end.

"I just can't handle being home all day," she said. "I can only vacuum the carpet so many times." This mentality would make anyone lose it. Maybe you used to catch up on cleaning during days off, but now you have several weeks to fill. You can do a lot more than dust the miniblinds.

You're home from work with time to yourself, at least until your infant wakes up for the next feeding. This is probably the most freedom you've had since you were in school. Remember those days, when you could take classes on everything from history to art, from biology to film studies—when a variety of interests was encouraged? Then we all got jobs, and our breadth of interests slowly narrowed as we focused on a specific field. Here's your chance to try something different again.

What would you love to try? Creating an infant scrapbook? Writing something more personal than a marketing plan? Finally reading those paperbacks you received for your birthday? Actually making caramelized pear tarts with cardamom cream? Pulling out your old guitar? Making a baby blanket—or perhaps, if you lose steam about the time I would, a lovely little baby scarf? Whatever strikes your creative fancy, this is the time to do it. Sure, it may need to be a home-based activity, but there are plenty of these to keep you busy.

Make the Most of Baby Time

But what to do with your infant when he's awake? Interactive playtime with the stacking rings is months away. If you haven't been around newborns for a while, you may be shocked by how little they actually seem to do. Sleep. Eat. Look dreamily at the side of the couch. Drift off to sleep again. You get the picture. So, how to stimulate your little one and enjoy baby time during those first few months at home?

Make like Anne Geddes.   Until your child can crawl, he's an ideal model. He's incredibly cute, he loves your attention, and he can't escape. And with a digital camera, you can have all the photo shoots you want without paying for film. Take advantage.

Pull out the playmat and mobile.   Newborns are fascinated by contrasting objects and patterns. Try not to get jealous as your baby falls in love with the dangly shapes rotating above his head.

Make some music.   Babies enjoy music from day one. Listen to your favorite CD or belt out a children's song while you're lounging together on the couch.

Get cultural.   Fill a few afternoons visiting local museums. Your baby will enjoy the outing and you'll get to look at something more interesting than the inside of your house. Just call ahead regarding stroller policies—some museums prohibit strollers during high traffic days.

Rub the skin he's in.   Infant massage can be calming, stimulate growth, and even facilitate digestion. Plus, it's so darn cute.

Do the new mom monologue.   Your infant won't be able to respond for months, but he still benefits from verbal stimulation. Narrate what you're doing throughout the day, read to him from simple children's books, and ask him questions. You may feel crazy at first, but it's so worth it.

Hit the road. (Or sidewalk.)   Walks around the neighborhood are great for your fitness and overall attitude, and newborns love the rhythmic motion and fresh air. Pull out the stroller or infant frontpack, and build regular walks into your baby-time schedule.

Try tummy time.   To minimize the risk of SIDS, pediatricians recommend putting newborns to sleep on their backs. This approach can, however, lead to underdeveloped neck muscles or slightly flattened heads. To keep your baby's noggin intact, build in daily tummy time. Simply lay your child on his belly—on the floor, on the couch, or even on your chest. Then engage him with an animated voice or sparkly toy. Most babies welcome this change in position.

Do lunch.   During the first two to three months, your newborn is as content in a restaurant as he is at home. Take advantage of his mobility and show him off to your friends during a well-deserved lunch out. He'll enjoy the change in environment, and you'll get some needed adult conversation.

Browse local websites for other baby-friendly activities in your area, and for additional ideas check out Chapter 16, "Ideal Toys and Activities for Every Infant Stage."

Plan Some Baby-Free Date Nights

From Malika's journal:

My sister called today looking for a romantic restaurant recommendation for her blind date this weekend. I asked her if the question was some kind of sick joke. The last time Robert and I tried a romantic dinner out, I was eight months pregnant and could barely squeeze into the "intimate table for two" they offered us. We probably should've requested a table for two and a half.

You're on maternity leave and you realize you haven't left the house without your baby (and his gear) in fifty-nine days. And you haven't talked to your significant other about anything *except* your baby in even longer. It's officially time to get out. By yourselves. That's right, I'm talking about a new parent date night. No significant other in the picture? Ask your sister to baby-sit and head out with a friend.

The Breast Feeding Challenge

Granted, if you're exclusively breast-feeding, the first few months it can be tricky to leave your child. A night out means advance pumping between regular feedings, and that's never fun. ("I just finished nursing him forty-five minutes ago, and I'm probably going to breast-feed him again in an hour. Do I really want to spend the next thirty minutes with suction cups attached to my chest? I don't think so.") But once you've gotten the hang of things at home, make the date night happen. He can't say it, but your child really needs parents who remember the last time they discussed something more intimate than the merits of zippers versus snaps on infant sleepers. We've all heard the scary stories of parents so passionate about their kids they gradually lost track of each other. Try to build in some couple time from the beginning—even if it's just running out for a quick dinner while your baby snoozes at home and your best friend baby-sits. I promise, she won't mind.

Baby-Sitting Budget Busters

You can always hire help, although baby-sitters aren't cheap. To save on sitters, try these parent-tested tips:

- Ask friends or relatives for baby-sitting "gift certificates" instead of store-bought gifts for holidays and birthdays.
- Join a baby-sitting co-op. For full details, check out the baby-sitting co-op guide in Chapter 7, "Living for Less and Loving It."
- Go out when you have family or friends visiting. They'll understand your need for date nights, and you can hit the town for free.
- Plan a date night schedule you can afford—once a month, every other week, whatever works with your budget.
- If no other option is available, simply bring your baby along. Perfect? No. A decent alternative to never leaving the house? You got it.

Friends, Family, Sex, and Romance

Not Necessarily in That Order

When my son was three weeks old, our friends Heather and Jason stopped by to meet him. The following five minutes went something like this.

Heather and Jason arrive and hug my husband Charlie. So far, so good. Heather spots my son in my arms and eagerly reaches out to hold him. He turns toward her, leans in, and promptly spits up on her face and new sweater. Horrified, I send Charlie off to get baby wipes and a towel. Heather stands motionless, stunned, still feigning a tolerant smile but clearly ready to bolt.

The family cat, who's always had a sensitive stomach, decides this is the moment to throw up beside the couch. We all turn toward the gagging noise in time to see her lunch hit the hardwood floor. I call for Charlie to double the wipes and get his butt into the family room. Hearing all the excitement, our dog bounds in and chases the cat up the stairs. "No!" I yell pointlessly as he barks after her and she hisses back without breaking her stride. My son, upset by the sudden commotion, lets loose his most melodramatic tears, turning a deep shade of crimson and throwing his head against my shoulder in hysterics.

At that moment, Charlie runs into the room with several dozen baby wipes and tries to remove the spit-up from Heather. Turns out, baby spit-up has the consistency of well-chewed bubblegum, and his attempts only make matters worse. She grabs a handful of wet wipes from him and slowly backs out of the room, saying, "You know what guys, we'll stop in another time, okay? He's adorable. Bye!" The next second, Heather and Jason are gone, and we're staring at each other in disbelief. Just another day in Babyville.

|•|

It's been said it takes a village to raise a child. Similarly, it takes a village (or at least a bunch of ridiculously patient friends and family) to thrive as a new parent. A newborn inevitably takes over your life, pulling you away from the outside world. Yet this is exactly the time you need your adult support system the most.

Eventually, however, it hits you. Life outside your baby's nursery has continued moving forward. You can still meet a friend for coffee. You can still enjoy a romantic dinner. You can still have sex. Right? And will you ever want to again anyway? (In a word, yes. In six words, just not for a little while.) Here's the inside scoop on relationship issues, from fun to frisky. Learn how to thrive as a couple while baby rocks your world, stay connected with old friends, manage the grandparents, and more.

Sex: Will You Ever Want It Again?

It's Saturday night, and your ten-week-old daughter is asleep in her crib. Despite your significant other's recent failed attempts at seduction using oysters, chocolate, and massage, you just watched your old *Love Actually* DVD (for the fourth time), and you're shocked to find yourself in a Colin Firth–induced mood for lovin'. You snuggle up to your guy in a way that says, "I'm not just falling asleep this time, so pay attention." He instantly takes notice, thanks the gods of romantic comedies, and makes his best move.

|•|

In the weeks just after childbirth, sex is the last thing on your mind. That much we know. But when will you be in the mood again? And what should you expect until that moment hits?

Your Body Deserves a Break Today; and Tomorrow and the Next Day

Childbirth is the most miraculous thing most of us will ever experience. Conception is miraculous; pregnancy is miraculous, and childbirth is beyond miraculous. It makes grown men weep in awe. It brings together far-flung families. It puts the rest of our lives in perspective. But it really does a number on your back. And your hamstrings. And all areas in direct contact with your baby during delivery. This is a short-term setback; your body will recover, the strain in your back will fade away, and your hamstrings will decramp. Just give yourself some time. Get through the ice pack maxipads phase, accept all the painkillers you're allowed, and take hot baths like you've never taken hot baths before. In a few weeks— maybe six, maybe sixteen—you'll be ready to jump in the sack again. And not just for those seriously needed zzz's.

Tears Typically Aren't a Terrific Turn-On

Cut to a cozy bedroom. The lights are dimmed. A bottle of champagne is chilling bedside, and a ruggedly handsome guy is waiting eagerly under the velvet duvet. A woman steps into the room, looks the guy directly in the eye, and . . . bursts into tears?

Right. As we've discussed, the weeks after childbirth tend to be a crying free-for-all. Between baby's tears and mom's tears, dad better hang tough and brace himself for some waterworks. On the upside, just like your physical recovery, the emotional melodrama is temporary. Your crazy hormones will get back in balance, you'll get some sleep, and before you know it you'll feel like your impressively stable prebaby self.

Bye-Bye, Bodacious Black Bra; Hello, Nerdy Nursing Nightie

Let's be honest here. The concept of breast feeding is really weird at first. Yes, it's good for both mom and the baby and can be a beautiful bonding experience. But it also requires us to think of our breasts, the most sexualized female body parts, in a completely new way after we've given birth. Suddenly they serve a purpose that is no longer decorative or sexual but utilitarian and practical. Expect something like this on the breast feeding front:

During pregnancy, you maintained a whimsical sex appeal by flaunting your bigger-and-better cleavage around the house—and not surprisingly, it worked. As far as you can tell, your guy's eyes never made it below your suddenly Salma Hayek–like chest to fully take in the swell beneath.

Hours after childbirth, things change. Despite your even more impressive new mom chest, your significant other is suddenly forced to the back of the line as your baby, the nurses, and lactation consultants swarm around you in a frenzy of breast feeding management. If he's lucky enough to get a peek at the cleavage, the fuzzy newborn head blocking his view inspires a secret stab of jealousy mingled with confusion. He's lost his two best friends, and he never even got to put up a fight. Of course, these emotions are quickly repressed, shoved behind the memory of getting rejected by Katie Jacobson at the seventh grade dance. Not to worry; guys are masters of emotion control. But the weirdness goes on.

Unless you're a topless dancer, you're not used to being seen unclothed from the waist up outside your bedroom. That changes too. Even in the hospital or birth center, you're supposed to pretend it's perfectly normal to have random medical students, friends, family, and flower delivery guys wander in while you're attempting to breast-feed. Suddenly it's as if you don't have breasts at all—just conveniently located bottles with skin. Maybe I'm hypersensitive, but I found this transition odd.

If you choose to nurse, you get over the initial weirdness. And yes, it can be a wonderful bonding experience. Then, right about the time you get the swing of breast feeding, your guy starts rubbing up against you in bed. And things get really wacky, for a couple of reasons. First, there's no off switch on nursing breasts. They think any stimulation means one thing: produce milk. So, there's the simple challenge of milk overflow. Second, it's nearly impossible at first to mentally transition from maternal feeding machine to sexpot. It just doesn't add up. Feel better knowing we all go through this transition. Give yourself time, settle into your new role, keep the nursing pads stocked, and eventually you'll be ready for action.

That Thing Is Going Where? I Don't Think So

Here's the unspoken fear we all have: A several-pound person just emerged from between my legs, and it wasn't comfortable. Now as a human being with a rational antipain response, why would I let anyone get within five feet of that area? (After a cesarean, you'll similarly want some space.) In the first few weeks after giving birth, sex sounds about as appealing as sticking a burned fingertip in the toaster. And you don't know when you'll ever crave toast again. But again, be patient. Eventually you'll feel your frisky old self returning. When you feel ready, give your partner the signals. Try things slowly; take time to see how everything feels. Burned fingers heal, and good toast is worth the wait.

Remember Those Periods You Missed the Past Nine Months? Well, They Found You

Not having your period for nine plus months while pregnant is fun. But you make up for those lost periods by experiencing a menstruation-like phase that lasts about six weeks after giving birth. Yep. Sorry to be the bearer of that news. Keep the maxipads handy and tell your significant other to touch base in about a month and a half.

Personal Space Never Felt So Good

One of the great things about infants is the physical affection—the warm, soft weight of your baby's sleeping body on your chest, the peaceful bundle cuddled into your arms during feedings. It's a palpable pleasure, a tangible experience of love. However, your need for romance may be at an all-time low. After twelve hours of carrying, feeding, and consoling your baby, your ideal night will probably involve two feet of extra space in bed. If you're feeling the need for space just when your significant other is trying to make his move, let him know it's nothing personal and assure him the time will come again soon.

In the Meantime, Perfect Snuggling

Yes, you may want personal space more than snuggling at times. But at other times, a good snuggle hits the spot. A hot bath, a massage, and hanging out together in bed should fulfill your physical needs during your presex phase. So, enjoy it and consider this a second courtship. You'll soon discover the baby love that takes over the bodies of all new moms provides a great distraction. It's a new type of attachment, expanding the family love, friend love, and romantic love you've experienced before. It's a buzz in itself, like the sweet high of romance, and it keeps your heart and mind full until you're ready to jump-start your sex life again.

From Cute Couple to Parents: Your Long, Strange Trip

FROM:	**Lana Schulte**
TO:	**Elaine Jesper**
SUBJECT:	**He's a keeper!**

Blind date so much better than expected. Despite his unfortunate retro name (Ward? Were his parents *trying* to get his butt kicked?), he turns out to be nearly perfect. Great smile. Good listener. Orlando Bloom hair.

Afraid to get my hopes up, but feeling really good about this one. Near-term trauma: To call him or wait? Calling would reinforce confident, forget *The Rules* attitude. Waiting for his call, while painful, may allow for innate guy need to hunt and gather. Send any words of wisdom my way.

Parenthood will transform your relationship with your significant other like nothing else.

When Life As a Couple Was Easy

You're sitting across the table from him at your favorite Italian restaurant. He asks about your job, your family, your ideal vacation destination. He really listens to your answers and laughs in the right spots. He's funny in a good way, confident but not cocky, and you realize you're obsessed with his hands. Or his shoulders. Or his mouth. You fake a ladies room emergency and secretly call your best friend to share the news: This guy is different. In a good way.

Whatever the details of your first date, it didn't include debating over whose turn it was to refill the diaper genie. My point? You fell for each other back when you were fancy-free singles living large and looking for love. It was easy. Okay, relationships are never easy, but it was *easier*. You dated, made couple friends, went to movies spontaneously, slept in when you felt like it, and had long, uninterrupted conversations about the important stuff like your aspirations and proudest moments and the most obvious implants at the Golden Globes.

Courting Conception: Parenthood's Preseason Training

Then you decided you were ready for the next step: a child. Your carefree Saturday evenings became scheduled baby-making sessions. You tried to keep things passionate, but by month six even he was faking headaches. After all that time fearing an accidental pregnancy, now conception seemed about as likely as Ashton Kutcher winning an Oscar. Then it happened. You stood together admiring the positive pregnancy test, and you felt like a new kind of team. You were closer than ever before. You were going to be parents.

When You Knew Things Were Altogether Different

You're lying back in a hospital bed with your knees pulled up like a sort of horizontal sumo wrestler. That cute guy from the Italian restaurant is supporting one of your knees and a nurse you met twenty minutes ago holds the other. Your doctor, fresh off the night shift, offers helpful commentary like, "We're going to need you to push *a lot* harder." And as the whole posse stares between your legs, it hits you—what a long, strange trip it's been since that first date. And you have a feeling things are only getting crazier.

Your Brave New World of Parenthood

Entering parenthood is like leaping together from a low-flying plane into Lake Superior. You try to holds hands going in, but there are moments when you're on your own. You're both, at different times, filled with excitement, fear, joy, and a sense of losing control. You panic just before hitting the water, but as you come up for air you realize the experience has brought you together in a new, inexplicable way. Only this rush is infinitely greater because you're creating a life together. And the adventure will be taking over your house for the next eighteen or so years.

Thriving As a Couple While Baby Rocks Your World: Six Irrational Relationship Fears More Common Than You Think

From Jane's journal:

I've finally mastered newborn care, but my libido is still on new mom hiatus. Plus, now that I'm on maternity leave, Paul is "too busy" to help with the laundry, dishes, or errands. Funny how he had the time when we were both working forty hours a week. In fact, I'm starting to suspect my lagging libido is directly related to my increasing housework bitterness. If I had a therapist, I'm sure she'd have a field day with that one.

Here's the scoop on some common relationship concerns and strategies for success:

Fear 1: My Significant Other Will Be So Horrified by My Ballooning Belly We Won't Have Sex Again Until We're Too Old to Care

Hypothetically, we know our guys should still find us beautiful as our love children flourish and our bellies take over the bedroom. But will they? And we aren't going to stand for any sympathy attraction; we need the real deal—the yes-your-massive-belly-makes-it-impossible-to-even-hug-but-I-still-find-you-ravishing kind of thing. Well, modern men are either truly sensitive or great actors. Odds are, even if you feel like a beached whale, your guy will be thrilled with your hormonally enhanced cleavage and pregnancy glow. (Okay, seriously, it's all about the cleavage.) And if you stay active, there's no reason you can't maintain a happy sex life while pregnant. Your first trimester nausea may slow things down, but the second trimester pregnant woman's libido is no urban myth. I don't really care why—it's probably hormonal—but I like to believe it's

Mother Nature's little gift for surviving morning sickness. Even third trimester, your growing belly doesn't mean you have to put the kibosh on your sex life. I don't suggest hooking up anywhere near a mirror. Let's face it, watching a seriously pregnant woman making love must be a wacky sight, even if it's you. But there's no reason to think your love life has to take a nine-month break.

Fear 2: My Significant Other Won't Think of Me the Same Way When I Become a Mother

Here's the deal with this concern: It's absolutely true. He won't think of you the same way. But this is not the June Cleaver generation—his new view of you will be even better. ("She's sexy; she's successful, and now look at her with a kid! Did I hit the jackpot or what?") The old ball-and-chain analogy is so last century. Keep the communication going, divide the baby tasks, and parenthood will be a shared adventure that brings you closer.

Fear 3: I'll Never See My Cute Prebaby Body Again, and My Significant Other Will Leave Me for a Nineteen-Year-Old Cameron Diaz Lookalike with a Teeny-Weeny Torso and Belly Button Ring

Something like this may have crossed your mind in a moment of pregnancy insanity. Your significant other signed on when your body was a little less weeble-wobble shaped, if you know what I mean. But never fear; your prebaby body will return. And it'll still be cute even as a weeble-wobble, so keep up the confidence. You can help things along by staying active and eating well during and after your pregnancy.

Fear 4: Despite the Fact That We're Both Working Full-Time, My Significant Other Won't Contribute Much to the Baby Care or Increased Housework

This situation is a classic. Mom brings home half the bacon and is expected to fry it up in a pan while folding everybody's laundry, changing the dirty diapers, and putting the baby to bed. If this sounds like your life, pull that guy of yours into the twenty-first century and hand him a diaper pail. And a dust rag. If you want some backup, here you go: Disagreement about the division of household tasks is one of the leading causes of stress among parents. Mothers who feel most supported at home tend to be the happiest, and dads with happy significant others report feeling more fulfilled in their personal lives. Kinda puts that dirty diaper in a whole new light, doesn't it?

Fear 5: My Significant Other Won't Respect Me As Much If I Cut Back at Work (Or, Worse Yet, I Won't Respect Myself As Much, And I'll Become a Bitter, Psycho Mom and Wife)

First, let's deal with your significant other. *He will still respect you regardless of your job situation*, assuming one little thing: You're happy. And that brings us to the second part of this concern. A bitter mom running around the place is a direct route to parental tension. If you're energized and excited by your days, your self-esteem will be high and your relationships will thrive. Whatever you choose to do career-wise, build in the support, socialization, and stimulation you need to make the most of your working and nonworking days.

Allow yourself time to transition. If you decide to cut back at work, you know you'll be giving up some income. And possibly benefits. And responsibilities. And maybe even your old title. Career sacrifices will be made. This process is never painless ("Sure, I'll move from the window office to that cubicle down the hall. After all, I am only here three days a week."), but you can do it. I've talked to many part-time moms who initially struggled with this shift but ultimately found a happy new groove. You may have to redefine your ambition and accept some temporary blows to the ego, but it can be done without (too much) bitterness.

Focus on the parts of the job you enjoy—maybe you're not managing a team anymore, but you're still working with great people and getting to use your brain. Create new expectations for yourself at work and be satisfied when you meet them. And know your career sacrifices can be temporary. Many part-timers switch back to full-time when their kids are in preschool. Others enjoy the new lifestyle so much they never go back.

*Fear 6: Good-Bye Laptop, Hello Laundry. If I'm No Longer
Working Full-Time, My Significant Other Will Assume I
Should Take Over All the Housework. And I'm Not Excited
About Reducing My Paid Workload Just to Increase My
Unpaid Workload at Home*

Prebaby, you're both working full-time and attempting to divide household stuff (relatively) equally. Maybe you straighten, cook, and throw in
the laundry, and your significant other does the dishes, fixes things
around the house, and takes out the garbage. He manages the home
maintenance projects; you manage the selection of cute picture frames.
Then your baby hits the scene, and you shift to part-time work. Now
what? You're working less for pay, so should you take over everything at
home plus the new baby-related tasks? And do you really want to reduce your *paid* workload just to increase your *unpaid* workload? Welcome to the tricky world of new parent household labor, where no easy
answers exist.

If you're at home more, you could take over some tasks, but both
parents should pitch in or somebody's going to get bitter. (That would
be you.) Even if you're home full-time for a while, you deserve some
help. Make a list of household tasks and plan who'll take what. When
the roles are clear, there's no need for daily debate. Include baby care
and give yourself triple bonus points for any time spent attached to the
breast pump. If your significant other doesn't believe you're busy during your "nonworking" days, record your activities over a typical
twenty-four hours and show him your schedule. And if he's still giving
you a hard time, offer to let him take over breast pump duties and you'll
call it even.

Getting By with a Little Help from Your Friends

"No, seriously, I'm listening," Shantell climbed the stairs, attempting to
quiet her shrieking infant while balancing the phone on her shoulder.
"Just tell me again. Did you say you got fired or you're tired? Because if
it's sleep you need, I can totally relate."

She heard a faint click and then a dial tone. And as her baby's hysteria ramped up to fever pitch, she forgot about returning her best friend's call.

|•|

Parenthood is as emotional as life gets. It's joyful, humbling, scary, confusing, and often, if you keep the right perspective, hilarious. In other words, it's a time when you really need your friends. Get lots of advice on networking with new moms in Chapter 5, "Making the Most of Your Days at Home." For tips on keeping your old friendships going as you hit Babyville, read on.

Old Friends in Your New World

Yes, it's tough to keep up your weekly coffee dates in the early days of parenthood. And your baby's unpredictable mood swings make even phone calls complicated. But don't be daunted by complication. Think of it as the relatively painless price you have to pay for the invaluable opportunity to vent, brag, and transform your hardest days into funny stories. Try these strategies for finding friend time in a baby-centered world:

Sweat together.   Once your health care provider has given you the green light on postpartum workouts, plan a Saturday morning yoga class or Sunday afternoon runs. Exercise + friend time = Happy body, happy mom.

Volunteer.   No, volunteering to assist each other shoe shopping doesn't really count. But that would be fun too.

Join a book club.   A great excuse to partake in appetizers, good wine, and dialogue more stimulating than, "Look, you made a big poopy!"

Plan a monthly dinner date.   Another excuse to partake in appetizers and good conversation, and you can never have too many of those.

Battle the Babyville black hole.   Keep up the regular phone calls, e-mails, and spontaneous drop-ins. Make friends a priority. Your resulting sanity is so worth it.

Hopefully you have someone you can beg, pay, or bribe into watching your child on occasion for some quality friend time. You and your significant other could take turns—one parent stays home, the other heads out for some baby-free fun without having to pay a baby-sitter. (Note to significant others everywhere: Monday night football is *not* a valid cop-out here. The beautiful mother of your child is leaving you in charge of diaper duty and crying control. Deal with it.) If help isn't an option, bring the little one along. Those first few months, newborns are typically easy (i.e., sleeping) dinner companions. And as your infant grows, you can always shift to baby-friendly get-togethers like afternoon walks or evenings in watching a movie while your child snoozes happily in his room.

Managing the Grandparents: It Can Be Done

"Honey, are you putting Jacob's diaper on without any baby powder?" Arianna's mother asked as she walked into the nursery. "You know, he's going to get diaper rash if you aren't careful."

Arianna glanced at her mother, silently noting the fact that the woman had enjoyed exactly twice the amount of sleep she had the night before. "Mom," she replied, "the doctor told us baby powder isn't necessary."

"Really?" her mother looked down at her grandson with a sort of indignant pity, clearly anticipating a lifetime of parental incompetence. "Well, I used baby powder on you and your brother from day one, and we avoided diaper rashes almost entirely. I don't know what that doctor was talking about."

|•|

You've been eagerly anticipating your baby's arrival for nine months, but your parents have been waiting for this moment since you hit puberty. Their reactions to becoming grandparents may be somewhat over the top. Don't get me wrong, some grandparents beautifully transition into their new roles—offering help as needed and providing space when appropriate. If this describes your situation, feel free to skip this section and consider yourself lucky. Others fall into the more extreme ends of the grandparent spectrum—becoming either overly involved or strangely apathetic.

Common Grandparent Challenges

The critic: Some grandparents snap into superparent mode and offer critiques on everything from diaper selection to sponge bathing techniques. And while their intentions may be good, constructive criticism quickly gets old when you're living on four hours sleep.

The comparer: Others make constant comparisons to children in the family. And does it really matter if cousin Hailey was walking by eleven months? I don't think so.

The stalker: Some grandparents overwhelm you with constant visits, questions, and involvement. A little help is great. Spontaneous hourly drop-ins, not so great.

The missing in action: And others are unexpectedly apathetic, rarely visiting or showing an odd indifference to your child. (They're supposed to live for this stuff, right?) Similarly, if your siblings already have children, you may have to fight to get any attention for your new addition to the family tree.

And things get even weirder when dealing with the grandparents-in-law. Your relationship with your in-laws is by nature more sensitive, and it can be harder to set them straight if you're uncomfortable with their approach. But that's exactly what you have to do. One direct conversation is a lot better than a lifetime of awkward moments.

Setting the Grandparent Ground Rules

If your mom's constant advice is making you feel inadequate, or you're overwhelmed by your father-in-law's daily drop-ins, it's time to set the ground rules. Grandparents just wing it, like the rest of us. They'll be relieved to have some clear direction from you. If you have a significant other, get him onboard. Then have an honest conversation with the whole gang—like those scary family meetings you had growing up, with the roles finally reversed:

Describe your parenting philosophy.   Start with your preferred approach for infant feeding, sleeping, playtime, exposure to TV, gifts—whatever seems relevant.

Explain your hopes for their role in your child's life.   We all have visions of our parents' relationships with our kids. Explain yours so expectations are clear.

Define the ideal timing and frequency of grandparent visits.   You may want daily help, or you may have a bimonthly limit on tolerable parent time. Better to set the stage in advance than find yourself waging an unspoken war of passive-aggressive comments during unwanted visits.

Tactfully discuss any concerns you have.   You may have already noticed a problem area. Obviously it doesn't help to throw this stuff in anybody's face, but try to gracefully raise your concerns.

Make a specific plan of attack.   Every productive meeting ends with clear next steps. Conclude your discussion with a plan for upcoming visits and involvement.

Extended Family:
The Good, the Bad, and the Just Plain Crazy

"Wait, you're saying Connor still isn't sleeping through the night?" Tracy's sister-in-law looked stunned.

"No, I'm still feeding him at least once," Tracy replied, shifting on the park bench.

"You guys have to nip that in the bud. We had Matthew and Joey sleeping through the night by four months, and it made life so much easier."

Tracy looked over at her nephews, the apparent sleep prodigies, just as Matthew shoved Joey's face into his meticulously constructed sandcastle.

"Uh-huh. Well, I guess Connor's just a more challenging kid."

|•|

You've known your extended family forever—your crazy cousins who now have kids of their own, your aunt who sends a $20 check every birthday, your siblings who mysteriously evolved from playing T-ball to coaching baseball, from wrestling with the family dog to studying for the MCAT. They are your history, your home base. Yet your family feelings may shift when you first hit Babyville.

Like those grandparents who get it, many extended families offer ideal support from day one. They listen to your endless baby stories, lend you hand-me-downs you actually want, and offer to baby-sit just when you desperately need a night out. Others assume their familial status and parental experience make them experts on your child as well, and family barbecues become town meetings of uninvited parenting advice.

Keeping the Commentary in Check

If you're reaching the end of your family-involvement rope, take control.

Nobody knows your baby better than you do.   Parenting is more art than science, and what worked for one child may not work for yours. Heed the good advice but always trust your instincts.

Don't be afraid to speak your mind. Obviously your family isn't holding back, and neither should you.   If you're consistently upset by family comments, let people know your perspective.

Minimize family time for a while.   If the annoying comments continue even after you explain your concerns, feel free to skip a few family gatherings. You're a new mom. You deserve a serious break.

Remember, you're an amazing parent.   No really, you are—one of the absolute best. Feels good, doesn't it? That's a problem with parenthood: nobody offers official performance appraisals. Well, there's yours. So keep up the confidence; you're doing everything right. As Dr. Spock said to new parents over fifty years ago, "Trust yourself. You know more than you think you do."[1]

Living for Less and Loving It

Tips for Cutting Baby Costs and Getting a

Head Start on College Savings

"**Y**ou're kidding me, right?" Kristin's husband was talking to no one in particular, but his meaning was clear. His eyes were locked on the large yellow price tag attached to the white sleigh crib. He looked back at Kristin smiling, like this was some kind of inside joke. "Did you see this? Hilarious. I can't wait to check out the prices on the changing table and dresser."

| • |

Whether you're continuing to work full-time, cutting back, or leaving work for a while, baby gear isn't cheap, and every dollar counts. Try these parent-tested strategies for reducing your family's expenses on everything from toys to taxes, and start to save for your child's future college costs. Many of these strategies will apply during your maternity leave, and others will become more relevant over the following months.

Minimize Your Life-with-Baby Expenses

The average U.S. family forks over about $6,300 on year one baby costs.[1] But there are plenty of creative ways to spend less and still provide everything your little one needs.

Start a Baby-sitting Co-op

This is a formal name for a simple concept. Partner with another family and agree to take turns baby-sitting every other Saturday night. Or Friday. Or Sunday. Whatever you prefer. You go out every other week without the scary costs of a baby-sitter (typically $8 to $17 an hour), and you get practice managing multiple kids at once.

For a more complex version of the co-op, rotate baby-sitting with several families to build up credits. When you need a sitter, cash in one of your credits and an available family cares for your baby while you hit the town for free. This approach requires more coordination and works best if someone volunteers to be the point person. This role can rotate quarterly, or if one person is particularly organized, she may not mind maintaining the responsibility.

Relentlessly Pursue Hand-Me-Downs or Borrowed Clothes, Toys, and Baby Gear

Ask friends, family, and friends of friends for baby items their children have outgrown. You'll save hundreds of dollars. This works particularly well for sturdy, short-term gear like bouncy seats, exersaucers, and baby backpacks—just make sure they meet current safety codes. Also, check your phone book for children's consignment shops; these stores usually offer clothes and baby gear at less than half the retail price.

> **QUICK TIP FROM DR. NIED**
>
> If you receive a hand-me-down car seat, it should be in good condition with no cracks in the frame, no missing parts, and a label with the date of manufacture and model number. Use the original installation instructions or request them from the manufacturer, and confirm the car seat hasn't been recalled. How? Contact the U.S. Department of Transportation Auto Safety Hotline at 888-327-4236 or go to nhtsa.gov and enter "car seat recalls" in the search engine.

Rediscover the Library

Many of us haven't visited a library since we were required to back in school. It's a strange phenomenon, the proliferation of mega-bookstores selling expensive hardcovers out the wazoo while less visited libraries distribute books for free. Most libraries have excellent children's book sections and the librarians can recommend the best for your child's age. While you're there, ask about weekly story times and other free activities.

Hit Yard Sales and Online Exchanges

I know new moms who've found huge bins of perfect three-year-old wooden blocks for $2, great plastic toys for under a dollar, and children's books for pennies at local yard sales. And others who've purchased high-quality, supercheap baby clothes and gear on websites like craigslist.org, eBay.com, and urbanbaby.com. When families are ready to unload their baby gear, they want to do it fast, and you can benefit.

Minimize the Store-Bought Toys

Developmental toys for infants often run $10 to $25 a piece. And as any parent will tell you, your baby is as likely to enjoy the box as much as the toy inside. If you're trying to cut costs, look for child-friendly items around the house like plastic spoons, measuring cups, funnels, bowls, or empty boxes. Run empty shampoo or water bottles through the dishwasher and let your little one go crazy. Fill a baby-accessible drawer with plastic food containers and keep your child entertained for hours. He'll never know the difference between household items and store-bought toys.

Pass Up the Big-Ticket, Temporary Gear You Can't Borrow

I'm talking about pricey, short-term entertainment like the swing (costs $50 to $120, lasts about four months), the exersaucer (costs $50 to $100, lasts four to six months), and the play mat (costs $30 to $80, lasts about three months). If you can afford them, these things can be great, but they're definitely not essential. Your baby will outgrow them quickly, and then they require serious storage space.

Buy Clothes a Year Ahead to Get Sale Prices

Children's clothing is reduced in price at the end of each season. When you find cute kids' clothes on sale, buy for the following year. Your eighteen-month-old will never know you bought his toddler bathing suit half-price the previous summer.

Buy Last Year's Models

Strollers and other big-ticket baby items often go on sale for up to half price in January and February as retailers phase out last year's models. And we're talking about strollers here, people, not laptops; have no fear about missing out on fast-breaking innovations. Last year's model may have a navy and ice blue color scheme instead of this year's navy and white, but it'll still beautifully transport your baby around town.

Be Patient

Wait for holidays and birthdays, and get baby stuff for free.

Think of it this way: You're surrounded by toys and itsy-bitsy clothing all the time, but your family and friends have fun just wandering into the baby stores. Spread the word on items you love but feel guilty buying. Adorable outfit at your local babyGap? Tell the grandparents before your child's birthday. Great activity center at Toys R Us? Drop a hint to your siblings before the holidays. It is hard to resist when you're at the store, but exercising patience can save major cash. And if you're hoping for help with several items, you can register for baby gear at most major retail chains. Subtle? No. Effective? Yes.

Make Your Own Baby Food

Before your infant is ready for finger foods, he's living in the world of pureed peaches and peas. You can either buy little jars of the mushy stuff or make it yourself. Homemade baby food requires a certain level of motivation ("I just worked a full day, and I need to feed Eli, give him a bath, and put him to bed before I can focus on the three other things I have to do tonight. Should I pull out a handy jar of prepared baby food or make pureed sweet potatoes by hand? Hmm, this is a toughie."). But many new moms swear by this approach for the nutritional value and savings, so I wanted to mention it. And to be fair, you can save time by making a large portion in advance and freezing baby meal-size quantities in an ice cube tray.

Literally, Make Your Own Baby Food

Similarly, nursing saves money. A typical six-month-old consumes $15 to $40 worth of formula each week. Breast feeding is clearly a personal decision, but from a purely monetary standpoint it can be a source of savings.

Take Advantage of Your Family

Okay, don't actually *take advantage* of your family; you know what I mean. If you have family in town, they're your best, free baby-sitting source. Don't wait for them to offer; be proactive. Ask if they're interested in some weekly quality time with your child, or suggest baby-sitting gift certificates instead of store-bought gifts (assuming you're not counting on the gifts to avoid paying for baby items you need). You could schedule Saturday afternoons at the park with Grandpa, Friday nights with the cousins at Aunt Maria's, or occasional get-togethers with the godparents. Your baby will benefit from family bonding, and you'll enjoy gloriously free evenings out or occasional afternoons at the gym.

Start Saving for Future College Expenses

"I should have known the brainwashing would start early," Talisa said, smiling as she picked up her six-week-old son. He was casually sporting a University of Michigan cap, T-shirt, shorts, and socks, and her husband was grinning slyly, clearly proud of himself.

"Just getting him excited for the game this afternoon. It's never too early to start cheering for his future school."

"Assuming we can afford to send him. You're not going to believe what I was reading about projected college costs."

|❋|

By the time our children reach college, tuition costs will have surpassed the GDP of many small countries. Offset future sticker shock by starting to save now.

Select a Tax-Deferred College Savings Plan

For example, 529 plans allow you to invest now toward your child's college costs—and the earnings will never be federally taxed as long you spend the money on tuition, books, room and board, or school supplies. (No, you can assure your future college student that weekly dorm room keg parties don't count.) These plans are state-sponsored, but most don't require the student to attend a school in that state. And you don't have to use your state's plan, but you may receive tax benefits if you do. You're always in control, and you can start by investing less than $100 or up to $12,000 year one without incurring a gift tax. And don't forget to tell grandparents, aunts, and uncles that you have a plan in place. Each contributor can give up to $12,000 a year without gift tax penalties.

By the time your child reaches college, you could have $250,000 in his 529 plan—or more if it performs well. If he doesn't need the money (yes, I think my son will be on a full basketball scholarship too), you can roll it over to educational expenses for another child, relative, or even yourself. Some plans allow you to withdraw funds without penalty if your child receives a scholarship. If you pull the money out for other purposes, however, you will incur federal income tax and a 10 percent penalty on the earnings. To learn more about 529 plans, talk to a broker or your bank, call the College Savings Plan Network toll-free at 877-277-6496, or check out these websites: collegesavings.org, savingforcollege.com, sayplanning.com, or morningstar.com.

In addition to 529 plans, also consider:

Prepaid tuition plans: As the name implies, these plans allow you to pay a portion or all of your child's college costs now at *today's prices*. This is serious savings; if college costs continue to increase at current rates, we can expect annual tuition prices to *triple* by the time our babies are ready for higher education. You have to purchase an individual state plan, however, and your investment is generally accepted only at public universities within that state.

Education IRAs: You can invest up to $2,000 per student per year tax-free. You'll need to use the funds on private precollege or college expenses before your child turns thirty (just hope he's not on the ten-year college plan), and as with 529 plans, you can transfer these funds to another family member for education expenses. There are some restrictions based on parents' earnings, and you'll pay taxes and a 10 percent penalty if you pull the money out for nonacademic expenses.

Roth IRA Accounts: These accounts allow you to take money out before the age of fifty-nine years and six months to help with your children's college costs.

EE and I Bonds: Some savings bonds offer tax-free interest if the funds are used for college.

Keep in mind, many financial advisers recommend taking advantage of your employer's retirement plan at least up to the match each year before investing in college savings. Otherwise, you're giving away free money. And there are a lot of ways to pay for college, but your child will feel really guilty if you can't afford to retire because you spent all your savings sending him to school.

Maximize Your College Savings Returns

Once you've selected a specific 529 plan or other college savings vehicle, follow these expert tips for maximizing your investment returns:

Start now.   Year one is the perfect time to set up your college savings plan. You'll benefit from compounding interest acceleration—your best bet to offset skyrocketing college costs. Baby expenses are always high, but cut back on other areas before you skimp on savings.

Take a risk.   If you start saving now, you have almost eighteen years until the college bills hit. Given this long-term time horizon, many investors recommend focusing on riskier, higher-return vehicles. Then, as your child's college days get closer, you can shift to a lower-risk strategy.

Invest monthly rather than annually.   Financial advisers call this approach dollar cost averaging, and it minimizes the risk of a fund value dropping just after a bulk amount has been invested. Set up an automatic monthly deposit that safely spreads your investment across the entire year.

Plan for perfect college timing.   Calculate the month and year your child will start college and schedule your investments accordingly. Any savings bonds you purchase, for example, should mature at that time to maximize returns.

Get personalized guidance.   Most advisers these days have software with projected costs of every college in the country to give you a personal estimate. To find a financial planner, ask for referrals from relatives and friends, meet with at least two, and then go with the one you feel best understands your needs.

Work:
The Road Ahead

Your Simple, Step-by-Step Guide to Making the Hardest Decision of Your Life

To Work Full-Time, Flextime, Compressed Weeks,

Flexplace, Part-Time, Job Share, Freelance,

Start Your Own Business, Extend Your Leave,

or Stay Home for a While

"It first hit me like some high school crush," new mom Chandra explains. "Cedric reached out and grabbed his toes for the first time, and I was hooked for life. Complete and utter infant attachment. I couldn't get enough of him. And, of course, that was the day I was supposed to start looking into day care centers."

Chandra, a fund-raiser for an environmental nonprofit, initially planned to return to her old full-time schedule. Then the toe incident occurred, and all former work-related bets were off. She debated asking for flextime. She thought about shifting to part-time. She fantasized about taking off six months and then starting her own business. She knew there was an ideal way to combine career and motherhood—she just had to figure out how.

|•|

You're a working woman moving happily along your career path. You believe—take for granted, really—there will be a way to beautifully integrate professional fulfillment and parenting when the time comes. Then the time does come, and things quickly get a lot more complicated.

Welcome to the new mom work conundrum—the nearly impossible decision we all have to make when parenthood hits. Need your full-time salary? You could return to your old schedule or try to negotiate flextime, compressed workweeks, or a work from home arrangement. Can you afford a lower income? You could cut back to part-time, job share, freelance, start your own business, take an extended leave, or focus exclusively on parenting for a while. There are more options than ever before, and yet the ideal blend of career and momhood remains elusive. We all know what we want: a comfortable household income, intellectual stimulation, social interaction, and quality family time. The question is, how to get it?

Heading back to work after maternity leave is emotional, challenging, and just plain tricky. Your hormones are still on overdrive, you're harboring a serious case of infant infatuation, and you're making a wild guess at the work arrangement that will meet your new mom lifestyle requirements while covering family costs. Defining and negotiating your near-term career path would throw anyone for a loop, and you're doing it while juggling diaper duty and overnight feedings.

Where to begin as you consider your options? How to assess them all without losing your mind? Here's a start. This step-by-step guide is designed to be a sort of in-house career counselor. It walks you through the process of reviewing various work arrangements from flextime to freelancing, defining your year one priorities, determining which work options you can realistically afford, identifying your mom/work baggage, and pinpointing the ideal approach for your new mom reality. If you need additional inspiration, you can check out success stories from the working mom front.

Review Your Options

FROM:	**Dana Skolnick**
TO:	**Roxy Klier**
SUBJECT:	**Who knew an eight-pound girl could wreak such havoc?**

I loved my job. You know I did. I loved the mental challenge, the people, the income. It was all beautifully simple. Then Marissa was born, and new mom mania took over my body and soul. Now I have three weeks left in maternity leave, and my career game plan is up for grabs. How does job sharing work? What is flextime, exactly? And if I shift to part-time, will I have *less work* or just *less time* to get everything done?

No, you're not the only one feeling crazy out there. It's never easy to decide what to do about work when your baby hits the scene. Start the process by assessing your options.

● ● ● ● ● ● Full-Time Work Arrangements ● ● ● ● ● ● ●
With Full Salary and Benefits

Return to Your Old Schedule

This is the easy one. If you want to keep your old full-time schedule (and not insignificantly, your old full-time salary), head back to work with confidence—ready to show off your new baby photos and actual waistline. And know you're in good company. Of the 68 million women in the U.S. labor force, 54 percent work full-time.[1]

To ease your adjustment back after maternity leave, you could request a phased return to work—starting three days a week or working from home at first and then gradually ramping up to your full-time schedule over a few weeks. Your salary will likely be reduced during this period, but it can provide a great transitional time for you, your infant, and your child care provider.

Flextime

You'd love to break out of the 9:00 A.M. to 5:00 P.M. routine, but you need your full-time salary. What to do? Ask for flextime. There are two ways it can work:

Negotiate a new schedule and follow it consistently.   Work 8:00 A.M. to 4:00 p.m. every day instead of 9:00 A.M. to 5:00 P.M., for example. Officially shifting your starting and ending times can allow for easier child care pickups, those mom-and-baby activities, or simply early evenings at home. Some couples even schedule complementary work shifts (maybe mom works 7:00 A.M. to 3:00 P.M. and dad works noon to 8:00 P.M.) to minimize child care costs.

Adjust your timing as needed day to day.   This approach offers even more flexibility. Your baby has a pediatrician appointment at 9:30 A.M. one morning? Come to work at 11:00 A.M. and then stay until 7:00 P.M. Other days you might prefer working 7:30 A.M. to 3:30 P.M. or even 9:00 A.M. to 5:00 P.M. Simply meet with your management in advance and come to an agreement on the total number of hours you'll be at the office each day—or week. Your presence may be required during a core daily period, such as 11:00 A.M. to 3:00 P.M., to ensure some coordinated face time between team members. Once those parameters are defined, you're in control.

Sound too good to be true? It's not—flextime is currently offered by 60 percent of U.S. employers.[2] While some jobs will always require a traditional schedule, think creatively about what might work for you. This kind of flexibility is the no brainer of new parenthood. Take advantage of current offerings and try to negotiate for flextime even if it isn't a formal policy. Employers are often open to this type of accommodation. There's no out-of-pocket cost, and studies have shown employee satisfaction and retention improve considerably when flextime is made available.

Compressed Workweeks

How about all the salary with permanent long weekends? You may be able to negotiate compressed workweeks, which squeeze a full-time load into three or four longer workdays (four 10-hour days instead of five 8-hour days, for example). This approach is not as common as flextime because some managers want daily accessibility, and it just doesn't work for some jobs. But if you can shift your responsibilities, compressed workweeks can be a great scheduling option. They're available to 22 percent of the workforce.[3]

Flexplace

This is the latest human resources lingo for a simple concept—working from home (or wherever you choose to work). Flexplace, also called telecommuting, is offered by 30 percent of employers,[4] and it saves hours wasted commuting to work, allows you to spend breaks with your baby, and can provide schedule flexibility if you aren't needed by phone or e-mail throughout the day. To be successful, you need a job that can be accomplished remotely and a trusting boss. Depending on the nature of your position, you may need to go into the office one or two days weekly for meetings and updates, and you're expected to have child care during your workdays at home.

As you consider working from home:

Assess your job.   Certain jobs require face time; others can be accomplished remotely without missing a beat. Make a list of your responsibilities and brainstorm about how some or all could be completed from home. You may find a partial work-from-home arrangement is your best bet.

Assess your space.   Depending on the nature of your job, you may need a quiet home office area with a separate phone line, appropriate wiring, and room for the basics: your work space, computer, printer, fax machine, daily materials, and ongoing files. Think through your work requirements and space at home. If you're going to meet with clients, for example, a professional-looking work space is key unless can you schedule meetings at your local Starbucks. (You always wondered who those people were reviewing business materials over lattes. Now they could be *your* people.)

Assess yourself. Working in your pajamas may initially sound like career nirvana, but think honestly about your personality and productivity. If you'd go crazy without the socialization of colleagues or you focus best with a manager down the hall, flexplace may not be ideal for you.

● ● ● Work Arrangements with Reduced Hours ● ● ●
Salary Reduced Relative to Schedule, Benefits May Be Dropped or Cut, But Try to Negotiate to Keep Them

Part-Time

If you can afford the income reduction, part-time work could be the promised land—offering a relatively low-stress balance of career and parenting responsibilities. You're still making good money, you can still enjoy the socialization and structure of work, and you still have a perfect excuse to delegate diaper duty a few days a week. Part-time positions are offered by 46 percent of employers,[5] and they should (I repeat *should*) involve a clear, specified workload reduction. Most often, part-timers downshift from five eight-hour workdays to three or four eight-hour workdays, with designated responsibilities redistributed and a relative salary decrease. Other scheduling options, such as five half days, may be negotiable.

Unfortunately, part-time workloads aren't always well defined. In a Catalyst study, over 60 percent of participants who switched from full-time to part-time positions reported their workloads remained the same or increased.[6] Three-fourths were mothers who made the switch to have more time with their children. Don't fall into this trap. If you're interested in part-time, take steps to ensure your position is fairly structured and managed from the beginning:

Clearly document your part-time role in advance.   Include your shortened hours, reduced responsibilities, adjustments to your compensation package, and a specific plan for delegating prior tasks. (If no one is assigned to take over your work, guess who'll continue to handle it? Hint: Not your manager.) If you need to leave every day by 5:45 P.M. to let your baby-sitter go at 6:15 P.M., include this timing in your written job description. Expectations need to be thoroughly detailed.

Get management on board.   Set up a meeting and have everyone sign off on your revised job description. Your reduced compensation package should be explained. Everyone should understand they're *paying you less* now, so you'll be *doing less.*

Be honest about your workload.   Once you make the switch, maintain open communication with your manager. If your workload exceeds your reduced salary, she should know. This is no time to be a martyr, and she can't reallocate your work if she isn't aware of the problem. If your part-time workload remains unmanageable, you'll need to make a decision. You can (1) stay patient and hope things improve, (2) officially move back to full-time so your compensation matches your workload, (3) try to find another part-time position in the company, or (4) look elsewhere. Some corporate cultures simply fail to support part-time roles.

Job Sharing

You want to cut back to part-time, but your job requires full-time coverage. Find a job share partner, and your problem could be solved. Two employees with proven track records split one full-time job. Typically, one job share partner works Monday through Wednesday and the other works Wednesday through Friday. Wednesday provides time to touch base in person and transition projects.

Each job share partner generally receives 55 percent to 60 percent of her previous compensation, so you'll need to either justify an overall salary increase for the position or accept a 50 percent/50 percent salary split (not so exciting when you're *working* at 60 percent). Job sharing is often effective for sales or client service roles, and it's your best bet for maintaining a truly part-time workload and peace of mind on your days off. It's offered by 27 percent of U.S. companies.[7]

Intrigued? Keep in mind these strategies for job sharing success:

Find a compatible partner.   Your job share partner's work ethic, track record, and communication style should match yours. Your career success now depends on her, and you need to feel completely comfortable with her abilities.

Establish clear, consistent processes from the beginning.   The job share should be managed seamlessly from your clients' and your management's perspectives. In other words, welcome to the world of increased paperwork. Phone calls and meetings should be well documented and next steps always defined so they can be handed over to your partner each week. Deadlines must be tracked continuously, and e-mails should be organized consistently. Before beginning your job share, meet with your partner to set up documentation and project management processes from day one.

Use the same contact information.   Before you shared a job, you and your partner each had unique contact information—two e-mail accounts, phone numbers, and possibly pagers. Once you split a job, this needs to change. Consolidate all communication to keep contact simple for clients and management.

Get client feedback in advance.   Before shifting to a job share, call your key clients to explain the upcoming arrangement and request suggestions for facilitating the transition. Generally clients won't mind the change, but they'll appreciate your foresight and may offer useful process advice.

Part-Time Flexplace

The flexibility double whammy, part-time flexplace allows you to reduce your hours and work from home.

●●●●●● Other Fun-Filled Options ●●●●●●●

Freelancing

You may have been a full-time administrative assistant or graphic designer, journalist or brand manager, speech therapist or CPA, but you're ready to exchange full-time security for flexibility. You want to keep your work skills current, make some money and avoid a gaping hole in your résumé, and you're willing to tolerate erratic work and income. Freelancing may be for you. But how to repackage yourself as an independent provider?

Decide what services you want to offer.   As an administrative assistant, you could add value to a variety of projects from efficient data entry to creating PowerPoint presentations. As a journalist, you could pitch work from Internet copywriting to freelance magazine reporting. Brainstorm with your skill set in mind.

Create a killer résumé or portfolio.   Be ready to succinctly demonstrate your skills to potential clients. Maintain samples of your work and an updated résumé, either on hard copy or a personal website. Domain name, development, and hosting fees can be relatively minimal, and a website allows you to e-mail your link as you seek new business.

Pitch your old management.   Begin with an easy pitch. Your former employers know your skills—meet with them and offer your services. If they can't use your help, they may at least offer references for other project work.

Work for free.   As you're getting started, build your résumé and make new connections by volunteering your services for local non-profits or small businesses.

Get the word out.   When you're feeling established, invest in some targeted advertising in trade journals or local publications. Have business cards made and pass them out at industry events.

Promote your services online.   There are a variety of websites connecting freelancers with projects. Do your own industry-specific searches, check out the major job posting sites, and don't miss freelancing hubs like guru.com.

Starting Your Own Business

You've spent years acquiring impressive career skills, and then your baby arrives and autonomy becomes a top priority. How can you cash in on your skill set without your manager's penchant for last-minute requests and required face time at the office? Strike out on your own.

Almost 20 percent of employed Americans work for themselves,[8] and there are currently 10.6 million women-owned businesses in the United States, according to the Center for Women's Business Research.[9] In fact, the recent growth rate of women-owned companies is almost double the national average.[10] To thrive as an entrepreneur, you should excel at creating structure for yourself, developing work plans from scratch, networking, and making decisions independently. And you should be able to afford a serious income loss while you're ramping up. Feeling the entrepreneurial spirit? Follow these strategies for success:

Begin with a great idea.   This is the fun part—be as creative as possible. Draw from your work and personal experiences to identify opportunities in the market, from new products that could be offered to services needed in your city. Or look into existing franchises that could be introduced in your area.

Do your homework.   Search online for competitive businesses and read up on related industry news. Know your market before jumping in with a new venture.

Create a business plan.   Once you've identified a niche, document your plan of attack. This process helps you clarify your thoughts, assess the competition, and develop strategies for revenue growth. It's also essential if you require funding. If you need help creating a business plan, there are websites that will walk you through the process, or you can pick up a guide at the bookstore.

Start slowly.   You're a new mom—you have your hands full. Transition into your entrepreneurial role part-time and from home at first, ramping up and acquiring office space as needed.

Network.   Connections will often lead to unexpected new clients, employees, ideas, and growth opportunities. Don't be shy. Call acquaintances who work in related fields, set up lunches with old work colleagues, plan brainstorming sessions with friends over coffee, join professional organizations, and attend industry events or conferences.

Multitask.   If you're working from home, there are ample opportunities to be productive throughout the day. Work on the computer during your infant's nap times or go through paperwork while waiting at the pediatrician's office. Keep a to-do list with you and check off tasks when you have free time.

Taking an Extended Leave

Hoping for a five- or six-month maternity leave? Talk to your manager. Official parental leave policies vary by company and are usually open for discussion. Even if your employer's standard maternity leave is twelve weeks, you may be able to negotiate additional time off. Once your paid leave runs out, you'll be taking unpaid days off—but your job should be held and ideally your benefits will continue. Write up a proposal and make the request.

Taking a *Really* Extended Leave

Interested in doing the full-time parenting thing for a while? For a year? Two years? Or until your kids hit school? This approach, called sequencing, is a common strategy for moms hoping to strike that ideal balance by focusing on career and parenthood in stages. How to make the leap? You have two choices: Resign your job or try to negotiate a really extended leave with your management. Essentially you'll be asking for alumni status, which means your employer may cover your continuing professional education costs, occasionally keep in touch, and try to find a position for you when you're ready. The folks in human resources often call this kind of boomerang approach flexcareer (you knew they'd get the "flex" in there if they could), and it beats quitting without a safety net unless you hate your job. So, give it a shot if this is your ideal scenario—your employer may be more open-minded than you think. For lots of advice on sequencing in and out of the workforce, check out Chapter 12, "June Cleaver Be Damned."

Forget the Five-Year Plan—For Now; Focus on the Next Twelve Months

"I just can't do it," Lindsey muttered to herself, looking down at her two-month-old daughter.

"Can't do what?" her husband Greg responded, walking into the room.

"I can't make this decision. Think about it. If I quit now and take a year or two off, how will that look on my résumé? I'll never get a job in software development again."

"Then don't quit," Greg responded, the rational man trying to be helpful. "Work part-time."

"I could, but the part-timers in my division are never promoted. How will I feel in three or four years when less senior people are moving over me and I'm stuck at this level?"

"Okay, so don't shift to part-time," Greg piped up cheerfully.

"Right." Lindsey continued. "So I keep my full-time job and things just keep getting crazier at the office. Five years from now I look around and realize my work–life balance is completely out of wack, and I kick myself for having spent so much time on the job."

Greg was suddenly at a loss. "I see what you mean. The long-term possibilities can be sort of scary regardless of what choice you make."

"Yes," Lindsey responded. "Yes, they can."

|•|

Now you know your work options. You're ready for the next step—focusing on your immediate priorities. The most decisive people on earth can be overwhelmed by the long-term career possibilities when parenthood hits. Just keep in mind, we're all trying this for the first time—we're all winging it. And unlike other major life choices (think getting married, having a child, getting a tattoo), your job decision doesn't need to be permanent. So let the long-term fears go. You've got a decision to make.

Think Through Your Professional and Personal Priorities for This Year

What's most important to you this year? Keeping your full-time salary so you're in great shape to cover those baby bills? A more flexible weekly schedule? Maintaining your career trajectory so you return home fulfilled and energized for quality baby time? Additional days off? Getting that promotion so you can afford the down payment on a house? Easy access to your child? Keep these priorities in mind as you calculate your year one salary requirements.

Give Yourself Annual Deadlines to Stop, Assess Your Life-Fulfillment Meter, and Make a Decision for the Following Twelve Months

Feeling unsatisfied by a part-time role this time next year? Talk to your employer about increasing your responsibilities and get back to the fast promotional track. Burned out by full-time work? Revisit the family budget and consider options for cutting back or starting your own business. Getting restless after a year at home? Jump back into the working world you know so well. (No, despite your fears, time at home will not permanently atrophy your working mind.) You can easily make a change in the future to ensure your extended career path is rewarding.

It may feel like a leap of faith, but living without a definite long-term plan can be fun. And in the short term, this approach keeps you from completely losing it. Some alternative work arrangements may initially feel like a major career sacrifice. Until you've tried these approaches, however, you'll never know how they could work for you. You may find one offers the perfect balance, or you may ultimately want to shift back to your old schedule. Similarly, it's less intense to take a year off from your career than to go cold turkey on work. Even if your year off stretches to two years off and then a few years off, it's easier to make the transition when you do it gradually and consciously each step of the way.

For now, you're ready to calculate your year one salary requirements, so you know which work options you can realistically afford.

Determine What Options You Can Afford

"This decision would be easy if we'd recently won the lottery," Deirdre announced as she opened her front door for her friend Liz, stopping by with a baby gift.

"You're still obsessing about work, aren't you?" Liz replied, following her into the house.

"Here's my latest idea: job sharing. I know another salesperson in my division who might be interested in cutting back. I'm thinking about calling her and suggesting a job share arrangement. I'd love the reduced schedule; I'm just afraid money would be too tight without my full-time income."

"Have you put together a budget?" Liz asked. "Maybe you guys can actually afford it. Once you subtract taxes and child care costs, your full-time salary may not add as much as you think."

"We haven't done that yet. You're right; at least then I'd know my options."

|•|

Of course, the new mom work decision would be a lot easier if we all had bank accounts like Oprah's. But for most of us, money is the elephant in the nursery as we consider our career options for the first year of parenthood.

The average U.S. family spends $6,300 on year one baby expenses,[11] and basic costs like housing and health care are at an all-time high, making it increasingly difficult for families to feel financially secure. And while our politicians excel at family values rhetoric, they aren't so hot at setting policy to support working families. In other industrialized countries, child care is largely or entirely subsidized. In the United States, we pay for child care ourselves, and it's typically our second highest annual expense after housing. The United States and Australia are the *only* developed countries without federally funded parental leave, and even the

Aussies get fifty-two weeks unpaid leave.[12] The best new parent national entitlement we've come up with is the Family and Medical Leave Act of 1993, which offers only twelve weeks of *unpaid* job protection for less than half of U.S. workers.[13] You can do the math on that one. Bottom line, brace yourself for some sticker shock as you head into Babyville.

On the upside, there are lots of great work options these days—even if you need your full-time salary. And it's much easier to choose one when you have a handle on your finances. Interested in cutting back at work? You may think you can't afford to reduce your hours when you actually can with some creative expense management. Fill in the life-with-baby budget calculator on the following pages. It will tell you if you can afford to cut back at work or if your full-time income is essential this year.

(Not in the mood to focus on family finances right now? You could skip the budget calculator and go straight to the next step on page 164. When you're ready to think about a budget for this year, just flip back to this life-with-baby budget calculator and use it as a resource any time.)

LIFE-WITH-BABY BUDGET CALCULATOR

Income

First, fill in your aftertax household income. Want to shift from full-time to part-time after maternity leave? Or freelance? Or leave work for a year? Estimate your *new* aftertax salary and bonus—keeping in mind unpaid weeks during maternity leave—and include that total here. Part-timers shifting from five to three days a week typically make 60 percent of their full-time salaries. Freelancing and entrepreneurial incomes vary significantly, so use your best estimate. If you want to stay home year one, leave your salary and bonus line blank.

	Annual	Monthly
Aftertax salaries and bonuses		
*For you	_____	_____
*For your significant other	_____	_____
Income anticipated from investments or gifts	_____	_____
TOTAL INCOME:		

Expenses

Babies are never cheap, but there's a wide range of potential costs based on your spending style, where you shop, and money-saving hand-me-down opportunities. And if you plan to work this year, child care will likely be your second highest family expense after housing. The following pages walk you through the calculations for basic baby costs, child care, and everything else. Include your totals here.

	Annual	Monthly
Basic baby costs	_____	_____
Child care	_____	_____
Everything else	_____	_____
TOTAL EXPENSES:		

	AVAILABLE CASH	
TOTAL INCOME–TOTAL EXPENSES:		

Now subtract your expenses from your household income. Then turn to the results page to interpret your family finances.

BASIC BABY COSTS

Review the typical costs below, then write in your personal estimates based on your shopping style and hand-me-down opportunities. These should be annual costs; you'll divide the total by 12 at the bottom of the page for monthly expenses. Upper-end costs with a plus (+) could go even higher if money is truly no object (think $2,000 cribs and $750 strollers).

Shortcut: The average family spends $6,300 on year one baby expenses.[14] To skip the details, use $6,300 for your basic baby costs annual total and $515 for your monthly total on the next page.

	Your Estimated Cost	Typical Annual Cost
NURSERY		
Crib, mattress, pad, waterproof liner, bedding, receiving blankets, decor	_____	$350–$1,100+
Rocker and potentially an ottoman	_____	$150–$700+
Changing table, changing pad, and/ or dresser	_____	$150–$400+
Baby monitor	_____	$30–$100
CLOTHING (total cost for year one)		
Sleepers, onesies, soft tops and bottoms, hats, socks, sleep sack	_____	$250–$500+
Seasonal/specialty items (bunting, sweaters, bathing suit, sun hat, other cute outfits)	_____	$100–$400+
Maternity and nursing clothes/bras for mom	_____	$350–$1,200+
DIAPERING (total cost for year one)		
Diapers and wipes (assume lower end for cloth, upper end for disposable)	_____	$100–$875
Diaper rash ointment, petroleum jelly, diaper covers if using cloth diapers	_____	$10–$25
Diaper pail and refills	_____	$40–$80
HEALTH AND GENERAL CARE		
Thermometer, infant pain reliever, bulb syringe, brush or comb, baby lotion, first aid kit, and humidifier	_____	$50–$70
BATHING		
Plastic infant tub and inflatable baby tub	_____	$30–$40
Baby shampoo, washcloths, bath toys, hooded towel, soft cover for spout	_____	$35–$50

BABY ON THE GO

Car seat	_____	$50–$300
Stroller (cost here is per stroller)	_____	$20–$350+
Front carrier, sling, or baby backpack	_____	$40–$120
Portable crib	_____	$60–$150
Diaper bag	_____	$20–$125+

FEEDING

Nursing pillow, breast pads, lanolin cream, burp cloths	_____	$50–$150
Breast pump (manual = cheaper, electric = pricey) plus carrier and milk storage	_____	$50–$350
Bottles, nipples, dishwasher caddy, bottle warmer, burp cloths	_____	$60–$100
Formula ($15–40 a week for 9 months, adjust using your needs and timing)	_____	$550–$1,450
High chair or booster seat with infant-appropriate setting	_____	$30–$225
Baby utensils, bowls, sippy cups	_____	$30–$40

CHILDPROOFING

Safety gates, toilet locks, cabinet locks, electric outlet plugs, furniture fasteners, miniblind cord pulls, soft pads for table edges	_____	$50–$300+

PLAYTIME AND READING

Bouncy seat, toys, books, fun baby classes	_____	$75–$300+

PRESERVING THE MEMORIES

Camera, film, scrapbooks, etc.	_____	$50–$300+

BASIC BABY COSTS ANNUAL TOTAL: [   ] $2,800–$9,800

Divide by 12

BASIC BABY COSTS MONTHLY TOTAL: [   ] $235–$815

Heading back to work comes with an incremental price tag—the cost of paying someone to care for your baby while you're away. Factor in this huge expense; it often puts your working income in a new perspective.

1. Start by identifying a child care option below. Child care costs vary significantly depending on the type of care you want, where you live, the number of infants you have, and your caregiver's credentials and responsibilities. (For help with this decision, check out Chapter 10, "Nine Simple Steps to Great Child Care.")

2. Then refer to the corresponding "typical monthly cost" benchmarks. Want an in-demand day care center or superexperienced nanny who helps with housework in an expensive urban area? Assume the middle to higher end of these price ranges below. Looking for affordable options in a small town? Assume the lower end.
Shortcut: Despite these wide ranges, most new parents these days pay about $10 to $13 an hour for an experienced baby-sitter and about $600 to $1,000 a month for full-time, licensed infant day care, so you could use these rates for your initial estimate.

3. Write your estimated monthly child care costs in the boxes on the next page, and use it to calculate your life-with-baby budget today. When you're ready to nail down specifics, call a few parents or providers in your area.

If you're hoping to stay home during year one, you could still assume a small monthly baby-sitting cost for occasional weekend date nights or daytime help (bringing a ten-month-old to your annual OB-GYN exam is never fun).

FULL-TIME CHILD CARE (assumes coverage 45 hours a week)

In-Home Options:	Typical Monthly Cost
Live-in nanny or au pair*	Room, board & stipend
Experienced daytime baby-sitter/nanny*	$1,440–$3,060+
Share care* (You share your baby-sitter with another family, splitting costs.)	$720–$1,530+
Relative care	Typically free

Options Outside Your Home:	
Day care center	$300–$1,300+
Home-based day care	$275–$1,100+
On-site child care at your place of work (Ask human resources.)	Varies

PART-TIME CHILD CARE (assumes coverage 27 hours a week)

In-Home Options:	Typical Monthly Cost
Experienced daytime baby-sitter/nanny*	$860–$1,835+
Share care* (You share your baby-sitter with another family, splitting costs.)	$430–$920+
Relative care	Typically free

Options Outside Your Home:	
Day care center	Possibly less than $300–$1,300**
Home-based day care	Possibly less than $275–$1,100**
On-site child care at your place of work (Ask human resources.)	Varies

HOURLY

Experienced daytime baby-sitter/nanny	$8–$17 an hour x your monthly needs

CHILD CARE MONTHLY TOTAL:

Multiply by 12

CHILD CARE ANNUAL TOTAL:

 * You should offer paid vacation and you may be expected to subsidize health insurance.

** Day care centers generally consider thirty or more hours a week full-time, and many require full-time rates even if you only need care three or four days a week. Call providers in your area for specifics.

Now calculate your monthly nonbaby expenses, from housing to haircuts. If already have a monthly budget defined using software like Quicken or your own system, feel free to use that total instead of this sheet. If you need some help, this walks you through the process.

	Your Estimated Monthly Expense
HOUSING	
Rent or monthly mortgage payment	_____
Home insurance payment	_____
Monthly assessments, dues, etc.	_____
Furniture and decorations (divide annual expenditures by 12)	_____
Lawn, exterior maintenance, and home repairs	_____
LOANS AND FINANCES (excluding mortgage)	
Average monthly credit card payment	_____
Average monthly school loan payment	_____
Average monthly home equity loan payment	_____
UTILITIES AND PHONE	
Electricity, gas, and water	_____
Phone (local, long distance, cell)	_____
TRANSPORTATION	
Car payments and car insurance	_____
Gas	_____
Public transportation, taxis, etc.	_____
HEALTH AND BEAUTY	
Fitness club membership (monthly dues)	_____
Other fitness (tennis, yoga classes, etc.)	_____
Health insurance and copayments	_____
Other medical expenses	_____
Haircuts, highlights, manicures, etc.	_____
LEISURE	
Entertainment	_____
Eating out, morning coffee purchases, etc.	_____
Hobbies	_____
Magazines and books	_____
CLOTHING (average monthly cost, excluding maternity and nursing wear)	_____
GROCERIES (food, toiletries, cleaning supplies, etc., each month)	_____
PETS	_____
GIFTS (annual expenses divided by 12)	_____
VACATION (annual expenses divided by 12)	_____
OTHER (miscellaneous items)	_____

EVERYTHING ELSE MONTHLY TOTAL: [_____]

Multiply by 12

EVERYTHING ELSE ANNUAL TOTAL: [_____]

Once you've subtracted your expenses from your income in the life-with-baby budget calculator, you know your family's available cash monthly and annually. Get your results interpreted here.

Is Your Available Cash a Negative Number?

If so, you have two options: decrease year one costs or increase your income.

Cutting costs: Review your expenses, looking for opportunities to save. Could you bring lunch to work every day? Freeze new clothing purchases? Drop your gym membership? Scale back on your dream nursery? Skip the family trip this year? Child care is often a budget breaker; are there less expensive alternatives in your area? For lots of ideas, check out Chapter 7: "Living for Less and Loving It."

Increasing your income: Did you use a reduced part-time salary for yourself because you want to cut back at work? Or did you leave your salary line item blank because you're hoping to stay home for a year? If so, don't give up yet. Revisit your expenses and look for opportunities to save. Once you've minimized your family expenses, it's reality check time. Calculate how much salary you need to bring your family finances into the black. Maybe you could afford a 20 percent income reduction, so you can cut your work schedule from five days a week to four (assuming your employer will agree). You may find your full-time income is essential to cover your household costs this year. If so, head back to work feeling confident about your contribution to the household budget and revisit your job options next year.

Is Your Available Cash a Positive Number?

That's a great start. Is it a comfortable monthly surplus? Keep in mind that your available cash needs to fund your savings (like a 529 plan to start saving toward college tuition) and any unforeseen expenses. Many financial advisers recommend maintaining an emergency fund to cover family costs for three to six months if needed. You don't want to be scrambling to make your mortgage payment one month after an unexpected layoff. Once you're comfortable with your life-with-baby budget, it's go time.

If you were testing a reduced salary for yourself because you want to cut back at work or stay home this year, congratulations—you can afford this option! Now you're ready to take the next step toward making your final work decision.

Identify Your Mom/Work Baggage

"So, what's your plan work-wise?" Leslie's mother-in-law Carol asked as the family ate dinner. Leslie managed a local fitness center, and she was the primary breadwinner. She and her husband Jake were in the process of adopting a son.

"I plan to keep working full-time," Leslie responded. "I love my job, and we need the money. It's a pretty clear choice."

"I see," Carol glanced over at Jake. "Is that what you think is best for the baby, honey?"

Leslie cringed, knowing Carol stayed home with Jake and his brother.

"Yes, Mom," he responded, giving Leslie a supportive nod. "Yes, we do."

|•|

"Monique is doing really well, Dad. She's two months old today," Katrin said cheerfully into the phone, patting her daughter on the back as she talked. "And I've made a big decision. I'm going to quit my job and stay home with her for a year."

"You're what?" Her father was clearly stunned. "After your promotion in September? And all your hard work?" Katrin understood her father's perspective. He saved for years to send her to college and bragged to his friends about her career success.

"Well, yes," she answered, suddenly not so certain about her choice.

|•|

"Okay, people, Pilar is cutting back to part-time, so I'm going to need you to step up and take on more responsibility," Ann's manager stood at the front of the conference room, addressing her team. "We obviously can't afford to hire anyone else at this point."

"Great," a colleague murmured beside her. "Our hours are already too long. Now we get to take over Pilar's work as well."

Ann looked down at the table. She was pregnant, although she hadn't made the announcement yet at work. And she was hoping to switch to part-time herself when the baby was born. As she looked around the room, she started to question her plan for the first time.

|•|

The arena of work and motherhood remains controversial. It's one those things, like politics and wars and movie rental selections, that divides families and threatens friendships and generates lots of passive-aggressive comments around kitchen tables everywhere. Everybody has an opinion, and you've likely heard plenty of them.

Maybe your mother has suggested real moms stay home, or your Dad has said leaving work for a while "would be a real waste of that college degree." Maybe your manager has implied part-time workers aren't respected, or your college friend has wondered why anyone would give up a great job to change diapers. Maybe your husband has said you can kiss family vacations good-bye without your full-time salary, or your neighbor has gossiped about the horrible nanny next door. If we were completely rational beings, we could ignore the running commentary and make our decisions independently. But in the real world, a lifetime of comments is impossible to dismiss. In fact, it's hard to even identify where others' opinions end and our real feelings begin—to unearth the sources of our assumptions.

The layers of influence from our families, friends, and the media create what I call mom/work baggage. We all have it. It's the source behind those unspoken, often highly irrational fears that make the work decision so difficult. Until you get a handle on yours, it's nearly impossible to make your choice with clarity. There are lots of ways mom/work baggage can confuse you. Here are just a few of the big ones.

Am I Just Being Selfish? Paranoia

Is it selfish of me to (shift to part-time/leave my job for a while/try to freelance) when we could really use my full-time income? Is it fair to put more financial burden on my significant other just as the baby expenses are hitting? *Or* . . . Is it selfish of me to keep my current position now that I'm a mom? I know I like working, and I know we need my income, but am I a horrible mother for leaving my child?

Yes, ironically, our guilt can be just as powerful regardless of the work decision we make. Know this tendency and let yours go; you will make the best choice for yourself and your family.

Worst-Case Scenario Worries

If I take an extended leave from my job, will I completely lose it while I'm home with this tiny, nonspeaking person all day? Will I get hooked on soaps, start quoting Oprah at cocktail parties, and never again read a book without pictures? Or if I work full-time, will my child be forever traumatized by my daily departures and end up on *Dr. Phil* sobbing earnestly about her fears of abandonment?

It's easy to let your imagination run wild at this stage. Your hormones are still on overdrive and any baby-related decision is highly emotional. Channel your rational prebaby self and try to remain optimistic.

Exaggerated Financial Fears

Will we end up homeless and destitute without my full-time salary? Or, even scarier, will I be forced to cancel my *People* subscription and drink home-brewed coffee for the rest of my life?

Get your financial fears in check by creating a realistic family budget.

Absolute Ambition

I've worked incredibly hard, I'm smarter than my boss, and it sure would be sweet to have vice president added to my title the next time I run into my ex from high school (when he will, of course, ask for my business card just to "keep in touch").

After years of working, it's always weird to reevaluate your career ambitions. They may remain exactly the same, or your priorities may shift. Good luck getting a handle on your goals.

Daddy Loves Me Best: Sibling Rivalry

My sister just finished med school and is offering vaccines to poor children in Guatemala while training for her third marathon, and my brother is running his own investment banking firm while playing cello in the local symphony on weekends. Do I really want to face these people over the holidays without a full-time job?

Okay, nobody's siblings are that perfect, but you get the idea. Don't let family pressures unduly influence your career decision.

Keeping Up with the Joneses: Competitiveness

Friend X is staying home with her twin girls for a year and they started speaking like three weeks out of the womb. She's grown an organic garden in her backyard, taught the kids sign language "just for fun," and last I heard the girls were making shockingly realistic sculptures of past presidents out of Play-Doh. Friend Y kept working and just got that great promotion with the amazing company car. Plus, her son is perfectly well-adjusted and learning Russian from his baby-sitter. I'm lucky if I get a shower in every other day. What does everyone else know that I don't?

Don't even start down this road. You know we all have challenges, regardless of how perfect things seem from the outside. Make the choice that's right for your family and don't look back.

"I Never Wanted to Be June Cleaver" Paranoia (The Fear You Will Suddenly Personify Icky Media-Driven Stereotypes)

If I work full-time, will I become like those stressed-out moms in the TV ads and start wearing a bad business suit circa 1982, nude panty hose, and cross trainers while rushing a screaming infant through the grocery store and yelling into an oversized cell phone? Then again, if I cut back at work or stay home for a while, will I start living in cable-knit cardigans and spend endless emotional hours dwelling on the relative softness of different toilet paper brands? Will I morph into a *housewife*?

Recognize the subtle influence of media and pop culture images, then leave those stereotypes in the cereal aisle.

Somewhere under all this baggage are your authentic feelings on the issue of working while parenting. If you're incredibly intuitive and possibly spending truckloads of money on therapy, you can identify those feelings and make the decision with conviction. The rest of us take our best guess at the right personal approach, then we change our minds, then we change our minds again, and eventually time runs out and we do something. We put an end to the madness and make a decision—to work full-time or part-time, to take an extended leave or freelance, to work at home, stay home for a while, or start our own businesses. Hopefully, you can avoid the madness altogether.

Identify Your Mom/Work Baggage So You Can Approach
Your Career Decision with Clarity

How? It's easier than you think. Just write it down. List the names of a few of your closest friends, family members, and colleagues—anyone who may have influenced your feelings about work. After each name, briefly describe that person's stance on working moms. Try to remember any work-related comments, messages implied or explicit. The great thing about mom/work baggage is this: By identifying it, you take control. Once you understand the influences in your life, you decide which opinions to accept and which to ignore. You may even find your confusion isn't as complicated as you think, but simple dissonance between your desires and others'.

Go Beyond the Baggage:
Assess Your Alternatives with a Fresh Perspective

From Eve's journal:

Okay, here goes: I want to work. Full-time. As a mom. When I consider money, benefits, and the fact that I really like my job—I know it's the right decision.

I can admit that to myself now, despite my mother's recent guilt trips about leaving her precious grandson in day care. (And let's face it, while her intentions are good, she does have a track record of conveniently ignoring certain aspects of the big picture. This is the woman who wanted me to date her best friend's son based primarily on his flawless skin and perfect teeth postbraces. His lack of any discernible personality was apparently considered a nonissue.)

You've identified the influences in your life. Now consciously forget them; this is your choice to make. Complete the following thoughts on a new piece of paper and your gut feelings should become clearer. (Yes, this is where the book starts to feel strangely like a self-help seminar—minus the free coffee and bagels. Just go with me here; this stuff can be really helpful.) If you notice yourself articulating someone else's opinion—your mom's, your best friend's, your husband's, your colleague's—then stop. Try to keep an open mind and pinpoint your real preferences.

Returning to Your Old Job

- When I think about going back to my old job, I feel . . .
- The best parts are . . .
- The worst parts are . . .

Shifting to a New Position or Staying Home for a While

Flextime, compressed workweeks, flexplace, part-time, job sharing, freelancing, starting your own business, staying home for a while—whatever you're considering

- When I think about [*work option*], I feel . . .
- The best parts are . . .
- The worst parts are . . .

Identify Your Ideal Work Scenario and Come to Terms with Any Underlying Fears

"I think I've made a decision," Alexis said quietly to her friend over dinner.

"About your job?"

"Yes. I'm going to request a shift to four days a week, working from home on Mondays."

"That sounds great!"

"It does, doesn't it?" Alexis said, looking down at her hands. "Then why do I feel like I'm going to throw up?"

|*|

You've pinpointed what career options you can realistically afford. Your mom/work baggage has been tossed. And you've articulated the preferences that were in the back of your mind behind those infant CPR instructions

and the thank-you notes you still need to send. Now go with your gut reaction and make a choice.

Write at the Top of a Blank Page, "My Ideal Work Arrangement for the Next Year Is . . . "

Then finish the sentence. It should be affordable for you—this is the real
thing. Would you love to work from home to minimize your commute?
Work five half days to stay involved at the office? Start your own small
business selling children's clothes at trunk shows? Take this year off,
keeping in touch through e-mails and lunches? Run from your current
job and never look back? Write it down, and then include a list of benefits for this scenario. Nothing's too random—if you want to work part-
time because you'd really miss your new laptop, include it on your list.

Now Give That Option the Sick Stomach Test

Let it seem real, like it's a decision you've already made. How do you feel?
Energized? You may have nailed it. Sick to your stomach? Not a good
sign. This may not be the best choice, or you may just need to think
through your concerns. Every option has negatives, no matter how small.
You may love the idea of taking off a year but hate the lifestyle adjustments required with the loss of your income. Or you may want to work
full-time but fear leaving your child in someone else's care.

Consider Any Underlying Concerns You Have About the Choice You Just Made, and Think Through Strategies to Minimize Those Risks

Summarize each concern at the top of a new page. Then, under each one,
jot down ideas for minimizing that risk. If you want to work from home
but you're afraid of becoming isolated or falling out of the office loop,
brainstorm about ways you could socialize each week and stay connected
with colleagues. For lots of suggestions, check out common concerns and
strategies to overcome them in Chapter 11, "Loving Life as a Working
Mom," and Chapter 12, "June Cleaver Be Damned."

If needed, follow this same process with other work arrangements until
you pinpoint one that feels right. The postmaternity leave job decision is al-

ways emotional, but you should feel (relatively) calm, confident, and ready for the next step—making your ideal position a reality. Or, if you want some additional encouragement first, check out the following success stories.

Get Inspired by Success Stories from the Working Mom Front

Looking for inspiration as you make your final work decision? Learn how new moms are combining work and family in lots of different arrangements—from full-time to freelancing, from starting a business to sequencing out of the workforce for a while. Their names have been changed, but their stories are real. Do these women "have it all"? That's a tough one. The new moms I spoke with were honest about both the benefits and the challenges of their lifestyles. But at the end of the day, they were all happy—and that's the best measure of success I've come up with so far.

Full-Timer: Abby

Position: Attorney

Schedule: Monday to Friday, 8:00 A.M. to 6:00 P.M. or so, plus some work from home

Child care: Day care center

As a new mom, why did you want to work full-time?

I had been an associate for seven years, and I knew I was close to making partner. If I had shifted to part-time, it would have delayed that long-term goal. Plus, my salary really helps us financially and my firm tends to be family-friendly—focusing on the end product rather than face time—so I felt comfortable continuing my full-time commitment after my daughter was born.

At law firms, it's often more accepted to work fewer hours but remain full-time than to officially switch to part-time—because clients often need to reach you five days a week. I felt like I would be more sane, and better compensated, if I spread my workload over a five-day week, rather than cramming everything into four days and worrying about clients calling me on day five. And I've been lucky so far that my five-day week hasn't been supercrazy.

Has your full-time job allowed you to meet your current career and life goals?

I was recently elected partner, so I feel great about my career accomplishments. As a mom, my dream is to have a happy, well-adjusted child—and my daughter is doing really well. She loves her day care center, and I'm thrilled that she's receiving such wonderful care and benefiting from the socialization. I know she's happy during the day, so I can focus at work and then head out in time to focus on her and enjoy our evenings and weekends together.

What are the greatest benefits of keeping your full-time job?

Knowing myself, I wouldn't be as happy without my job. It's important to me to get positive feedback outside the home and have my own income. And I love being part of a team. Plus, I like being a strong role model for my daughter. Hopefully, as she gets older I can help inspire her to achieve her own goals.

What are the greatest challenges?

I feel a sort of tension between my career and family responsibilities. As a new partner, I should be attending client dinners and events—the kinds of things that eat away at family time. And when my daughter gets sick, my husband and I have to figure out who can stay with her or work from home. Some days are crazy, but I know this is the best approach for us right now. Overall, I feel like it's a great balance.

Do you have any tips for other new moms working full-time?

I think the key to success is a strong support network. If you have a significant other, work together to tackle your parenting and household responsibilities. Start researching your child care options early so you can find a provider you love. If you're interested in a day care center, you may need to put your child on the waiting list months in advance. Ask for help from family and friends when you need it. And keep your expectations in check. You can't do everything perfectly—you have to give your-self a break some days and just know you're doing your best.

Flextimer: Vanessa

Position: Technical support sales representative

Schedule: Monday through Friday, forty hours a week with a variable daily schedule

Child care: Day care center (with a webcam, so she can check in anytime)

As a new mom, why did you want flextime?

My company doesn't offer any work-from-home arrangements, and flextime allowed me to keep my full-time salary with some accommodation for my daughter's needs.

How did you negotiate for flextime?

Flextime is not an official company policy; it's informally approved by individual managers. I've been at my company for five years, and I have a good track record. Plus, my job involves a lot of e-mail, so it can be done anytime. I approached my manager with a flextime request when I re-turned from maternity leave, and she approved it. Although I was the only new mom in my department, there are a few older women who care for their parents, so my manager was used to making accommodations for family care. And she knew she could trust me to get my work done re-gardless of my hours at the office.

Has flextime allowed you to meet your current career and life goals?

My flexible schedule has been great. I have to work eight hours a day, but I can come in when it's convenient for me. I initially planned to work 7:00 A.M. to 3:00 P.M., but I've found my morning schedule often varies depending on when my daughter wakes up and how organized I am. When she has pediatrician appointments, I can take her to the doctor and then go into work without worrying about calling my manager or miss-ing meetings.

What are the greatest benefits?

The flexibility makes my daily life so much easier, and I appreciate the income, sense of independence, and social interaction of my job. If I was home all the time, I'd be afraid my whole world would focus around my daughter. It's nice to have a break and then head home excited to spend time with her.

What are the greatest challenges?

As a new mom, I don't have time for fun little work perks like catching up on personal e-mail or grabbing lunch with friends. I'm focused on getting my work done, and then I pump during my lunch break. We have a designated nursing room at my office, which is great for privacy, but it's not the most exciting place to spend my free time.

Do you have any tips for other moms interested in flextime?

I highly recommend flextime if you can negotiate it with your employer. Just ignore unsupportive comments from others working full-time. I used to work late fairly often, but now I head out as soon as I've put in my eight hours. And as I'm packing up—usually before 5:00 P.M.—a colleague of mine likes to say, "Oh wow, is it time to go already?" I just respond, "For me it is," and head out without letting her get to me.

Compressed Workweek: Kylie

Position: Administrative assistant

Schedule: Tuesday to Friday, 8:00 A.M. to 5:00 P.M. (considered full-time)

Child care: Her mother-in-law (day care for twins isn't cheap)

As a new mom, why did you want to compress your workweek?

I love my job, but when my twins were born I wanted to spend more time at home. Plus, my mother-in-law offered to baby-sit for us, and I felt like I couldn't ask her to help more than four days a week.

How did you negotiate your new schedule?

My team needs secretarial support all week, and I wanted to work four days—so I knew I'd have to find someone to cover my day off. I called one of the floating secretaries who was filling in during my maternity leave and asked if she'd like to continue in the position one day a week. We figured out the details over the phone, and then I talked to my supervisors. I focused on the fact that I'd be coming in earlier than I used to because I knew they'd like the additional productivity. And they were able to work it out so the floater was assigned to Mondays in our group. It worked out well for everyone.

Has the compressed workweek allowed you to meet your current career and life goals?

Yes, I'm able to get out of the house, stay mentally challenged, keep my friendships at the office, and make money. And I love having long weekends with the twins.

What are the greatest benefits?

I'm able to keep my full salary and benefits, be home three days a week, and feel comfortable that my mother-in-law is happy with her baby-sitting commitment. The compressed schedule is really the best-case work scenario for me during this stage.

What are the greatest challenges?

It's not easy leaving the twins in someone else's care four days a week, but I feel lucky that we have a relative staying with them. They adore her, so that makes the process a lot easier.

Do you have any tips for other moms hoping to compress their workweeks?

Be upfront and honest from the beginning. In my case, I realized I needed a shorter weekly schedule to make the baby-sitting easier for my mother-in-law. And when I explained the situation to my supervisors, they understood. They also knew I had a strong commitment to them, so they were willing to work around my schedule as long as everything got done. Before you meet with your boss, think about how the shorter week could work with your position. Try to come up with a plan in advance so you can explain exactly how you'll do your job. And during your days at home, really focus on your child. When I'm home on Mondays, I try not to spend too much time catching up on housework or errands. I want it to be a fun day with my kids.

Position: Marketing manager

Part-Timer: Maria

Schedule: Tuesday through Thursday, usually 8:00 A.M. to 5:00 P.M.

Child care: Started with on-site day care, then shifted to a three-way baby-sitter share

As a new mom, why did you want to work part-time?

Before we adopted my daughter, my full-time hours could be long, and I was in a relatively stressful role. I knew as a parent I'd be happier if I could cut back my work schedule and responsibilities. I wasn't interested in leaving work entirely; if I was home all the time I know I'd start obsessing about random domestic things like the fact that my husband didn't do the dishes after dinner. I needed my own projects to focus on; I just wanted a balance between work and parenting. Part-time seemed like the best solution.

How did you negotiate your part-time position?

I could have gone to my director, but she had chosen to work full-time as a mom and I was afraid she might not be the best advocate for a part-time role. So I met with a human resources manager. I explained my track record and desire to take a six-month maternity leave and then come back part-time. I had positive performance appraisals and good business results as a full-timer, so I assumed they would want to keep me. We had an informal discussion about potential part-time roles in the company, and she said they would keep me in mind for the next opening. A few months into my leave, she called with news of a part-time position doing new product development. I would no longer be managing a core business, but I actually preferred the lower stress level as a new mom anyway.

How was your transition from full-time to part-time?

The first six months were challenging. I was used to working long hours, beating deadlines, and generally overdelivering, and I didn't have a good role model or mentor to help me set new expectations for myself as a part-timer. My director at that time also had unrealistic expectations for my productivity. She really wanted full-time output from me, so I often felt like I wasn't doing well enough. It was very frustrating. After six months, a new director was assigned to our group. She had worked part-time in the past herself, and she gave me more realistic goals. Plus, I had gotten the hang of the reduced schedule, and since then I've been thrilled with the part-time lifestyle.

Has part-time work allowed you to meet your current career and life goals?

I used to be focused on achieving at work and moving up in the company. My career success fulfilled a certain need I had; it gave me confidence and was closely tied up with my self-esteem. Now, work plays a different role in my life. I still want to do well, and I appreciate the mental stimulation, but I can leave at 5:00 P.M. to pick up my daughter without stressing about work I could be completing. I'm very efficient while I'm at the office, and I know I add value at least relative to my salary, if not more. Then I look forward to heading home. It's an ideal combination for me.

What are the greatest benefits of working part-time?

I love the fact that I'm home more than I'm at work; I have a great outlet to use my brain, and I still make enough money to feel comfortable about our family finances. My income allows us to afford certain things that make life easier like flying home to visit my parents rather than driving eight hours. I feel like I'm buying myself quality time with my family.

What are the greatest challenges?

It's interesting; the restrictions that my part-time peers might complain about don't really bother me. My career path is in a holding pattern; I've been told point-blank I won't be promoted to director until I switch back to full-time. That could be frustrating if I wanted more responsibility right now, but fortunately I don't. There's a premium on benefits for part-time employees at our company, but I can use my husband's benefits. I have fewer direct reports now; as a full-timer I managed three marketing associates and now I manage only one. If I was concerned about expanding my managerial experience, that could be a problem, but I'm not. I'm just happy to come in, get my work done, and head home without unnecessary stress.

Do you have any tips for other moms hoping to work part-time?

Before making the switch, ask other part-time employees at your company for advice and try to find a mentor. My transition would have been much easier if I could have talked to someone about managing a reduced workload and establishing realistic expectations with my director. I've joined an informal network of part-time employees at our company. It's cross-functional; there are part-timers from administrative support, sales, marketing, and customer service. About twenty-five of us meet quarterly in a conference room over lunch. We discuss policy issues like standardizing part-time benefits, and we share strategies that help with work/life balance. We also put together case studies of successful part-time positions to share with directors who may otherwise resist alternative work arrangements. It's been a great support system for me, and I definitely recommend trying to join or establish a network of part-timers in your own company if possible.

Also, you have to create boundaries from the beginning. When I started in my part-time position, I went around and introduced myself to my new team members by saying, "Hi, I'm the part-time gal. I'm here Tuesdays through Thursdays." I was very clear, but some people still tried to schedule meetings with me on my off days. I really try to avoid coming in Mondays and Fridays because I think it sets a dangerous precedent. If I absolutely have to come to the office for a Monday meeting, I comp myself the time and leave early another day that week. You have to be very strong about protecting your part-time schedule or your colleagues will assume it's fluid, and you'll end up resentful.

Job Sharer: Natasha

Position: Advertising salesperson for a women's magazine

Schedule: Monday through Wednesday, 9:00 A.M. to 5:00 P.M.

Child care: Two-way baby-sitter share

As a new mom, why did you want to job-share?

We need my income, so I never considered leaving work altogether. And my job requires full-time coverage; clients call with requests or questions throughout the week, so I knew I couldn't just cut back to part-time. After my maternity leave, I returned to work full-time, but I was traveling quite a bit and feeling torn between my job responsibilities and parenting. When my daughter was six months old, I started looking for a job share partner so I could still make 60 percent of my salary but cut my travel in half and spend four days a week at home.

How did you negotiate your job share?

First, I found a colleague interested in a job share. She was pregnant with twins and liked the idea of coming back part-time after her maternity leave. She and I were a great fit; we had similar experience, track records, and working styles. We talked to other job share partners at the company, discussed how we would manage the logistics of the job share, and wrote a proposal outlining our request. The proposal included our plans for communicating with clients and management, handling ongoing projects, and meeting annual goals. We were each asking for 60 percent of our full-time salaries, so we included revenue projections that made the case for an overall salary increase. Then we scheduled a meeting with my manager and presented the proposal. She seemed impressed, and ultimately she approved our request.

Has the job share allowed you to meet your current career and life goals?

Yes, it's been great. I feel like I'm even more productive than I used to be because I want to prove to my manager that the job share approach can work and I don't want to let my partner down. It's an interesting dynamic; as job share partners you depend on each other for your career success. I want to uphold my end of the team, so I try very hard to make sales, document calls and meetings well, and maintain smooth communication. And I really appreciate my days at home.

What are the greatest benefits of job sharing?

You don't have to worry about work on your days off. You know your partner is handling everything at the office so you can be relaxed and 100 percent focused on your child.

What are the greatest challenges?

Job sharing does require extra time each day to document everything so there won't be any questions or misunderstandings. Your paperwork increases, but it's definitely worth it. Also, you depend on your partner, so if she decided to quit you would have to find a replacement or temporarily take over her work. That could be really stressful.

Do you have any tips for other moms hoping to job share?

Find a compatible job share partner. If you split responsibilities with someone who isn't meticulous about documentation, for example, you aren't going to be successful. Some job share teams we spoke with kept two phone numbers and e-mail accounts, and that approach often required clients to make multiple calls to get questions answered. To avoid that confusion, we used one phone number and e-mail account. We didn't have any privacy, but that was fine—it was just for work. Plus, we created our own processes and paperwork. Our manager and clients have never had to repeat themselves, and we've received great feedback about our performance.

Flexplacer: Lisa

Position: Mortgage broker

Schedule: Variable

Child care: Primarily works during naps, weekends, and evenings, and does free baby-sitting swap with neighbors during busy periods

As a new mom, why did you want to work from home?

When my son was born, my top priority was spending time with him, but I also needed to make some money, so I started looking for jobs I could do from home on my own schedule.

How did you get your work-from-home position?

I knew I couldn't work from home in my old job, and I didn't find any great leads in the classifieds or online—so I had to get creative. Initially, I earned extra money by making sales on eBay, and then I started offering daytime baby-sitting services to families in our neighborhood. But eventually I wanted a different type of mental challenge.

When we refinanced our house, I became intrigued by the industry. After working with a mortgage broker, I realized it was a job I could do from home, and I knew I had the skills to be successful. I called a few brokerage firms and asked a lot of questions, basically just following my natural curiosity. Once I understood the career opportunities, I called the company we used to refinance and told them I was interested in working for them from home. I didn't have direct brokerage experience, but I outlined my background and explained how I could add value to their company. They hired me, provided some basic training, and now I've built up a steady business.

Has your position allowed you to meet your current career and life goals?

For now, this is a perfect way for me to meet the needs of my family. I get to exercise my brain even beyond the daily challenges of parenting, and I help pay the bills.

What are the greatest benefits of working from home?

I love being at home. I can see my son throughout the day, I don't have to waste time commuting to work, and my schedule is completely flexible.

What are the greatest challenges?

It can be hard to make client calls from home with a child potentially making noise in the house. And even on weekends, I could be walking around the zoo with my son in the stroller but thinking about an upset client I should call as soon as we get back. There's not a clear separation between work and family life.

Do you have any tips for other moms hoping to work from home?

If you can negotiate a work-from-home arrangement with your employer, I think that would be ideal. You'd be in a position you know well with more convenience. If your employer won't let you work from home, look for other options. I just kept trying things and asking questions until I found a job that suited me. Follow your curiosity and don't be afraid to ask questions. A friend of mine received a welcome basket, and she asked the delivery person about the company. Now she makes and delivers welcome baskets in our area. You could also look for opportunities with small businesses. The mortgage company I'm working for is run by a husband and wife team, and they completely understood my interest in a flexible, at-home schedule. I didn't have to negotiate with a human resources department; I just defined the position I wanted and they approved it.

Freelancer: Stephanie

Position: PRN (per required need) occupational therapist

Schedule: Generally three days a week with variable daily appointments

Child care: Her mother

As a new mom, why did you want to freelance?

I knew I needed to work to pay our mortgage, but I wanted control of my schedule after my son was born.

How did you establish yourself as an independent contractor?

Before I left my full-time job, I called several local hospitals and nursing homes and asked about their needs. I let them know I was thinking about going PRN—offering my services as an independent contractor—and I wanted to gauge the opportunity in our market. I learned local supply and demand were on my side. Several people I talked to said they could use my help on a fairly consistent basis, so I knew I wasn't taking a huge risk. I have expertise in rehabilitation and acute care, so my skills are marketable.

Once I decided to go out on my own, I called around again and let everyone know my availability. I wanted to limit my work to three days a week, so I spread the word about my open days and hours. I had some clients right away, and once I established myself, the work just kept coming. Sometimes I have ongoing projects; now I'm covering for a full-timer on maternity leave at a hospital, so I know that's a steady job for three months. Otherwise, I keep in contact with the local hospitals and nursing homes to determine their upcoming needs.

Has freelancing allowed you to meet your current career and life goals?

I love it. I have complete control of my work schedule; I can take off a couple of weeks around the holidays, take vacation whenever my husband does, or work a shorter day if I need to get a haircut or take my son to the pediatrician. I just let my clients know my schedule, and they work with it. I don't have to negotiate with human resources to take off during busy periods or worry about letting my employer down to meet family responsibilities.

What are the greatest benefits of freelancing?

I can interact with adults, use my brain, and stay out of office politics. I just come in, work with my clients, and then head home. I feel like I have positive energy with my son because I'm not stressed at work. Plus, I've learned a lot by working at so many different sites. I've been exposed to different paperwork, different paces, and different people. I feel like I could work almost anywhere now.

What are the greatest challenges?

I do miss the close friendships I had in my full-time job. As an independent contractor, I'm not part of a team. Everyone is nice, but I don't have the same kind of social support system at work. Now I make more of an effort personally to get together with friends or schedule play dates on my days off.

Also, freelancing obviously doesn't offer the stability of full-time work. I'm a control freak by nature, so it took some time to get used to the uncertainty of this approach. One week I may be fully booked, and the next I may end up calling around to fill in a lot of open hours. I get paid by the hour now and my benefits aren't covered, so there's definitely pressure to stay busy. Fortunately the work has been consistent enough over time, and I've gotten used to the variable schedule.

Do you have any tips for other moms hoping to freelance?

Do research first. Call around to establish some contacts and make sure there's a need for your services. Then put yourself out there and see who bites. And don't be afraid to approach your full-time employer with a freelance proposal. It's easy to tell yourself your director won't be interested in a freelancer, but you never know what she might be willing to negotiate. Bring her a specific plan with your services, availability, and fees, and see what happens. You have to have the guts and confidence to sell yourself and accept rejection if someone isn't interested.

Entrepreneur: Isabella

Position: Cofounder of a company that offers cooking classes for new mothers

Schedule: Variable

Child care: Combination of her mom, baby-sitters, and bringing her son to classes

As a new mom, why did you want to start your own business?

I was running an adult cooking class program, and during my pregnancy I started thinking about options that would give me more autonomy as a mom. I talked to a colleague with a similar background, and we came up with the idea for our company. She had a toddler and was pregnant as well, and we collaborated on the business plan during our pregnancies. We decided we would use our instructional cooking experience to offer classes for new moms.

We realized mothers are so interested in meeting each other, but they often focus on baby-oriented activities to connect. Our classes range from easy dinner ideas to making baby food, and we design them so the babies can nap or play. We also provide interactive cooking activities at kids' birthday parties, and we're about to launch mommy-and-me classes for toddlers.

How did you found your company?

Once we wrote the business plan, we developed a class schedule, created a website, found an inexpensive space for the classes, established marketing alliances with local food sellers who could help us cross-promote, and then focused on spreading the word. I started going to a new mom seminar series mainly to meet new friends, but it ended up being a great way to market our company as well. Word-of-mouth among mothers is so much more valuable than dollars spent on advertising.

Has your company allowed you to meet your current career and life goals?

I love having control of my schedule, and we've hired chef assistants to help with some of the classes now, so I have even more flexibility. I do all the planning from home, which is great, and I'm meeting so many women with young children. It's fulfilling my professional and personal needs in a lot of ways. Also, I've been able to bring my eight-month-old son to some classes and let him hang out with the babies, which is a nice way to integrate the two worlds.

What are the greatest benefits of running your own business?

I'm able to use my experience and skills in a new way that works even better for me during this stage. And we can control the amount of time we want to put into the company, offering fewer classes or bringing in more people to help as needed.

What are the greatest challenges?

The income is not as stable as full-time employment, but I feel like there's great potential. We're in the early stages of the company now, and I'm hoping to expand over time—bringing in more instructors and offering classes for different age-groups.

Do you have any tips for other entrepreneurs?

If you can, create a website from the beginning to legitimize the business. When we were brainstorming potential company names, we checked to make sure the domain names were available for our favorites before settling on one. Establish as many marketing partnerships as you can. Networking and word-of-mouth are so important when you're getting started. Follow up with all your contacts from past jobs. Have business cards made; do what you can to appear professional. And start at a pace that works for your lifestyle, ramping up gradually if that's easier for you.

Sequencer: Lauren

Position: Former financial analyst, current full-time mom

As a new mom, why did you want to leave your job in finance?

I was working with great people, making a nice salary, and learning a lot. So in some ways, it was hard to walk away from my job. But my hours were long and I realized my working lifestyle would be difficult to manage as a new parent. Plus, there were no part-time role models at my company. There was basically an unspoken sense that the client service demands of our jobs required a full-time commitment. My husband also worked long hours and traveled quite a bit, so I realized something had to give. During my maternity leave, spending time with my son convinced me I was ready to leave work for a while.

How did you explain your decision to your employer?

I met with the director of our office and explained my feelings. He knew I always worked at 120 percent capacity, and I told him I was afraid of feeling like a failure professionally and personally—which probably would have happened if I had tried to balance my crazy work schedule with parenting. Although my office was male dominated, he was supportive and extended my leave for three months so I could fully consider my options. Toward the end of that period, I met with him again and explained my final decision to stay home for a while.

How was your transition to full-time parenthood?

At first, I had a major identity crisis. I remember the first time I brought my son to a mom-and-baby class at our gym. I looked around the room and thought, "I can't believe a couple of months ago I was working full-time with a bunch of guys." It was a surreal moment. Over time, I adjusted to the stay-at-home lifestyle, and I joined a playgroup with women who had similar backgrounds. We had all been focused on our careers and then decided to take off some time when our children were born. Their friendships made a huge difference in my experience of new parenthood. It made me realize I wasn't alone—that there were a lot of women who were trying a similar approach.

Has this time at home allowed you to meet your current career and life goals?

Yes, I've been very happy with my choice, and I love being home with my son.

What are the greatest benefits of sequencing?

I like to believe I'm experiencing the best of both worlds. I focused on my career for over ten years; now I'm focusing on parenting. The greatest benefit of this approach is all the time I've had with my son during this early stage. We plan to have two children, and when they're both in preschool I'll head back to the workforce again. I'd love to find a part-time or flextime finance position at that point. I'm not sure exactly where I'll end up, but I'm optimistic something will work out when I'm ready.

What are the greatest challenges?

I miss the intellectual stimulation and camaraderie of the workforce at times. Occasionally when I see women heading to work in their business suits I get a twinge of jealousy, but I definitely don't regret my decision.

And I am concerned that my work skills won't be as sharp when I return to the job market. After working so hard, it would be very disappointing if my résumé became irrelevant because I left the workforce for a few years. My dad has a small business, and I've helped him with a few projects so I have something for my résumé from this period. I hope that will make a difference.

Do you have any tips for other moms interested in sequencing?

Keep in touch with your old work colleagues. You don't want them to forget about you; they may eventually hire you back, or at least they can provide references when you're looking for a job. You could read the trades or check websites for your industry to stay current. And as you're making the transition away from work, definitely connect with other moms going through the same process.

Negotiating Your Ideal Position

Now You Know What You Want to Do;

Make It Happen

From Megan's journal:

> *Work decision finally made! My plan: Work part-time and shift*
> *responsibilities to Francie, who wants more client exposure anyway. Now*
> *just praying Mara will approve my request. Must explain how I can meet*
> *annual sales goals with three-day schedule. Should talk to Christy—*
> *part-time overachiever—for advice.*

You've pinpointed your ideal work arrangement. Now make it happen. If you've decided to return to your old full-time schedule, you're golden. When your maternity leave ends, you'll simply head back to known territory with assurance. If you want to extend your leave or negotiate a new arrangement with your current employer—flextime, compressed workweeks, working from home, part-time, job sharing, or freelancing for your company—it's time to sell your request.

Although some work environments are clearly more enlightened than others, 74 percent of U.S. employers offer some form of workplace flexibility, according to a recent Hewitt Associates survey.[1] And managers and human resources professionals are increasingly open to proposals for work/life accommodations—for full-timers and those hoping to cut back. Yet many of us never ask for flexible work arrangements because we assume the answer will be no, or we're afraid of being perceived as slackers. We all want to be respected, and after a lifetime of working at 110 percent, it can be gut wrenching for one's all-star status to take a hit. Plus, we're contending with the female instinct to keep everyone happy, and the idea of making life difficult for our managers or colleagues can be more painful than Braxton-Hicks contractions. But this is the time to look out for yourself.

Most employers will try to accommodate you if you come to them with a well-thought-out plan, says Natalie Gahrmann, work/life expert for BlueSuitMom and *Parenting* magazine. If your employer offers a flexible work arrangement that meets your new mom lifestyle and financial requirements, repress your fear of rocking the boat and make the request. If not, don't give up. Many employers understand the need for work/life accommodations but simply haven't allocated resources to create the programs, according to Teresa Hopke, director of WorkLife Strategy for business and tax advisory firm RSM McGladrey, Inc.

And it is hard. Designing the wacky work arrangements and emergency child care assistance is tricky enough, but for this stuff to stick, employers have to get down in the trenches and change the way people think. Every manager needs to understand how flexibility can work, and every employee needs to feel comfortable making a request. In the meantime, be your own advocate and push the envelope with your management, says Hopke. As a valued employee with a good track record, you're in control. Think creatively about what could work for you, submit an impressive proposal, and be persistent.

Fortunately there are several macrofactors pushing for workplace flexibility, according to Lisa Levey, director of Advisory Services for Catalyst, a nonprofit research and consulting firm that focuses on advancing women in business:

- Current family dynamics, in which the majority of moms work even year one
- Technology that allows for remote work and communication

- Globalization (You're dealing with colleagues in five different time zones anyway; why should you be required to work *at the office?*)
- Aging baby boomers hoping to stay connected but cutting back at work
- Gen Y heading into the workforce looking for the balanced lives their parents never had

Head into the process with confidence and know we're all out here rooting for you. The first year of parenthood, we can ask our employers to step up as needed, use the work/life supports that are in place, and fill in the gaps with creativity, resourcefulness, a slightly warped sense of humor, and realistic expectations of ourselves on every front. (Remember, supermoms went out in the 1980s.) Let's push for and then demonstrate the viability of flexible work arrangements until family-friendly accommodations become the new standard. And we'll consider that legacy a long-term gift to our kids. And their kids.

In the future, flexibility won't be a program, a policy, a benefit, or a perk. It will become the way we work.

FAMILIES AND WORK INSTITUTE, *When Work Works*[2]

We all have unique challenges to consider, but the following step-by-step guide will walk you through the process—from organizing your thoughts and writing your new job description to selling your proposal and responding to common employer concerns.

Organize Your Thoughts

FROM:	**Megan Quinn**
TO:	**Amy Hainen**
SUBJECT:	**Preparing My Part-Time Pitch—Day 1**

Amy,

Following weeks of indecision, yesterday had a glorious work revelation. (About time, since maternity leave is drawing to a close.) Finally reviewed family finances, determined reduced salary won't sink us, and decided to cut back to part-time—if I can get approval.

Planning to pitch new schedule to Mara this Friday; must harness killer sales techniques gone soft during cuddly weeks at home with Sam. Would love to charge into her office waving baby photos, but should probably go for professional vibe instead. Need to organize thoughts, think through logistics, and write up formal plan. Wish me luck! Will keep you updated daily.

Megan

P.S. Sam is currently enjoying an unrequited love affair with his voice. Though limited to an impressive range of gargling sounds, the kid may have a real future in competitive yodeling.

Don't risk a quick rejection from your employer by making your request before you've done your homework. Once you've chosen your ideal work arrangement, start building your case. Where to begin? Pull out your employee handbook or check with human resources to determine your company's official stance on flexible work arrangements. No current policy for your preferred approach? No problem. Someone has to be the first—just plan to write a thorough proposal. Organize your thoughts using the worksheets on the following pages. They explain the primary challenges in negotiating each position and walk you through the key issues. Flip to the worksheet for your preferred position and follow the steps.

Choose from:

- Flextime/compressed workweeks
- Part-time
- Job sharing
- Flexplace (work from home)
- Freelancing
- Extended leave

FLEXTIME/COMPRESSED WEEK WORKSHEET

Your challenge: Convincing your employer you can adjust your schedule without creating communication problems or disrupting workflow

You've decided you want to ask for flextime, officially shifting your daily schedule to better accomodate family obligations. Or you're interested in compressed weeks, which squeeze a full-time load into three or four longer workdays. In either case, your full-time compensation and benefits should not change (unless you plan to ask for additional benefits such as child care assistance). You just need to demonstrate your plan for continued accessibility and productivity. Use this worksheet (or your own paper if you need more space) to organize your thoughts and include this information in your final proposal.

Scheduling Plan

Interested in flextime? What is your ideal daily schedule? 8:00 A.M. to 4:00 P.M. for easy child care pick-ups? 7:00 A.M. to 3:00 P.M. to spend more time with your baby? 11:00 A.M. to 7:00 P.M. to have mornings at home? Consider your lifestyle priorities, and then list your preferred starting and ending times here. Or, if you want to shift your daily schedule as needed, note the total daily and weekly hours you'll commit to be at work.

Interested in compressed workweeks? Decide which days you'd like to work and for how long. Often compressed workweeks involve four ten-hour days, but you may prefer three even longer ones. Your new schedule should total the same number of hours you worked over five days. List your ideal workdays and timing.

FLEXTIME		COMPRESSED WORKWEEKS	
Daily Start Time	End Time	Days of Week	Schedule Each Day
TOTAL: Daily Hours	Weekly Hours		

Communication Plan

What if your manager has an urgent question at 4:00 P.M. and your workday ended at 3:00 P.M.? Or a client needs you one Friday morning and your compressed workweek ended Thursday? Head off this objection by developing a foolproof communication plan. Many flextimers use PDAs or cell phones to guarantee accessibility from home. Others check in at designated times. Although none of us wants to feel invaded during our time away from the office, small accommodations like this can make the difference in getting your request approved. Consider the needs of your position and write down your thoughts.

Transition Plan

How will you tell your colleagues and clients about your new schedule? A memo or e-mail may work, plus personal calls to important clients. Be prepared to include this plan in your proposal; your professionalism and foresight will add credibility.

Productivity Plan

You're still working full-time, so your workflow shouldn't change significantly. Just be ready to explain minor adjustments like weekly reports to be submitted Thursdays instead of Fridays.

Your challenge: Convincing your employer some of your
responsibilities can be delegated without creating workflow problems
and demonstrating your accessibility on days off

Use this worksheet (or your own paper if you need more space) to organize your
thoughts and include this information in your final proposal.

Responsibilities

First, think about your job. Does your weekly marketing report really add value, or
could it be completed monthly instead? Develop a suggested plan for adjusting responsibilities that are less important but time-consuming. Then divide the remaining
tasks into two lists: those you can keep and those that need to be delegated. If possible,
note another employee who could take over each delegated task.

TASKS TO BE COMPLETED LESS FREQUENTLY OR CUT	TASKS TO BE MAINTAINED	TASKS TO BE DELEGATED	DELEGATE TO

Transition Plan

How will you shift your responsibilities? What sort of documentation will you provide
as you hand over projects? Do clients need to be contacted? Will you offer training? Jot
down your thoughts.

Communication Plan

Many part-time employees use PDAs or cell phones to offer accessibility from home.
Others check in at designated times. Although none of us wants to feel invaded during
our time away from the office, small accommodations like this can make the difference
in getting your request approved. Consider your employer's needs and develop a plan
for open communication.

Compensation Package

If you're lucky, your part-time salary and bonus will be reduced relative to your workload reduction (cutting back from five days to three would involve a 40 percent drop in
compensation, for example). In some cases, employers try to offer even less and may
cut benefits. For lots of ideas on maximizing your work/life benefits, check out Chapter 11, "Loving Life as a Working Mom."

REQUESTED SALARY	REQUESTED BENEFITS

JOB SHARE WORKSHEET

Your challenge: Convincing your employer you can effectively split responsibilities and potentially justifying an overall salary increase

Use this worksheet (or your own paper if you need more space) to organize your thoughts and include this information in your final proposal.

Responsibilities

Typically one job share partner works Monday through Wednesday and the other works Wednesday through Friday, with Wednesday used to transition projects. Your employer needs to know how you plan to manage the split workload. Divide your current responsibilities into two lists: those you can keep and those your job share partner will take.

YOUR RESPONSIBILITIES	YOUR JOB SHARE PARTNER'S RESPONSIBILITIES

Transition Plan

How will you shift responsibilities to your partner? What sort of documentation will you provide as you hand over projects? Will you provide training? How will you update colleagues and clients regarding the change?

Communication Plan

Smooth communication between job share partners, clients, and management is critical. Start by consolidating your contact information; you and your partner should share a joint e-mail account and work phone number. Then decide how you'll document meetings and phone calls and track ongoing projects. Be ready to share your processes and paperwork with your management when you're negotiating the position. They'll be more likely to approve if they're impressed with the professionalism and thoroughness of your approach.

Compensation Package

Generally both job share partners work three days a week, so ideally you should each receive 60 percent of your full-time salary. That would, however, require an overall compensation increase for the position. Justify this cost by projecting improved productivity or revenue. Some employers will try to cut benefits such as health care coverage; be ready to request your ideal benefits package as well. For lots of ideas on maximizing your work/life benefits, check out Chapter 11, "Loving Life as a Working Mom."

REQUESTED SALARY	REQUESTED BENEFITS

FLEXPLACE WORKSHEET

Your challenge: Convincing your employer you can maintain productivity and consistent communication from home

Demonstrate how your work can be accomplished between home and the office and detail strategies for keeping in touch. If you're worried about major resistance, you could propose a partial work-from-home plan at first, starting with only one or two days away from the office. After a few months, when your manager is comfortable with your productivity, you could request additional at-home days. Your compensation package should remain unchanged unless you're also shifting to part-time. Use this worksheet (or your own paper if you need more space) to organize your thoughts and include this information in your final proposal.

Productivity Plan

TASKS TO COMPLETED AT HOME	TASKS TO BE COMPLETED AT THE OFFICE

Communication Plan

Consider offering daily progress reports, morning conference calls, or end-of-day e-mails during your workdays at home. You could guarantee accessibility by setting up designated work phone and fax lines or using your cell phone only to take calls from the office. Think through the type of communication your manager prefers and define a weekly process that should make her comfortable.

FREELANCING WORKSHEET

Your challenge: Convincing your employer you can add value cost-effectively as an independent provider

Ready to swap your full-time job for the flexibility of freelancing? Start by pitching your independent services to your employer, who already knows your talents and work ethic. Use this worksheet (or your own paper if you need more space) to organize your thoughts and include this information in your final proposal.

Your Services

Consider your skill set and your employer's needs, and make a list of projects you could propose from graphic design to data entry, from accounting to personal training.

Your Fees

Calculate the fees you'd like to charge per project. Don't know where to start? Divide your full-time salary by the number of full-time hours you used work (2,000 annual hours is a standard benchmark) to calculate your old hourly revenue. Now add a premium; freelancers generally make significantly more per hour than full-time employees because they're working less and paying for their own benefits. Multiply your freelancer hourly rate by the number of hours you think you'll need to complete each project. Unsure about the time each project will require? You could simply propose an hourly rate and bill your employer weekly for the amount of time you work. When pitching your fees, start by reminding your employer of your full-time compensation package, including salary and benefits, and point out the savings that would accrue from paying you on a project basis.

OLD FULL-TIME HOURLY RATE   NEW FREELANCER HOURLY RATE

PROPOSED FEE FOR EACH FREELANCE PROJECT

Your Availability

How much time do you want to allocate to freelance projects? You may be able to work from home 15 to 20 hours a week during your baby's naps, weekends, and evenings, while a greater commitment would require you to pay for child care. And what about trips to the grandparents or other vacation time? As a freelancer, you can take advantage of your newfound flexibility and build in some downtime. Look at your calendar. Mark out weeks you'd prefer not to work, and be ready to explain your availability when meeting with your employer.

HOURS PER WEEK   AVAILABLE WEEKS

Your challenge: Demonstrating how your responsibilities can be delegated for several months without straining the team workload or convincing your employer you're worth placing on alumni status

If you want five or six months at home before returning to work, you need to demonstrate how your job can be covered while you're away. You're taking maternity leave, so your employer has to reallocate your responsibilities temporarily. An extended leave simply requires more time. This may not be a problem, or it may be perceived as unnecessary strain on an already overworked team. Use this worksheet (or your own paper if you need more space) to organize your thoughts and include this information in your final proposal.

(If you're interested in a really long leave—like a year or two—the best you can expect from your employer is alumni status. This means subsidizing your continuing professional education, keeping in touch, and possibly accommodating you when you're ready to return. You likely won't get a guarantee, but a very loose safety net is better than nothing. If this approach appeals to you, make the request.)

Responsibilities to Be Put on Hold

Could some of your work be postponed until your return? Maybe certain reports could be temporarily eliminated? Business trips scheduled later in the year? Not so essential projects cut from the immediate team workload?

TASKS	SUGGESTED TIMING

Responsibilities to Delegate

Who could temporarily take over your remaining work? A junior person on your team looking for additional responsibility? Someone at your level interested in more client exposure? A manager who could complete some of your tasks with very little effort? Consider spreading your projects among team members to minimize each employee's workload increase.

TASKS	DELEGATE TO

Compensation Package

You're probably already maxing out your paid days off, so your extended time at home will likely be salary-free. You should, however, confirm that benefits like health care coverage carry over during your months at home. You may have to pay your regular monthly health insurance bill and send a check to your employer for the portion typically covered. (Don't expect any benefits if you're taking the really long leave approach.) For lots of ideas on maximizing your work/life benefits upon your return, check out Chapter 11, "Loving Life as a Working Mom."

EXTENSION OF CURRENT BENEFITS	NEW WORK/LIFE BENEFITS TO REQUEST

Write Your New Job Description

FROM:	**Megan Quinn**
TO:	**Amy Hainen**
SUBJECT:	**Preparing My Part-Time Pitch—Day 2**

Amy,

Starting to make progress on the part-time pitch. Laid out plan for delegating west coast clients to Francie. Picked up new BlackBerry so Mara can reach me by e-mail or phone during days off. Calculated savings from my reduced salary and benefits (can switch to Brett's health insurance). Just have to pull my thoughts together into some kind of document, a sort of new job description . . .

Megan

You've used the flexible work arrangement worksheets to develop plans for your productivity, distribution of responsibilities, communication, transition, and scheduling. And you've determined the salary and benefits you want to request. Use this information to write up a formal job description.

Include:

- Job title
- Responsibilities you'll maintain
- Weekly schedule
- Plan for keeping in touch during nonworking or work-from-home hours
- Transition plan
- Salary
- Benefits, including work/life benefits such as child care assistance
- Vacation allotment
- Travel requirements
- Plan for delegating or postponing prior responsibilities

Research Role Models

FROM: **Megan Quinn**

TO: **Amy Hainen**

SUBJECT: **Preparing My Part-Time Pitch—Day 3**

Amy,

Wrote up new job description last night. Now time to call Christy (part-time goddess, surpassed sales goals last year working three days a week). Must ask how she (1) got approval for the part-time schedule and (2) deals with client/Mara emergencies on days off. After Christy, need to call human resources and get list of other part-time employees. Currently in mad scramble for all the advice I can get.

Megan

Management is more likely to approve your request if you can demonstrate other employees working successfully in comparable roles. If you want to shift to a job share, for example, talk to other job share teams at the company. Ask them how they negotiated the positions, what responsibilities they maintained, how they managed the workload, and how they feel about their roles. If you can, speak to their managers or colleagues to assess the company's attitude toward job share productivity and challenges. Ideally, you'll gather useful tips and case studies to include in your proposal.

Step into Your Employer's Shoes

FROM: **Megan Quinn**

TO: **Amy Hainen**

SUBJECT: **Preparing My Part-Time Pitch—Day 4**

Amy,

Got great info from Christy and two other part-timers yesterday. Proposal starting to come together.

Today, thinking through Mara's likely concerns:

Her: Personal bonus tied to overall team revenue.

Me: Must prove I can meet sales goals even with reduced schedule.

Her: Obsessed with responsive client service.

Me: Must demonstrate plan to handle urgent (though often pointless) client calls on days off.

Her: Even more obsessed with weekly sales reports.

Me: Must offer assurance mind-numbingly boring report will still be submitted in timely manner.

Anyway, Sam says hi. Well actually Sam says "aauhhgfgrya," but he means hi. I think.

Megan

If you work in sales, this is a no brainer. When attempting to close any deal, you consider the decision maker to predict potential barriers and opportunities. By focusing on your audience, you can frame your argument around their needs. Sure, working from home or part-time may make life easier for you, but that personal benefit isn't relevant here—unless it also adds to your productivity.

You're trying to sell your ideal position. Who has the authority to approve your request? Your manager? Group director? The CEO? Depending on the size and hierarchy of your company, you may need to meet with a few people before your proposal can be approved. Consider the goals and likely concerns of each decision maker. Your manager may primarily need help with her workload, while the group director may be worried about setting a difficult precedent. Write out arguments that defend your position relative to each person's perspective. Yes, managers prefer full-time in-office employees, but they also hate to lose valued contributors. They waste time and resources hiring and training replacements. That's your trump card.

Create a Three-Point Proposal

FROM:	**Megan Quinn**
TO:	**Amy Hainen**
SUBJECT:	**Preparing My Part-Time Pitch—Day 5**

Amy,

Meeting is tomorrow. Located prepregnancy work suit that fits over new mom curves and finally got highlights to fill in scary roots. Have gathered all necessary info; today writing up highly impressive, impossible-to-reject proposal during Sam's naps. Thankfully, the kid's a great sleeper.

Megan

Now you're ready to prepare your sales pitch—otherwise known as the three-point proposal to make your dream job a reality. To receive serious consideration, create a formal document that can't be dismissed summarily. Your alternative work arrangement won't make your employer's life any easier; be prepared to convince her it's worth the effort.

Include:

1. Your new job title and detailed job description: Use the job description you just created, incorporating the specifics from your flexible work arrangement worksheet and any advice you picked up while researching role models.

2. The benefits of your proposed position from the decision maker's perspective: Skip the personal pleas. Share your infant infatuation with friends over coffee; keep this proposal purely professional. Be specific, focusing on key work issues such as productivity, reduced costs, and ongoing projects. For example,

- "My reduced salary will save the department [$X] annually, without a significant drop in our productivity."

- "I can continue to manage [project X], so you don't have to train a replacement."
- "I can utilize my established contacts to quickly acquire donors for the fund-raising campaign while working from home."
- "I can complete [responsibilities X, Y, and Z] during my three days in the office each week, so you won't have to delegate those tasks or take on additional work yourself."

3. *Next steps:*   Include the date when you'll return to work in your new role. Describe anticipated follow-up with human resources and include your plan of attack to transition old responsibilities to other team members. You may have more success suggesting a sixty- or ninety-day trial period at first. Schedule a follow-up meeting to review the success of the position and discuss opportunities for process improvements.

Sell Your Proposal and Respond to Common Employer Concerns

FROM:	**Megan Quinn**
TO:	**Amy Hainen**
SUBJECT:	**Part-Time Pitch Today!**

Amy,

Feeling prepared and ready to sell my part-time proposal. Work suit and styled hair helping to reclaim confident career gal vibe. Baby-sitter should be here any minute. Gotta run and get one last good luck hug from Sam. Wish me luck!

Megan

You know exactly what position you want, you've done your homework, you've considered your audience, and you've prepared an impressive written proposal. It's go time.

Making Your Pitch

Meet with the relevant decision makers and make your pitch. Emphasize your past contributions and desire to stay with the company. You know they love you, so act with confidence. If they seem hesitant, be persistent and passionate. While your alternative work arrangement may seem like a minor inconvenience to them, it will make a major difference in your quality of life. Don't give up the fight without your best effort, and be prepared to respond to common employer concerns.

Common Employer Concerns and Recommended Responses

"If we approve your request, it will set a difficult precedent." Some employers take the long view, fearing any alternative work arrangement may lead to an avalanche of similar requests. Explain every position is unique, so your work arrangement will not necessarily set a new precedent. Other employees should understand that management evaluates every request on an individual basis.

"A flexible/shortened schedule just won't work for your job." This knee-jerk management reaction tends to result from a lack of imagination. Certain aspects of your job may require face time, but you could break out the discrete tasks and demonstrate how each one can be accomplished in your new arrangement. Don't let your boss get off this easy.

"The team is already swamped, and no one can take over any of your work." Head off this objection by suggesting projects that could be eliminated or completed less frequently. Once you've exhausted opportunities for reducing your weekly workload, lay out a plan for delegating some tasks without putting too much burden on anyone. Is there a junior employee on your team who wants more responsibility? Offer to train her and slowly transition some projects. How about someone at your level who wants additional client exposure? She might be happy to take over some client service responsibilities. Think about what could work for your team.

"During busy periods we need everyone to work longer hours, so we can't approve a shortened schedule like this. It's unrealistic."   Crunch times are inevitable, with some jobs more than others, but the occasional busy period doesn't rule out an alternative schedule. You may be able to negotiate a flextime schedule that ends at 4:00 P.M., but offer to take work home or come in early during particularly crazy weeks. And as a part-timer, you could work full weeks a few times a year. Be creative—you want to maintain boundaries between work and home, but you also want your request approved. Good luck finding a manageable compromise.

"We need to be able to reach you at all times, so this just won't work."   You developed a communication plan when completing your flexible work arrangement worksheet. Be sure to explain your plan to your employer, and remind her if she voices this concern at the end of your meeting. PDAs, cell phones, and designated phone and fax lines can offer guaranteed accessibility.

"It could bring down team morale if everyone else is working long hours and you have a special arrangement to work part-time."   This is a toughie, and the right response depends on the personalities of your colleagues and your company's corporate culture. Point out your willingness to bring work home if needed, your strong relationships with teammates, and your track record. If you've proven yourself over time, your team should continue to respect your contributions even in a reduced role.

Sealing the Deal

When you've reached agreement on your position, follow up with a memo to your manager and copy human resources. The memo should reiterate your new job title, responsibilities, weekly schedule, compensation package, benefits, and your plans for delegating work, keeping in touch, and making the transition. Keep a copy in your files so you can remind management if your new workload far exceeds your agreement or if questions arise in the future. You could also send a short, informal e-mail to colleagues so everyone understands your new role.

Congratulations! And best of luck in your new position.

Returning to Work
with Confidence

Nine Simple Steps to
Great Child Care

From Assessing Your Options

to Closing the Deal

Maya, a nurse, and her husband Oliver, a paramedic, stared in stunned silence at the fifty-two-year-old baby-sitter candidate attempting to play with their three-month-old daughter. Elsa's application described her as "bilingual, enthusiastic, and in love with kids of all ages." She was currently lounging on the floor beside the bouncy seat, quietly singing an unintelligible tune and slowly waving a rattle over the child's head like a sparkler at a Fourth of July parade. She'd been at it for almost ten minutes, and the baby had slowly progressed from bored to completely pissed off. "Well, she may be bilingual," Oliver whispered to Maya. "But English definitely isn't one of her languages."

"And she may be enthusiastic," Maya whispered back. "But at this point I'd say she's stoned."

|•|

She should be shockingly smart and constantly cheerful, perfectly patient and fully flexible. She should fall in love with your baby instantly, recognizing without prompting his obvious genius and angelic personality. And during their days together, she should recite Dr. Seuss from memory, demonstrate mind-boggling wooden block formations (she also has a Ph.D. in physics), and teach your child to speak in three or four different languages. We all have high hopes for our child care providers. It's a huge decision and no small task—finding a nanny, baby-sitter, relative, day care center, or home-based day care to stimulate, comfort, entertain, feed, and care for our babies as well as we would ourselves.

But your efforts are worth it. Good child care is the secret sauce of contented working parenthood. This chapter guides you through the mother of all tough decisions—from assessing your options to interviewing top candidates and closing the deal. You'll also learn how to manage separation anxiety (your baby's and yours), keep your child care provider happy (always a good thing), and deal with sick baby days (inevitable, yes—but not so bad if you have a plan).

Learn Your Options

From Tina's journal:

Who knew child care was so complicated? I asked four friends for suggestions today and got four completely different recommendations. One swore by her neighbor's home-based day care. Another said I'd be crazy not to hire a baby-sitter. One said I should definitely go with the big day care center in town, and the last said I should beg my mom to move here and watch Caitlin. And I thought college applications were going to be the confusing stage.

Don't be frustrated by all the child care advice coming your way. There are two overall approaches: child care inside or outside your home. Here's the full scoop on the options and costs so you can make your choice with confidence. Keep in mind, child care prices vary *significantly* depending on the type of care you want, where you live, the number of children you have, and your caregiver's credentials and responsibilities. Want an in-demand day care center or superexperienced nanny who helps with housework in an expensive urban area? Assume the middle to higher end of the price ranges below. Looking for affordable options in a small town? Assume the lower end.

Child Care Options in Your Home

Live-in Nanny or Au Pair

This is the luxury-car-with-leather-seats-like-butter-and-extras-out-the-wazoo of child care. An actual person living in your house ready and willing to help with diaper changes and laundry at a moment's notice? Nice. Very nice. A bit over the top for most of us, but potentially great if both parents work long hours with unpredictable schedules and you have space at home for another person. You sacrifice privacy for convenience, and by offering room and board you may save somewhat on salary. Live-in nannies generally pitch in on serious housework as well. If this approach fits your lifestyle, personality, and budget, you know who you are. Contact a nanny or au pair referral agency.

Typical cost: Room, board, a negotiable monthly stipend, paid vacation, and possibly a health insurance subsidy (Also expect to pay a placement fee if you're using a referral agency.)

Baby-Sitter/Nanny

First, the semantics. What exactly do you call a woman who arrives at your house in the morning and cares for your child until you return from work? You have two options: nanny or baby-sitter, and as far as I can tell, the only difference between these terms is the mind-set of the person using them. To employ an actual "nanny" seems very nouveau posh, very "We're popping out to the country home this weekend, so alert the nanny. And the butler. And the rest of the household staff." It's a title with attitude. Baby-sitter, on the other hand, brings to mind Saturday nights back in high school giving the neighbor's kids pizza while their parents went bowling. Not pretentious, just practical.

I'm guessing the referral agencies may have had something to do with the popularization of "nanny." They probably realized early on they could charge a lot more to connect working parents with an actual nanny (So professional! So Mary Poppins for the new millennium!) than with your basic baby-sitter. And they would argue nannies have a certain level of experience, a certain career orientation to their child care role. But I know women with sterling credentials and a long-term kid care commitment who call themselves baby-sitters, so go figure. I still say it's marketing spin. In any case, either term is accurate, but let's keep it real and use baby-sitter here.

The upsides of a regular baby-sitter? Your child receives one-on-one care, and you don't even have to get him dressed before scrambling out the door in the morning. A baby-sitter may perform light housekeeping as well. Of course, by light housekeeping I'm talking about so light you barely notice it. Like putting the baby's bottle in the dishwasher after using it. And maybe, if she's really inspired, pressing the start button when the dishwasher is full. Don't expect her to do anything as viciously time-consuming as removing the clean dishes and placing them in the cabinets. That kind of so-called heavy housekeeping falls under the "I have to be free to focus on your child" copout. (Silent response in the mind of every working mom with a sitter: "If I'm able to care for this kid and get everything around the house done during naps, why can't you?") In any case, even the occasional dishwasher run still feels luxurious, so we all take what we can get.

The downsides? Cost and paperwork. You can call her a baby-sitter, but she still gets the salary with attitude: $8 to $17 an hour these days depending on her experience, education, job responsibilities, where you live, and the number of children you have. (And you thought twins were tough on the clothing budget.) Some parents fork over the premium price for solo attention year one, and then they switch to day care for more socialization and lower long-term expense. Beyond your baby-sitter's salary, legally employing her may feel like running a small business. Granted, many full-time sitters are paid under the table in cash, but this is illegal and really problematic if you run for president one day. (Hey, you never know.)

Typical full-time cost: $1,440 to $3,060 a month including paid vacation, plus potentially a health insurance subsidy (This assumes $8 to $17 an hour at 45 hours a week. Also expect to pay a placement fee if you're using a referral agency.)

Share Care

If you can locate a nearby family with compatible child care needs, share care is the secret sale of baby-sitting. You share a sitter by bringing the children together and rotating houses every other week. The parents split the exorbitant cost of in-home care, and the children enjoy built-in socialization in a comfy known environment. It works best when the families decide in advance how they'll provide ongoing feedback, performance appraisals, and raises to the baby-sitter. And you should agree on basic infant care issues such as feedings, naps, and recommended activities. The challenge? If the other family's needs ever change (mom decides to quit, they move to Peoria), you're forced to find another family pronto or cover the sitter costs yourself. To really save, coordinate a three-way share care arrangement.

Typical full-time cost: $720 to $1,530 a month and up including paid vacation, plus potentially a health insurance subsidy (This assumes you're splitting an $8 to $17 an hour rate, 45 hours a week. Also expect to pay a placement fee if you're using a referral agency.)

Relative Care

Relatives are the most popular nonparental caregivers in the United States, accounting for almost half of children under the age of six in child care.[1] If you're lucky enough to have a family member willing and able to care for your baby, take advantage of it. Free, loving, dependable help is like winning the child care lottery. Don't ask why you were the chosen one, just accept the prize and be grateful. There are some risks—mainly with your relationship. If you're not thrilled with your mother-in-law's approach to nap time or your aunt's love affair with daytime TV, you're in a tough spot. She's caring for your baby and saving you massive amounts of money. You owe her. Plus, you have a whole relationship and history outside of your child. You can't just fire her if the situation isn't perfect, and you don't want your frustrations to create unspoken tension.

To minimize these interpersonal risks, discuss your parenting philosophy in advance. A vast amount of infant care information has emerged since we were kids, and her thirty-year-old approach to baby feedings and naps may not be compatible with yours. Ideally, ask her to start coming over a couple of weeks before you return to work, and use that period to show her the basics—from opening the stroller and fastening the car seat to introducing new activities and putting your baby down for naps. Come to an agreement on basic infant care issues before you return to work, and then maintain an open, respectful dialogue as you settle into a weekly routine. Give her space to do some things her way, but let her know if you have significant concerns. Keep your feedback upbeat but clear, and your relationship should only strengthen.

Typical cost: Free or an agreed-on payment.

Overall Advantages of In-Home Child Care

Individual attention: Wouldn't it be great if we could clone ourselves at our very best? One self could head calmly and professionally to work and the other could spend her days at home happily playing peek-a-boo and never getting grossed out by lumpy baby food. Until that day, there are baby-sitters.

Health: Fewer kids' germs means fewer ear infections and colds for your infant. And that's what you call a work/life benefit.

Convenience: Your baby napping in his own crib: Sweet. Someone home with your child when you're running late from work: Really sweet. Leaving the house each morning without shlepping your bundle of joy: Priceless.

Disadvantages

Expense: Priceless doesn't come cheap.

The what-do-we-do-now factor: Your sitter calls Tuesday night with a weird rash and a fever. You're managing a four-hour training session the next day, and your husband is away on a business trip. You picture yourself leading the session with a Baby Bjorn secretly strapped under your shirt and suddenly feel a migraine coming on. And that's the moment I'm talking about. (Learn how to deal with child care emergencies later in this chapter.)

Less socialization: Not a big deal for babies, but important as your child matures.

Logistics: Organizing paperwork. Managing payroll. Supplying W-2 forms. Probably not your ideal weekend activities.

● ● ● ● ● ● Child Care Outside Your Home ● ● ● ● ● ●

Day Care Center

After relative care, day care centers are the second most common form of child care in the United States for children under six.[2] They're popular and they vary significantly. They're located in church basements, in stand-alone facilities with ample outdoor space, and everything in between. Some have twenty kids; some have two hundred. Some have been run by the same staff for over a decade, and others experience endless turnover. The number of infant spots is generally mandated by the state, and many centers don't allow infants at all. (Babies require more attention than older children, and some centers can't afford to maintain the necessary adult-to-child ratio. Generally, kids age two and up are welcome in any center.) Variations on your standard day care center include drop-in facilities for occasional help and centers for children with special needs. Day care tends to be more affordable and less likely to leave you stranded than a baby-sitter, and socialization is built in.

What to look for in your day care search? Your center should be licensed and accredited, providers should be trained in early childhood education, and staff turnover should be low. You typically get what you pay for in the world of day care—unlicensed providers have lower rates but generally don't offer the same quality of care or safety. There should be a one to four or lower adult-to-child ratio. They should be experienced with infants, conveniently located, and provide drop-off and pickup times that meet your work requirements. If you only need part-time care, make sure they'll accommodate your schedule at a reasonable price (some may charge a premium or require full-time rates). Assuming these basic criteria are met, go with your gut. Look for an environment that's safe, bright, stimulating, and comfortable. Talk to all the caregivers and make sure you have a personality match.

Typical full-time cost: $300 to $1,350 a month (This is the slightly higher range generally charged for babies and toddlers because of the lower required adult-to-child ratio. Your day care rates will generally decrease when your child is eighteen months to two years old.)

Home-Based Day Care

Yes, we're talking about someone actually setting aside part of her home—often a lower level or playroom space—for daytime baby-sitting. The options here are also endless—from a stay-at-home mom watching two or three extra kids to a family running a long-term child care business out of their basement and backyard. In many states, small home-based providers can have up to three children over the age of two plus your infant, and large providers (also called group day care homes) may have several more kids with additional staff. Given the greater capacity of most day care centers, home-based care can offer a cozy year one alternative.

Compared to centers, home-based care tends to be slightly less expensive, with fewer children, possibly more flexible drop-off and pickup times, and a homier atmosphere. (It is an actual home, after all.) On the downside, home-based caregivers in some states aren't required to have the same level of training or accreditation as day care centers. And some parents prefer the clear day care environment versus someone's home. If you're interested in this approach, visit a few in your area to determine the environment you prefer.

Typical full-time cost: $275 to $1,100 a month (This is the slightly higher range generally charged for babies and toddlers because of the lower required adult-to-child ratio. Your home-based day care rates will generally decrease when your child is eighteen months to two years old.)

On-Site Day Care

Many employers provide on-site day care these days. This can be a great arrangement, allowing you to spend more time with your baby during your commute and lunch break. Challenges? Waiting lists tend to be long, and during peak separation anxiety periods morning drop-off can be a stressful way to start your workday. If your employer offers on-site care, visit the facility and make the call.

Typical cost: Facilities and costs vary by company; talk to your employer for specifics.

Overall Advantages of Child Care Outside Your Home

Price: There's a reason day care is so popular. It starts with a dollar sign and ends with a number that's a lot smaller than what baby-sitters cost. Bottom line, in the premium-priced world of child care, day care is—for many us—the only realistic option. Still, day care rates vary significantly based on licensing, adult-to-child ratios, the cost of living in your area, and basic supply and demand. Certain communities have lots of home-based providers but few centers, for example, so those centers may have higher rates. Other communities have a significant proportion of unlicensed providers, so licensed care is in particular demand.

Socialization: Your child can learn about sharing even before siblings hit the scene. And there's nothing cuter than seeing your little one toddling around after his buddies when you arrive for pickup.

Disadvantages

Less convenience: Schlepping your baby out the door is required. And we all know what that entails.

The sick factor: The downside of all that fun socialization. Picture three-year-old Zach coughing into his hand and then innocently tickling your baby on the cheek. Enough said.

Less flexibility: Your boss needs you to stay late and your day care center closes at 6:00 P.M. And remember, cloning isn't an option.

High staff turnover: Consistent adult relationships give babies the confidence to explore the world. If your day care center's staff is always leaving, you should too.

Assess Your Budget

FROM:	**Sylla Ross**
TO:	**Leigh Christopherson**
SUBJECT:	**And I thought the crib was expensive**

Just learned the going rate for full-time baby-sitters around here is $11 an hour, which sounds really scary until you run the numbers, and then it's downright terrifying. We're talking about paying a cool $495 a week just so I can go to work every day. I made $2.50 an hour baby-sitting in high school— did I miss the part where baby-sitters unionized and established MBA-level wages? The radical baby-sitter rallies? The sit-ins for better pay? Given my desire to make an *actual profit* from my job after taxes and child care costs, I'm now on the day care center search.

Next we move to the three most powerful words in the world of child care: cold, hard cash. We all want caregivers who will educate, nurture, protect, and inspire our little ones, but ultimately cost drives this choice for most of us. The average working family spends 7.5 percent of its annual income on child care, and it's often the second highest household expense after housing.[3]

Money: The Root of All Child Care Decisions

You may already maintain a monthly budget. If so, you're ahead of the game. Subtract your expenses from your net income and calculate the amount you can afford to spend on child care. For help, fill in the life-with-baby budget calculator in Chapter 8.

Child Care Cost Cutters

And keep these child care cost-cutting strategies in mind:

Get an FSA ASAP.   Flexible spending accounts (FSAs) are a no brainer. They significantly reduce the annual cost of child care by allowing you to apply up to $5,000 of pretax income, and they're offered by 79 percent of employers.[4] Meet with someone in human resource and explain the amount you'd like to set aside.

Claim child care tax breaks.   The federal child and dependent care credit can help offset annual child care expenses, and many states offer additional credits or deductions. If you're setting aside pretax money in a dependent care FSA, however, you can't also claim the tax credit. (Let's face it, the IRS *isn't that* generous.) Contact your human resources department, an accountant, the IRS, or your state's Department of Revenue for specifics.

Let your employer pitch in.   Many organizations offer child care discounts or subsidies. If yours does, take advantage.

Do a thorough search.   Day care and baby-sitting costs often vary considerably even within communities. Explore your options until you identify one that meets all your key criteria—and offers an affordable price.

Schedule creatively.   If you have a significant other, you could minimize required child care hours by negotiating complementary work schedules. Or consider freelance projects that you could complete when he's home with the baby.

Choose a Child Care Approach and Research Local Providers

"Hey, Mom. Well, we finally settled our big child care debate, and we decided to use a day care center when I go back to work."

"Sounds good. Which one?"

"Well, we haven't gotten that far."

You Know Your Options and Budget; Start to Focus on a Child Care Approach That Could Work for Your Family

Consider priorities like your work schedule, your desire for one-on-one care versus socialization, and these key selection criteria:

Parent prerequisites

1. Affordable cost
2. Convenient location
3. Compatible hours
4. Infant care experience
5. Reliability

Baby benefits

1. Cognitive, verbal, and physical stimulation
2. Comfort, safety, and wellness
3. Socialization
4. A strong emotional connection (think low staff turnover or a non-flaky caregiver)

Identify Local Providers

Now you're ready to research caregivers in your community. Your goal: to make a list of four to six you can contact and interview. But where do you find them? Initially, network. Ask work colleagues, relatives, neighbors, friends from your gym—anyone you know with a child. Parents love to pass on child care references, and your best option is one that comes enthusiastically endorsed. You may hear of an ideal day care center in your area or a family who's moving and has a full-time baby-sitter now looking for work.

For additional baby-sitter and nanny candidates, try these sources:

International Nanny Association: The INA is a nonprofit organization offering a variety of free resources and state-level referrals. Check out nanny.org or call them at 888-878-1477.

Referral agencies: These agencies generally prescreen candidates and offer background checks. This kind of service does, however, come at a price—most agencies charge a fee in the range of several hundred to a few thousand dollars. Check your phone book or find free listings of local referral agencies online at nannynetwork.com and nanny.org.

Online referral agencies: As a less expensive alternative, some online agencies charge a lower fee for access to their database of available nannies and baby-sitters. Check out sittercity.com, 4nannies.com, and enannysource.com.

Free localized websites: Sites like craigslist.org connect baby-sitters and families in cities around the United States for free. You can either post a listing with your requirements or review the local baby-sitter postings. I had a great experience using craigslist to find a baby-sitter. I posted my free listing one afternoon, and several viable candidates responded in the next two days. I interviewed the most impressive ones by phone and then met my top choice in person. She was a local college student with excellent references and started working for us that week. Supereasy and no referral fee.

Places parents go: Look for postings in local baby stores, parks, pediatrician offices, fitness centers, or mom-and-baby classes. Baby-sitters often place handmade ads in these parent-populated spots.

Local publications: Some seriously savvy baby-sitters promote their availability in local newspapers and magazines. Check the classified ads, or pay for your own if you really want to spread the word.

Colleges: A local student may be a great fit at a slightly lower cost—especially if you're looking for part-time help or have variable needs (e.g., freelancers with superbusy and less busy periods). If there is a college in your area, contact the student employment office and ask how to post a position. Some use online career placement services and others may invite you to put an ad on their office bulletin boards.

For local day care centers and home-based day care, check out:

Child care aware: This nonprofit connects parents with over 850 local child care referral and resource centers. Call 800-424-2246 or go to childcareaware.org and type your zip code into the child care connector tool. Then contact your local referral center for options in your community. Many local centers offer referral services for free; some may charge a nominal fee to families with higher incomes.

NAEYC: The National Association for the Education of Young Children provides a free listing of accredited child care and educational programs, although some are specifically for older children. Check its website at naeyc.org.

Your phone book: Look for listings under "child care" or "child care referral agencies."

Localized websites and publications: Like professional baby-sitters, some day care providers place ads in community newspapers, magazines, and websites.

Interview Your Top Candidates

"So, Brenna the baby-sitter is coming by in the morning to interview."

"I thought you already talked to her. And loved her."

"I did, but that was by phone. This is the big face-to-face. And she sounds so perfect, I'm totally stressed. What if Noah cries while she's here? Or if she just doesn't like us? With her background, she could work for anyone. I have to remind Brian to break out the charm."

"Right. And whatever happened to interviews where the potential employee was the nervous one?"

|•|

You have your list of potential day care centers, baby-sitter candidates, or referral agencies compiled. Now you're ready to make some calls. Start by conducting informal phone interviews to refine your list, and then meet with your top candidates in person—either by inviting potential baby-sitters to your home or visiting day care providers around town.

Baby-Sitter/Nanny Interviews

When a potential baby-sitter comes to your house, hand her your infant about halfway through the interview and watch her interactions with him. Pay attention to her energy level, soothing skills, and personality. She may have impressive references and experience, but if she seems worn out by holding your supersquirmer for fifteen minutes, you should probably keep looking. Similarly, quiet babies may be overwhelmed by ultra-high-energy personalities. Go with your gut—your instincts will tell you when you've found the right fit. Once you feel good about a candidate, call her references and ideally conduct a background check. A listing of background check providers is available at nanny.org.

What to ask the candidates? Here are expert-recommended questions to get you started. Review them here and then flip to the pullout list of these questions in the appendix. It's designed to be removed and used as a reference during your interviews.

Training and child care philosophy:
1. Do you have training in early childhood education? Infant CPR? First aid?
2. Are you familiar with safe back-to-sleep practices?
    Babies should always be put to sleep on their backs, and the risk of SIDS is particularly high when infants begin child care. If a caregiver starts putting a back sleeper down on his tummy, he may not have the neck strength to shift his head from that position and he'll be at much higher risk for SIDS. Make sure your baby-sitter consistently follows safe back-to-sleep practices.
3. Why do you enjoy working with children? How would you describe your style of care?
4. What activities would you introduce to our child at this age? At six months? Nine months? A year?
5. How do you comfort a crying baby?

6. What would you do if our baby starting choking?

Here's the wrong answer to that question: "Call you and ask what you'd like me to do." Believe it or not, one of our child care candidates answered this in our interview. I attempted not to appear horrified and wrapped up that conversation faster than you can say disaster-waiting-to-happen. The lesson? Of course you want to be involved, but make sure your caregiver is comfortable taking action when necessary.

7. When would you normally put a baby this age down for naps? How do you feel about making sure naps are always taken at home? When would you provide bottles?

This is a great time to discuss the feed-to-wake approach described in Chapter 13. Some experienced caregivers have strong opinions about how feedings and naps should be provided; make sure her approach is compatible with yours.

8. How do you discipline older children? Please offer specific examples from past positions.

Job specifics:

1. What hours are you available?

If you have occasional late nights or weird hours, make sure she can accommodate your needs.

2. What is your hourly rate?

Or you could research the going rate in advance and tell her what you'd like to pay.

3. How long will you be able to keep this position? Do you have any plans or commitments that might take you away in the next year or two?

4. Would you be willing to take our child to activities and the park as he gets older?

5. We provide two weeks paid vacation. (This is standard.) Would you mind taking your vacations when we take ours?

If you're lucky, she'll agree so you're not forced to find alternate care during her weeks off and committed to pay her for nothing when you're on vacation. Some families suggest a compromise arrangement: They pick one vacation week and their baby-sitter requests one week.

6. How will you get here every day? Do you have a driver's license?
7. Would you like to baby-sit occasionally on weekend evenings? Overnights? On vacation with us? (If you're interested in any of these things.)

    Some would like the extra cash; others prefer the free time.
8. What type of housekeeping will you do during the day?

    As I mentioned, don't expect much. But do make specific requests now so she's committed to some regular tasks like emptying the diaper pail or changing soiled crib sheets as necessary.

Experience:
1. Describe your past child care positions. How much experience do you have caring for babies this age?
2. What did you enjoy most about each position?
3. Describe your typical day at a previous job. What did you do with the children? What did you do during their naps?
4. Can you think of any books the children particularly enjoyed? How often did you read to them?
5. Why did you leave those jobs?
6. Have you ever dealt with a medical emergency or sick child on the job? If so, what did you do?
7. How many days were you sick or unable to make it to work while at those positions?
8. Do you have children?
9. Can you provide a list of references?

    Call her past employers and ask for their impressions of her performance, reliability, child care style, and personality. Even if the first two are glowing, call all her references for comprehensive feedback. Also, ask them for tips on working with her. Normally you'll pick up some useful advice.

Day Care Center and Home-Based Day Care Interviews

Set up an appointment with your top day care candidates and plan to stay at each one for an hour or two to get a good feel for their approach. When you enter each facility, look closely at the surroundings. Is it a comfortable, happy environment? Do the children seem content and engaged? Are there ample toys and play equipment to keep your baby stimulated as he gets older? Where are the infants? Are they parked in baby swings or is someone keeping them stimulated? Do you click with the staff members on a personal level? During your visit, hand your baby to one of the staff members if there's an appropriate moment. If one adult primarily cares for the infants, make sure it's her. Watch the way she interacts with your child and look for a personality match.

What to ask as you visit providers? Here are expert-recommended questions to get you started. Review them here and then flip to the pull-out copy of these questions in the appendix. It's designed to be removed and used as a reference during your interviews.

Background:
1. How long have you been in business?
2. What type of licensing do you have?

    Licensing requirements vary by state, and the facility should follow your state's guidelines. Review your state's licensing requirements in advance using either of these sources (both have free online listings):

    Child Care Aware—Phone: 800-424-2246; website: childcareaware.org

    The National Resource Center for Health and Safety in Child Care—Phone: 800-598-KIDS; website: nrc.uchsc.edu

3. Are you accredited?

    Accredited facilities generally offer staff training and provide structured activities that surpass minimum state licensing requirements. Ask for details about their training and approach.

4. Do you accept infants? Toddlers?
5. How many children do you care for at any given time? What are the typical ages?
6. Do you have an opening?
7. What is the monthly cost? How do you bill parents? Are there any other fees we may incur?

8. What are your hours? What happens if I'm running late from work one evening?
9. Do you have written policies we can review?
10. Do you have a list of references?

   Call these parents and ask about their experience with the provider and any issues of particular concern. If the management can't provide a formal reference list, just talk to a few of the current families. (It never hurts to do that anyway.)

Staff:
1. How many adults do you have on staff? What's your adult-to-child ratio?
2. What kind of child care experience do the caregivers have? Experience with infants?
3. Are they all trained in infant CPR? First aid? Have they all passed background checks?
4. Are all caregivers trained in safe back-to-sleep practices?

   Babies should always be put to sleep on their backs, and the risk of SIDS is particularly high when infants begin child care. If a caregiver starts putting a back sleeper down on his tummy, he may not have the neck strength to shift his head well from that position and he'll be at much higher risk for SIDS. Make sure all staff consistently follow safe back-to-sleep practices.
5. What is your turnover rate among staff members?
6. Will one person be focused on our child? If so, describe her background and training.

Health and safety:
1. How often are the toys disinfected? How often is the center fully cleaned?
2. How do you deal with children who seem sick?
3. Do the caregivers wash their hands after every diaper change?
4. How have you child-proofed the facilities? Where are the cleaning supplies and other hazardous materials kept? Do you have first aid kits on hand?

5. What's your plan for handling emergencies?

6. What are your security guidelines? How do adults sign in during drop-offs and pickups?

Schedule and activities:

1. What is the daily schedule? When are naps given? Bottles? Diaper changes?

    Most day care facilities have specific schedules for infant naps and feedings. Make sure you're comfortable with their timing and approach. This is a great time to discuss the feed-to-wake approach described in Chapter 13.

2. Once my baby starts eating solids, what will you typically feed him for lunch? What snacks are offered?

3. What activities do you generally plan for the kids? How will our child be involved?

Child care approach:

1. How do you soothe crying babies?

2. How do you discipline older children?

3. How do you facilitate interaction and socialization? What kind of one-on-one time can we expect our child to receive?

4. How can parents become involved?

Select Your Favorite Provider and Close the Deal

FROM:	**Christina Saldana**
TO:	**Ana Cruz**
SUBJECT:	**The baby-sitter search has ended! Almost.**

After asking friends for references, contacting two referral agencies, scouring the handwritten baby-sitter ads posted around the city, researching online, interviewing five baby-sitter candidates by phone, and meeting three in person—I've found her. And she's perfect. Her references love her, I love her, Eva loves her. Now what?

After in-person interviews, reference checks, and potentially a background check, it's time to make your choice and sign a contract.

Legally Employing a Baby-Sitter/Nanny

If you're going to pay your baby-sitter over $1,400 per calendar year (as of 2006, this limit changes incrementally), you should establish yourself as an employer and report her wages on your federal income tax return. Yes, many parents forgo the paperwork and pay their baby-sitters in cash under the table. But that approach is illegal and it prevents you from taking advantage of child care tax breaks. (You can't use your FSA or claim a tax credit for a baby-sitter who's not officially on the books.) You'll need to manage payment of your baby-sitter's salary, Social Security, Medicare, and unemployment taxes, and supply her W-2 each year. You may also withhold a portion of her salary each pay period for her federal and state income taxes.

Eyes glazing over already? Don't worry; you can outsource the whole deal to companies like these:

Baby-sitter/nanny payroll and tax services providers:
- HomeWork Solutions
    Phone: 800-NANITAX
    Website: 4nannytaxes.com
- GTM Associates
    Phone: 888-4EASYPAY
    Website: gtmassoc.com
- PayCycle
    Phone: 866-729-2925
    Website: paycycle.com
- Breedlove and Associates
    Phone: 800-BREEDLOVE
    Website: breedlove-online.com

Managing payroll yourself:
If you're ambitious, you can do it all yourself by following these steps. Yes, they're scary at first, but feel better knowing your future political career will remain intact.

1. Confirm your baby-sitter's start date, salary, vacation, and health in-surance details.
2. Make sure she's eligible to work in the United States.

   If she moved here from another country, ask her for a copy of her passport, Social Security card, and driver's license.

   Together, complete a U.S. Citizenship and Immigration Services (USCIS) Form I-9 and keep it in your files. This form can be requested at 800-357-2099 or downloaded at uscis.gov. (This website is confusing; try searching for "Office of Business Liaison" and then follow the links to Form I-9.)
3. Become a legal employer.

   Call the IRS at 800-829-3676 and request the following:

   Forms

   - SS-4: You'll submit this to receive your federal employer iden-tification number (EIN).
   - W-4: You'll give this employee withholding allowance certifi-cate to your baby-sitter/nanny and ask her to fill it out before she starts work so you know how much federal income tax to withhold from her salary. (You aren't legally obligated to with-hold her federal or state income taxes, but it makes her life a lot easier come tax time if you do.)
   - W-2: As an employer, you'll fill in your baby-sitter's annual wages and withholdings and give her the completed W-2 by the end of January each year so she can submit it with her tax returns. You'll keep a portion of the W-2 to file yourself by February 28.
   - W-3: The W-3 simply reiterates the information from your baby-sitter's W-2. You'll submit it to the IRS in February as well.
   - 1040ES: You'll send in quarterly payments of your employer taxes with this form. Questions about this process? Ask the IRS representative while requesting these forms.
   - Schedule H (Form 1040): You'll file this summary of your household employment taxes with your personal tax returns by April 15.

Informational materials
- Household Employer's Tax Guide: Publication 926
- Employer's Tax Guide (Circular E): Publication 15

I know all of this sounds daunting, but you can order these forms and materials in one phone call to the IRS or download many of them at irs.gov (search for "employment tax forms") or 4nannytaxes.com.

Then, to get your state employer identification number (yes, you need that too) and report the impending hire—contact your state's Department of Labor office of employment or unemployment tax agency. The specific agency names vary by state and are listed at the end of the Household Employer's Tax Guide: Publication 926 (which you ordered in your call to the IRS). The phone number should also be in the government listings in your local phone book.

4. Decide how you're going to manage salary payments and taxes.

You're responsible for withholding 7.65 percent of your babysitter's salary for Social Security and Medicare each pay period, and some states require additional withholdings. You should also ask if she'd like you to set aside a portion of her wages for federal and state income taxes. This isn't required, but it ensures there's money withheld for her personal tax returns. Each year, you'll complete a W-2 and W-3 summarizing these annual wages and withholdings.

As an employer, you also have taxes to pay: unemployment insurance and your portion of her Social Security and Medicare (also 7.65 percent of her salary). These payments are required quarterly with the 1040ES form, and they should be summarized, using the schedule H (Form 1040), in your personal tax returns.

To calculate employer taxes and withholdings, check out the "nanny tax calculator" at 4nannytaxes.com. It's free and very helpful. Or, if you're brave and financially savvy, you can calculate this stuff yourself using the Household Employer's Tax Guide and Employer's Tax Guide (Circular E). For further questions, contact an accountant or someone from the IRS.

5. Sign a contract. (The sample contract on the next two pages includes explanations and comments. An abbreviated pullout version is provided in the appendix.)

Now you're ready to celebrate. You've survived the hard part and you can head back to work feeling great about your baby's care.

Day Care Centers and Home-Based Day Care

Closing the deal with day care providers is relatively simple. They should provide a contract outlining their licensing and accreditations, payment requirements, holidays, late fees, meal and snack plan, cancellation policy, and general child care philosophy. You'll simply sign this contract, provide updated medical forms and a deposit to hold your child's spot, confirm your timing, and celebrate. You've made one of life's toughest decisions—and you're ready to head back to work with confidence.

SAMPLE BABY-SITTER/NANNY CONTRACT

Employer

Names of parents: _____

Names of children: _____

Address: _____ Home phone: _____

Mom's work phone number: _____ Cell phone number: _____

Dad's work phone number: _____ Cell phone number: _____

Emergency contact information: _____

Baby-Sitter/Nanny

Name: _____

Address: _____

Home phone number: _____ Cell phone number: _____

Social Security number: _____ Driver's license number: _____

Emergency contact information: _____

Start date: _____

(If she's starting gradually, include her hours during this initial period.)

Job Description

CHILD CARE RESPONSIBILITIES:
Include your requests for your child's naps, feedings, playtime, reading, safety, baths, and any other specifics. Also list certification requirements such as infant CPR.

HOUSEHOLD CONTRIBUTIONS:
Include your housework requests. If you're lucky, she'll agree to change the crib sheets if they become soiled, put bottles and feeding supplies in the dishwasher after use, run the dishwasher when full, put away toys and items used during the day, and accept deliveries to the house. You could also ask her to do your baby's laundry during naps, but she may not want to take on the responsibility. Good luck outsourcing that one.

DAILY UPDATES:
Request end-of-day verbal updates and written logs of your child's napping and feeding schedule, demeanor, and activities.

TRANSPORTATION:
Clarify the use of your car, her car, and public transportation. Explain where she may need to take your child (walks to the local park, drives to play dates and activities, etc.).

ADDITIONAL POLICIES:
Detail your requests for visitors, TV restrictions, phone use, smoking, and managing emergencies. And explain your feelings about bringing your child to someone else's house. Include anything you really care about so expectations are clear.

Weekly Schedule

Days: _____ Hours:____ A.M. to ____ P.M. Total: ____ hours per week

Overtime policy: _____

(Her hourly rate should still apply; just confirm her availability.)

Salary and Benefits

Employer will provide $____ gross per hour, to be paid at the end of each week.

Employer will pay one-half of Social Security and Medicare taxes (7.65% of employee's gross salary), and all unemployment insurance and Worker's Compensation insurance. Employee's half of Social Security and Medicare taxes will be withheld each pay period and, if desired, employer will also withhold federal and state income taxes.

Other benefits: (Room and board, meals, health insurance subsidy, etc.)

Performance Reviews and Termination Notice

Performance reviews will be provided ____ times a year, and salary increases will be provided annually if warranted by performance.

Baby-sitter should provide at least four weeks notice before leaving position.

Paid Days Off

Employer will provide ____ paid holidays (specify), ____ paid sick days, and ____ paid vacation days.

Baby-sitter must provide ____ weeks notice prior to vacation days.

Confidentiality

The baby-sitter may become aware of personal, financial, legal, health, or work-related information about the employer's family. All family information is confidential and should not be shared without the employer's written consent. If this confidentiality is breached, the baby-sitter may be discharged. (Makes you sound really important, doesn't it? Even if you aren't hiding Swiss bank accounts, it's always a good idea to ensure your privacy.)

SIGNATURES

Employer:_____ Date:_____

Baby-sitter: _____ Date:_____

Set Up a Trial Period

Start your child care a week or two in advance to give your baby an opportunity to gradually acclimate and you a chance to confirm your choice. Give your caregiver an emergency contact sheet so all vital information is on hand. Include parent phone numbers, other emergency contacts, your pediatrician, and even local poison control and police. If you feel uncomfortable with your child care provider during this period, try to line up another option before work begins. (Yes, this is a complete hassle—but it would be a much bigger hassle if you were already working.)

Baby-Sitters/Nannies

On your baby-sitter's first day, take the lead. Let her watch you and explain the tricks that keep your baby happy. Over the next few days, allow her to gradually take over and offer advice as needed. She could work half days at first, gradually shifting to full days. Stay with her as much as you like, increasing your time away each day. Return unannounced so you can see her natural interactions with your child. Occasional spontaneous drop-ins are a great idea after you return to work as well.

Day Care Centers and Home-Based Day Care

Start by bringing your baby to day care for an hour or two. Watch the caregivers and share strategies that work well with your child. Over the next few days, leave him for longer stretches and gradually phase yourself out. Return at different times so you can get a sense for their daily routines. (Some facilities discourage parents from staying so the other children aren't distracted. Just do what you can.) Once you head back to work, try to drop by unannounced every once in a while to ensure your child is receiving high-quality care throughout the day. Sneaky? A little. Effective? Very.

Your First Full Day Away

Try to leave your baby in child care at least one full day before heading back to work, and make it a fun day. Meet a friend for lunch, get a haircut—whatever you want. It's always gut-wrenching to leave your infant that initial full day. Ideally, do it on your own time so you can process the emotions of heading back to work separately.

Manage Separation Anxiety (Your Baby's and Yours)

From Becky's journal:

> *Mornings have suddenly become a complete drama. As I leave*
> *Samantha in day care, she starts to sob like she'll never see me again. It's*

nice to be appreciated—but why now? And how can I bring back our easy morning routine?

Separation anxiety is a natural response for infants. It generally hits in an obvious way by six or seven months and peaks by month ten or eleven.

Separation Anxiety: Baby Style

You'll most likely return to work after about three months—prior to the onset of major infant separation anxiety. That's the good news. And as this stage initially hits, it's primarily flattering. Finally someone recognizes you are, in fact, the most fun person in the universe. Your baby becomes your own personal fan club—even your trips to the bathroom are clear justification for tortured sobs. (If only guys could be so out there with their emotions, they'd save a lot of money on flowers.) As separation anxiety peaks, however, you may have real challenges. Don't be surprised if your well-adjusted child morphs into a mommy-obsessed lunatic. And even if he's settled into child care, he may regress for a while.

To minimize your baby's separation anxiety:

Be consistent.   Try to follow a similar routine each morning so he knows what to expect. (I know, who am I kidding? Just do your best.)

Stay upbeat and concise.   As you leave, briefly explain you're going to work and will be home that night. Offer a casual good-bye like, "See you later, sweetie."

Don't dawdle.   The longer you drag out your departure, the longer he'll cry. Feel better knowing his torment will likely end as soon as you're out of sight.

Don't go back.   After heading out, try to avoid trips back in the house or day care facility to grab things you forgot. No need to repeatedly jump-start your baby's emotions.

Separation Anxiety: Mom (and Dad) Style

It's the final evening of your maternity leave and you head to bed with a queasy feeling reminiscent of the last day of summer vacation back in third grade. You're already nostalgic for your baby's constant presence, and you're fearful your impending work/life balance may not be exactly balanced. But you're also excited to see work friends, ready for some non-sleeping-feeding-or-pooping-related challenges, and driven to get back up to speed.

You're managing a belly full of contradictory emotions, and underneath it all is disbelief. Will you actually be separated for full days at a time from this new center of your universe? If entering motherhood is a crazy twilight zone, reentering your old working life as a mother is like a twilight zone déja vù. It feels familiar and yet somehow unreal.

To minimize your separation anxiety:

Find great child care.   If you know your baby is happy, you'll be happy. End of story.

Prioritize and conquer at work.   Try to focus on essential tasks, delegate when possible, skip the long lunches, and minimize the watercooler chats. Streamline your workdays like never before to be ultraproductive and then head home. Feeling in control of your work schedule is your best bet for anxiety-free days.

Focus on the positives.   There will be mornings when your baby cries as you head out to work. And you'll feel like ripping your heart out, quitting your job on the spot—or both. Guilt will override all rational thought and you'll practically cry yourself as you slowly walk away. When these moments hit, remind yourself of the advantages of your job—your health care plan, your contribution to the family finances, your sense of fulfillment—and the quality time you'll spend with your baby as soon as you get home.

Allow yourself baby brag time.   No, your colleagues don't need an update every time your little guy overcomes constipation. But don't be afraid to share an occasional milestone or funny story. Sharing some parental pride at work may help integrate your two worlds.

Put your baby's melodrama in perspective.   When your child's separation anxiety hits, remind yourself his intense reaction is part of a normal developmental phase. He'll outgrow it quickly, and you might even miss the days when you had your own fan club.

Maintain a Positive Relationship with your Child Care Provider

"Joan brought Hayden a birthday present yesterday. Do you think that's strange?"

"Why would it be strange? She baby-sits Hayden three days a week, and she adores him. You've said yourself Joan seems like part of the family."

"I know. But as her employer, I hate when she spends her money on us."

"She's just being thoughtful. You probably gave her something small around the holidays, right?"

"Well, that would have been a good idea."

|•|

Yes, it is a job for her. But your child *loves* this woman, and you want her to be happy.

Consider Your Child Care Provider a Parenting Partner

Exchange strategies that have worked successfully, ask for advice, and share stories of your baby's little triumphs. You've got the maternal bond—your child care provider has the experience. You're the infant care dream team.

Recognize Good Work

A thank-you note after that week of late nights. A holiday gift or bonus. An enthusiastic story about your baby doing something she taught him. Simply pointing out the obvious: She's amazing with kids. A few thoughtful gestures can help maintain your child care provider's enthusiasm and loyalty, which ultimately benefits everybody.

Donate to Day Care

Day care facilities, like schools, always benefit from parental support and any contribution is appreciated. Surprise them with snacks, supplies for a simple craft project, or a new toy for the kids to share. Help plan a holiday party or put together an end-of-year newsletter. Even small contributions can go a long way in maintaining a positive long-term relationship.

Keep Everyone in the Loop

Let your child care provider know in advance about upcoming pediatrician appointments, anticipated busy periods at work, and planned vacations.

Deal with Problems Fairly and Calmly

Your baby-sitter seems strangely incapable of cleaning up after herself. You find your child temporarily unattended in the day care center's infant swing. Your home-based caregiver doesn't seem to be disinfecting the toys. Dealing with conflict is never fun, but don't internalize your child care frustrations. Tactfully communicate questions and concerns as soon as they arise, and together define next steps to remedy problems. And if the situation just doesn't feel right, trust your instincts and make a change.

Deal with Child Care Emergencies

"This cannot be happening," Stacy muttered quietly, hanging up the phone and turning to her husband. "A pipe burst at the day care center last night, and they'll be closed for at least two days."

"I'm fully booked with meetings today, and you're presenting your fiscal year recap this afternoon."

"Thank you for pointing that out."

"Okay, it's time for Plan B."

"I didn't know we had a Plan B."

"Oh yes. Plan B it is. My sister said she would watch Chloe if we ever had a day care emergency, and I think this qualifies."

"Perfect."

|•|

Unexpected child care challenges are an inevitable part of working parenthood, but they can be easily managed with advance planning.

The No-Show Scenario or Sick Baby Syndrome

Your baby-sitter comes down with pneumonia. Your home-based day care provider is closed for two weeks so the family can take their annual vacation. Your mom, who watches your baby year-round, wants to visit her brother for a week. Your baby has a fever and can't go to day care. What do you do?

The Beauty of the Backup Plan

This is the kind of child care emergency that sends working parents into a tailspin. To avoid undo stress, create a backup plan from day one. Your best bets for child care emergencies are:

A backup baby-sitter: Make an arrangement with a family member, friend, or stay-at-home mom neighbor who could baby-sit for a few days if needed. You could even ask to share a colleague's or friend's baby-sitter during emergency days. Set this up in advance so you're covered.

An advance employer agreement: If backup help isn't an option, you could request working from home during emergency days. Obviously this only makes sense if your job can be accomplished at home. If so, discuss this possibility with your manager when you return from maternity leave. Otherwise, you may have to take sick or personal days, or set your baby up with some stacking rings next to your desk. (Kidding. Although that would be tempting.)

chapter
11

Loving Life As a Working Mom

Year One Strategies for Making
Work and Family Work

From Gretchen's journal:

Afraid of jinxing myself but feeling like the master of the single working
mom universe:

- *Despite all fears, Annie seems content in day care.*
- *I'm not obsessed with Annie while at work or with work while at*
  home.
- *I'm actually leaving the office on time for evening pickups, and*
  Richard has been great about my 5:00 P.M. departures. (The cute
  Annie photo on my computer wallpaper can't hurt.)
- *The day care ladies finally agreed to keep it to themselves if Annie*
  has any firsts (first step, first word) during her time there. I much
  prefer living in denial versus daily regret at missing the good stuff.
- *Overall stress level and happy daily routine so much better than*
  expected. Must casually mention this to Aunt Louise, who predicted
  the worst.

New mothers find working for pay fulfilling, mentally challenging, lu-
crative, and a really nice way to delegate diaper duty. But few of us
head back to work worry free. Here's the good news: As you balance parenthood and a paying job, you won't live in a constant state of stress,

your child care provider won't be a secret psychopath, and you won't miss every one of your baby's firsts. Yet we all have fears like this. We gamely head back to work after maternity leave and hope for the best.

This chapter goes a step further. It offers strategies for success during that wacky first year—so your risks can be minimized and your lifestyle fears thrown out with the diaper genie refills. Learn how to pump at work without feeling like an overpaid dairy cow in cute shoes, feel hip to be mom, minimize morning chaos, negotiate the ideal work/life benefit package, and lots more.

Make Work and Breast Feeding Work

FROM:	**Molly Whitman**
TO:	**Elaine Barnett**
SUBJECT:	**And I used to think a really bad hair day was embarrassing**

First two weeks back on the job had been perfect. Was effectively emitting confident working mom vibe—generally impressing colleagues with gorgeous newborn photo on desk and continued mastery of Asian markets. Until today, which shall now be known as The Day I Lost All Credibility At Work.

Locked office door, pulled out breast pump, unbuttoned blouse, held breast shields in place, pressed on button with elbow, and leaned back in chair—trying to visualize Caroline's little face. Suddenly nineteen-year-old mailroom guy wandered in with interoffice memo and froze midstride just as new group director charged in with client update. Quickly deduced door was never actually locked (easy mistake on five hours sleep), and made mental note to request transfer to Denver by end of day. Currently considering escape routes that would minimize exposure to additional colleagues without requiring me to climb out office window and rappel down three stories in recently purchased Jimmy Choo slingbacks. Send rescue party asap.

Breast feeding can be complicated even during maternity leave, when you have all day to master an effective latch-on. Then you head back to work, and it gets even crazier. But never fear. If you want to continue nursing, you can.

If You Decide to Keep Breast-Feeding, Master the Pump Now; It's Going to Become Your Best Friend

Following your maternity leave, you can continue to breast-feed while at home and pump during the workday. Drink lots of water to maximize your output, pump during breaks or at lunch, refrigerate your expressed milk at the office, and bring it to your child care provider to be given to your baby in bottles the following day. Check out Chapter 3, "Breast Feeding and Bottle Feeding," for comprehensive guidance on choosing a pump plus expressing, storing, warming, and serving breast milk.

I Am Dairy Cow; Hear Me Roar

Beyond these pumping logistics, which can be learned quickly, there is the larger issue: How to attach a pump to your chest and express milk at work without feeling like an overpaid dairy cow. How to stride confidently out of the designated nursing room, jauntily toting your expressed milk like any high-powered career gal nonchalantly sporting a grande soy latte.

This is, of course, a rhetorical question. The dairy cow self-image, as far as I can tell, is an inevitable part of the pumping reality. You can, however, justify the weirdness very easily by reminding yourself that pumping (1) is good for your baby, (2) burns a few hundred calories without even having to break a sweat on the treadmill, and (3) minimizes any residual working mom guilt. (You're willingly strapping a motorized suction cup to your chest when you could be catching up on personal e-mail; your maternal devotion is clearly beyond reproach.) And feel better knowing we're all out here doing it too—pumping away behind locked office doors and in employee break rooms, teacher lounges, and bathroom stalls around the country. Which brings us to the next great pumping quandary: Where to do it while at work?

Claim a Private Pumping Station

If you're really lucky, you have an office with a lockable door, or you work at a company that has designated nursing rooms. In either case, pumping is a snap. Otherwise, you'll need to claim an unused space or head to the ladies room for pumping sessions. Are these options ideal? Not even close. But they can work.

A colleague of mine used to pump in a small conference room down the hall. The room was used for meetings throughout the day, and the door didn't lock—she simply kept out potential intruders by taping up a handmade "Pumping in Session" sign. I always thought this was very, very brave. With my luck, the spacey IT guy would miss my handmade sign and walk in on me midpump. And what about the random guys in the department who saw the sign perfectly? They'd stop, let the meaning slowly sink in, and then acquire a scary mental image of me pumping just beyond the door. I don't think so. As a feminist, I realize I'm a complete wimp. To further the cause of supportive workplaces, I should be willing to brave midpump drop-ins and colleagues picturing me with suction cups attached to my chest somewhere in Conference Room C. Hypothetically, I'm right there with you. In reality, I'd find it a tad awkward. Good luck finding a neutral, nondescript, and secure pumping place in your working world.

Explain Your Pumping Plan to Your Manager

Granted, this can be a slightly uncomfortable conversation if your boss is one of those uptight guys who successfully shirked diaper duty in his house or, worse yet, doesn't even have kids. But it should be done—unless you can subtly fit in pumping over lunch without being missed. Explain when you anticipate pumping each day, where you'll be, and how much time you'll need. Establish a clear plan so there's no confusion over your whereabouts during pumping sessions. And *don't feel guilty* about your time spent pumping. You could be taking smoking breaks, right?

Invest in Nursing Pads, Lots and Lots of Nursing Pads

You're sitting in a meeting, attempting to pay attention, but the guy up front has a seemingly endless series of PowerPoint slides and a seriously distracting arsenal of hand gestures. Eventually your mind wanders to a happy place: your baby. You picture her engaged in her latest hobby—

earnestly attempting to stick her toes into her mouth—and suddenly you recognize a warm, tingly sensation in your chest.

"Message received. All systems go," your milk ducts announce proudly, kicking into overdrive. And before your brain can respond ("Abort mission! I repeat, abort mission! It's just a daydream, you morons. The baby's back at home!"), they've dutifully produced enough milk to feed your child for days, and half of it has leaked onto the white cotton shirt you just purchased on sale at Ann Taylor Loft. You stifle a scream, pull your notepad to your chest, and make a mad dash for the door.

Right. To prevent moments like this, wear absorbent cotton nursing pads 24/7 until the day you stop breast-feeding. And then wear them a few more days just to be on the safe side. Keep extras at work to use after emergency soakings.

Double-Pump

At the risk of stating the obvious, you can express milk a lot faster by pumping from both sides at once. And unless you have one of those leisurely jobs where they pay you to sit around and read magazines, you'll understand the merits of this approach. I'm assuming you'll be using an electric breast pump, which is almost essential for pumping efficiently at work. The double-pump strategy requires practice and coordination, but it's worth the effort. You can now purchase hands-free pumping accessories, which hold both breast shields in place and allow you to multitask while pumping. If you find double-pumping awkward, pump one side at a time and use your free hand to catch up on paperwork, e-mail, or calls.

Dress for Success

I've never been a fan of those tops designed for breast feeding. The subtle flaps are not really so subtle, and the style quotient is usually decades behind the times. You've just survived several months of maternity clothes—do you really want to extend the torture with nursing wear? Even the logic doesn't add up. Either I'm at home, where my husband is always up for the cheap thrill of a little exposed cleavage, or I'm out and I simply drape a baby blanket over my shoulder during feedings. The baby's body covers my belly, and nobody sees a thing. While pumping at work, you'll be in a private spot so there's no need for modesty. Just wear tops that can be unbuttoned or pulled up easily.

Save the money you would have spent on breast feeding clothes, and invest in a couple of comfy nursing bras and a sweater or jacket you can leave at work and pull on in case of leakage. Allegedly patterned tops also help hide leakage, but if I'm featuring a milk stain at work, I'm heading straight for the layered look regardless of any distracting prints.

If You're Working Part-Time, Try to Pump on a Consistent Schedule Each Workday

I say "try" to pump on a consistent schedule because very few jobs allow for regular pumping times. Ideally, pump when you feed your baby on your days off. This approach will help you maintain your milk supply and minimize discomfort.

If you, like many of us, are lucky to squeeze in a couple of random pumping sessions between meetings, sales calls, or typical work chaos, don't stress. Keep the nursing pads in place and take ibuprofen if needed to minimize achiness.

If You Want to Drop the Daytime Feedings, Give Yourself a Few Weeks to Wean Your Baby Before Returning to Work

Some moms decide not to pump during working hours but continue to breast-feed first thing in the morning and overnight. If you want to try this approach, plan ahead. Weaning is typically most successful (and less painful) when you drop one feeding per week. If you usually breast-feed three times during working hours, you need about three weeks to shift from nursing to formula for those feedings. This approach can offer a nice balance, but nursing pads are critical during the day, and your milk supply may diminish over time.

Don't Fret Over Firsts

"Look! She's smiling! It's her first smile!" Alex called his mom over to the baby's bassinet. She looked down at her granddaughter's face and then glanced at her son.

"Honey, she's making a definite expression, but I don't know if I'd describe that as a smile."

"What do mean?"

"Honestly, I'd say the baby has gas."

| ※ |

You're on maternity leave. You're staring at your infant twenty-four hours a day, with no risk of missing a memorable moment. Then you head back to work, and your constant baby watch takes a several-hour reprieve daily. What, you wonder, will he do today while I'm at the office? Something miraculous, surely. Something that clearly demonstrates his impressive intellect, his physical prowess, or his artistic sensibilities. In any case, maybe he'll discover his hands, and I don't want to miss it.

Let Go of the Sanctity of Firsts

As a new mom, I'm about to make a highly controversial claim: Firsts are overrated. I'm not a cynical person. My husband can tell you I always tear up at those "Having a Baby Changes Everything" Johnson & Johnson commercials, and I'm as sentimental about my child as anyone. But the reality is, the major baby firsts—the first smile, the first word, the first step—are very hard to pin down.

Despite what we've been led to believe by the baby books requiring us to place a specific date next to each first event, they're not single events at all. Infant milestones are better explained as gradual occurrences. Who can really differentiate between those gas-induced lopsided grins and the real first smile? My son made mammama sounds for months, but can I call mama his first word? He'd look right at me, grin like an angel, and utter "Mama." Then, just as I reached down for him, bursting with maternal pride, he'd continue, "Mamfgyham ama dadafgd mmmaaa dadadafgd." What was that? Does it count? Do you see where I'm going with this? Eventually his "mamamama" evolved into Mommy and his "dadadafdgfdadad" evolved into Daddy, but in the meantime his "words" were a bit vague. Even his first step was anybody's guess. He cruised around on the edges of the furniture for weeks, and it was impossible to tell if he made an unassisted step or two as he moved about.

So, release your anguish about missing that first step. You're going to see a version of it, and that moment will be perfect.

Tell Your Child Care Provider to Keep a Few Secrets

Yes, firsts are hard to pinpoint. But that doesn't prevent your caregiver from deciding she's been the singular witness to every major milestone during your child's first year. A friend of mine had a creative strategy to avoid this situation. She asked her daytime baby-sitter not to mention any firsts she witnessed that day. Know your baby is close to walking? Just ask your child care provider to keep it to herself if she sees the little dude take an independent step. You don't have to dwell on the missed moments, and the steps you see will seem like the first.

Establish Boundaries; Really Firm Boundaries

"Finish the proposal by tonight? Okay, sure. No problem. I'll drop it off on your desk before I head out." Carmen hung up the phone and dropped her head into her hands. She was supposed to pick up her ten-month-old daughter at day care in forty-five minutes. Finishing the proposal would normally take almost two hours. And her husband was at a client meeting over an hour away.

"I really have to learn more about cloning," she thought to herself, turning to her computer.

|•|

You're working. You're a new parent. You're going to make some major sacrifices on one front or the other, right? Not necessarily. The secret to less stress and a feeling of greater success both at work and at home may lie in establishing boundaries and sticking to them.

The Families and Work Institute, Catalyst, and the Boston College Center for Work and Family collaborated on a report that offers a fresh perspective on work–family balance. Researchers found that executives who placed equal priority on work and family—people they called dual-centric—achieved greater success at work, felt more successful at work *and* home, and reported lower levels of stress than executives who consistently sacrificed one aspect of life for the other.[1] These dual-centrics offer a few tips for the rest of us.

Be a Rebel; Tell Your Manager When You Need to Leave Each Day, and Then Actually Go Home at That Time

As you return from maternity leave, explain your scheduling requirements. Be clear. Be bold. If you need to head home regularly by 6:00 P.M. because your baby will be asleep by 7:00 P.M. and you'd like to see her eyes open once a day, just be honest. You could go in early or take work home to complete while your little one sleeps. The occasional late night at the office is normal. A corporate culture that expects a constant routine of late nights may not satisfy your new lifestyle requirements. Ideally, find a working environment that allows you to meet your family responsibilities guilt-free. And yes, these places do exist.

Of course, this kind of request can be stressful. We're all hardwired to do our best. We want our colleagues to respect us; we want to contribute to the team; we want to demonstrate our diligence and overdeliver on every task. We've spent years working overtime without complaint, and we don't want to disappoint anyone. Fortunately our babies make the process easier.

"My children helped me create boundaries in a way I never could for myself," says Lisa Levey, director of advisory services for Catalyst, a non-profit research and consulting firm that focuses on advancing women in business. "It's been one of the great gifts of being a mom, and a complete paradigm shift for me. I used to be able to throw time at a problem and spend many hours making something perfect—or near perfect—in my eyes. The time spent was often not worth the incremental improvement. I worked very hard but not always very smart." As a mother, she now tries to prioritize tasks and maximize her productivity during the workday, so except in rare circumstances she can be home at night with her kids—in mind and body. She's become comfortable telling herself, "It's time to go. This is good enough, or it can wait until tomorrow." Levey's advice for new moms heading back to work? Go easy on yourself and be realistic about what is possible—and desirable—in this chapter of your life. Know you'll need a new rhythm in terms of how you do things, and be satisfied with your daily accomplishments.

When You're at Home, Be Home

Don't let work stress disrupt your quality new mom time. Give your baby your undivided attention—at least until she's asleep. And when you're at work, prioritize, conquer, and hit the road. With the right boundaries, you should feel energized by your job *and* your time at home.

Admit It; Working Can Be Fun

Yes, it pays the bills. And offers health insurance. And makes that 529 plan possible. But have no guilt admitting the truth: Your job is also fun (at least sometimes). It gets you out of the house; it offers mental exercise; it entails adult conversation and gives you a sense of accomplishment even beyond the pure joy of parenthood. In a recent Executive Moms survey, 97 percent of working moms believed being a working mother helped them feel like a better mother, according to founder and president Marisa Thalberg. So, establish a work schedule you can live with and then enjoy the ride.

Feel Hip to Be Mom

"I'm actually getting the hang of this working mom thing," Liza thought, smiling to herself. She had finished her sales calls with time to spare and even fit in pumping over lunch. She packed up to leave and stopped by the employee break room to grab her thermos of expressed breast milk from the fridge. "See ya Tom," she said to her boss as he walked out sipping his end-of-day decaf.

"Bye, Liza," he responded. "And if you're getting coffee for the road— we're out of the regular cream, but I found some in the refrigerator. It's in that silver thermos."

"Uh-huh," she replied, stopping in her tracks and watching him go. "The silver thermos. Thanks for the tip."

|•|

The first year of working parenthood will have its share of crazy moments, but you can survive with your confidence intact. Here's how to make your way through Babyville without losing your cool, calm, and collected self-image.

Get Creative to Make Your Favorite Stuff Happen

Mothers are busy—that's part of the job description. And the premium on personal time is at an all-time high as workweeks expand to keep pace with the global economy and the lines between career and personal time blur. (You've got a BlackBerry in your pocket; *why not* respond to that client request while your baby plays in her exersaucer after dinner?)

Can't make it to the gym anymore? Strap on the baby backpack and start a new routine of Sunday morning walks. Missing afterwork dinners with friends? Suggest Saturday lunches instead. Your new baby reality may require some creative scheduling, but try not to forgo the things that make you feel like, well, you. When you're happy, everybody benefits.

Keep Up the Mom Bonding

Mom bonding begins during maternity leave, but try to keep it going when you return to work by participating in some kind of mom's group, play group, or mom-and-baby activity. We're talking about any gathering that allows you to interact with other new moms, rant about the stuff that's hard, brag about your baby's latest tricks, share funny stories, and exchange advice. You might feel odd discussing the sheer thrill of your infant's first front-to-back rollover with work colleagues, but tell a new mom and she'll fully understand your excitement.

Infant activities offer the perfect opportunity. We can all argue little Aidan is gaining a deep appreciation of the transcendent power of music in that Wiggleworms class, but the mothers are secretly just thrilled to have thirty minutes to chat while the babies steal each other's shakers. And don't underestimate the power of chatting. I can hear you now, thinking, "That's all I need—a wasted half hour of small talk with women I don't really know." These women may remain acquaintances, but those quick conversations can make a huge difference in your experience of early parenthood. There's nothing better for the stress level than empathy, and these women offer it. You'll get practical tips far better than any pediatrician's and hear stories that make your life seem easy. Crazy things happen in Babyville, and nothing is more helpful than letting go of your anxiety through stories—both hearing them and telling them. You should be able to find an evening or weekend group or class that doesn't conflict with your work schedule.

Pay Attention to the Good Days

There will be wild and wacky moments. There will also be nearly perfect days when your prepregnancy suit actually fits without stretching, your big meeting goes flawlessly, and your baby sleeps through the night. On those days, stop. And notice your surroundings. These days can easily get you through the crazy ones, and before you know it you won't even remember that scary breast milk as creamer incident.

Minimize Morning Chaos

Heidi had never been a morning person. Dragging herself out of bed and getting to work by 9:00 A.M. had always been an impressive feat. Then her daughter Mia was born, and the situation didn't improve. Now her typical morning goes something like this:

- Alarm goes off, hit snooze button for the first time.
- Nine minutes later, hit snooze button again. Curse alarm clock and ridiculously short snooze button allowance.
- Twenty-seven minutes later, finally give up on multiple snooze button reprieves and pull weary bones out of bed. Note time and hustle into bathroom.
- Take scalding hot shower in unsuccessful attempt to wake up.
- Locate relatively wrinkle-free clothes. Get dressed. On a good day, all items match.
- Drink scalding hot cup of coffee in slightly more successful attempt to jump-start brain.

- Hear Mia waking up, go into nursery and assess scene. She's peed through her diaper and pajamas, per the usual, and is clearly unhappy with pervasive dampness.
- Pull off wet sheets, change and dress Mia, bring her downstairs for breakfast. Offer a bottle while mentally reviewing baby gear still to be assembled and meetings planned for the day.
- Burp Mia and, distracted by busy day to come, forget to use burp cloth. Suddenly realize shoulder is covered by sticky pool of baby spit-up.
- Run upstairs—toting infant—to find fresh, relatively wrinkle-free top. Pay no attention to color combinations at this point; desperate measures are required.
- Again check the time and make a mad dash downstairs.
- Assemble now crabby child in infant carrier, frantically locate paraphernalia for day care, grab work paperwork from kitchen counter, and head out the door—making a mental note never to hit the snooze button again.

|•|

Mornings in Babyville are the true test of your parenthood patience. You have ten things to do, your time is tight, and your coffee is just starting to kick in. Throw a baby into the mix, and even the perkiest morning person could start to feel frazzled. Try these strategies to keep your mornings under control.

Do Everything Possible the Night Before

We all get it. Plan ahead. Before going to bed, pull out your baby's clothes and pack up the diapers, the bottles, the various accessories required by day care. Have the diaper bag ready and waiting. Select your outfit, find your shoes under the living room couch, locate a relatively clean bra. If you're prone to forgetting things you need at the office, tape a "bring to work" checklist—with everything from your cell phone to your clean breast pump shields—on the inside of your front door. Then, impressively, you awake the next morning and whip through dressing and breakfast in record time. You double-check the items on your list and head out early, relaxed and ready for action. We all understand the merits of advance preparation, but somehow it's still nearly impossible to make this happen every evening. Best of luck in your preplanning attempts.

Create a Morning Routine for Yourself and Your Baby

Babies thrive on relatively predictable routines and, let's be honest, so do we. There will be days your child wakes at the crack of dawn and other days she sleeps right through breakfast, but do your best. It doesn't have to be anything elaborate, just try to keep the basics in a predictable order—bottle, diaper change, clothes, breakfast, five minutes of playtime, into the infant carrier, out the door—whatever works.

Expect Delays

No, you're not imagining it. Your child really does have a sixth sense that alerts her to pull out her best procrastination techniques when you're in a hurry. On the morning of your big presentation, when you've dragged your good suit out of the hall closet and actually tried to style your hair, she will sense your urgency like a heat-seeking missile and suddenly produce three explosive dirty diapers in a row. Or, for the first time in her life, refuse the bottle. Or have the meltdown of the century. Know this now, and keep your wits about you when these mornings hit. Try to channel your calm prebaby self, remain flexible, and follow your morning routine as quickly and quietly as possible. We've all been there, and we've all survived. You will too.

Don't Be a Martyr

From Eileen's journal:

> Crazy day at work and at home. To top it off, Joe was watching baseball while I did the dishes, put Lucas to bed, paid the bills, and folded clothes. I'd talk to him about it if I had the energy to put together a coherent sentence. Maybe tomorrow . . .

Women now run departments and companies and states, but we're also doing the laundry and getting the kids dressed every morning. As

Ann Crittenden explains in her book *The Price of Motherhood*, moms in the paid labor force work over eighty hours a week between home and the office, "Time-use surveys confirm that as women enter the workplace, they take on the equivalent of two full-time jobs, forcing them to cut back on everything in their lives *but* paid work and children."[2]

Even the most helpful significant others may fumble in the infant care department. Despite the Family and Medical Leave Act, which passed in 1993, many men take off only a few days after their babies are born, so mom quickly takes over child care on top of her other work at home and the office. What's your best bet for household balance?

Three Words: Delegate, Delegate, Delegate

Create a list of tasks that can be delegated and then make it happen. This can start when you're on maternity leave, but it should kick into high gear when you head back to work. If you have a significant other at home, he should get a list of weekly jobs. Maybe you used to do the dishes each night, but now he can take over that task while you're feeding the baby. Then get creative about enlisting additional help—whether it's using online grocery shopping and delivery or a Saturday afternoon baby-sitting swap so you can tackle your errands at warp speed. When you're working and parenting, your time is precious. You deserve some assistance.

Reduce Your Expectations

At the beginning of the past century, women spent forty-four hours weekly on meal preparation and cleanup.[3] Today, we whip out dinner in fifteen minutes and still have time to pay the bills and check e-mail before putting our babies to bed. Working moms have learned how to do it all with maximum efficiency, accomplishing more in a week than many Fortune 500 CEOs. So give yourself a break.

Prebaby, you may have exercised two or three times a week. Your first year in Babyville, this could become impossible. Don't beat yourself up—create a new exercise plan that works with your lifestyle (yes, carrying your infant upstairs counts as upper body toning and cardio) and be satisfied when you make that happen. Similarly, find a happy balance between household maintenance and downtime with your family. Sparkly floors may become less important than hanging out on the floor for an hour with your little one. (Hey, dust bunnies wouldn't have such a cute name if they were really dangerous, right?)

Be Less Than Perfect

Many women these days are high achievers, which is a good thing. Absolutely. But when you apply the same work ethic to every aspect of life—trying to be the best worker, the best spouse, the best friend, the best mom—something's gotta give, says Natalie Gahrmann, work/life expert for BlueSuitMom and *Parenting* magazine. This drive for perfection is a natural extension of years in the workplace, Gahrmann explains, but it's also the fast lane to new mom burnout. This year, give yourself a break on every front as you settle into your new routines.

Keep an Eye on Your Week

Malia hurried in from work, said good-bye to the baby-sitter, and checked on her peacefully sleeping son. Her stomach was audibly grumbling, and she headed to the kitchen to assess the dinner options. As she swung open the refrigerator door, she suddenly remembered the list of errands she'd scribbled somewhere and immediately misplaced. "Groceries," she said to herself, staring into the empty fridge. "We have no food. And we have no laundry detergent. Nice. Well, who needs clean underwear?"

|•|

Looking for an easy way to feel organized? Try keeping a weekly calendar in a visible spot, block out hours for work and commuting, and then fill in essential and fun stuff—from key errands to writing holiday cards, from calling friends to paying bills. Of course, daily life will inevitably veer from your plan. But at least you'll start with a sense of control. And you may even remember to keep that fridge stocked.

Negotiate the Ideal Work/Life Benefit Package

FROM:	**Erica Kleinfeld**
TO:	**Latisha Williams**
SUBJECT:	**Just a bunch of questions about work and life with a baby**

Happy Birthday to Mika! I can't believe she's one. And you've survived so far with both your job and your sanity impressively intact. Speaking of sanity, I need your help. I just hit month six of my pregnancy, and I already have a ton of questions about the details of working parenthood:

1. I just heard about a great day care center with 5:30 P.M. pickups, but I usually don't leave work until 6:00 P.M. Heard any recent updates on time travel?

2. What if the baby gets sick and can't go to day care for a few days? I have a feeling people would notice if I tried to stash her infant carrier under my desk.

3. Will I ever see the gym again? It's twenty minutes from our house, and they don't offer baby-sitting. I'm starting to think these extra pregnancy pounds may be permanent.

4. How will I make all those year one pediatrician appointments during business hours? I can only take so many long lunches before somebody catches on.

5. Do you know any secrets to saving money on child care? David has started buying lottery tickets. (No, I'm not kidding.) Please help.

Yes, you always *had a life* outside of work, but the need to head out for dinner with friends doesn't instill a real sense of urgency in employers. Prechildren, most of us put in the hours on the job without complaint, impressively matching and surpassing the pace of our chosen work cultures. Then our babies hit the scene, and our career commitments become more complex. We mentally create boundaries, we fantasize about flexible scheduling, and we could really use child care assistance. Many of us are still dedicated to our careers, but we need help.

And we're not alone. The number of women in the U.S. civilian labor force climbed from 18.4 million in 1950 to over 68 million in 2005.[4,5] Moms and dads used to play a sort of zone defense—specializing in discrete spheres of work and home. Today parents do it all. Almost three-quarters of American moms with children under eighteen work for pay,[6] and 62 percent of working women earn *at least half* of their family incomes.[7]

Work/life programs provide needed flexibility in terms of when, where, and how employees meet their career responsibilities. The goals? Improved quality of life and diminished work-related stress. Employees are happier and employers benefit from high levels of productivity, reduced turnover among experienced talent, and a competitive edge in recruiting. (We're talking about Corporate America—you knew they'd have an upside.)

Typical options:

- Alternative work arrangements
- Child care solutions
- Emergency family accommodations
- Adoption assistance
- Benefits that just make life easier (on-site gyms, referral services)

How to negotiate a work/life benefits package that meets your family's needs? Start by learning the lingo and context of today's offerings.

Understand Your Work/Life Benefit Options

Employee benefit packages vary significantly. The following work/life accommodations are currently available at many U.S. organizations. Some may be out of your employer's budgetary league, but others may meet your needs without undue financial strain—even for smaller organizations. And if your ideal benefit package falls outside your employer's current offerings, never fear. Work/life programs are typically fluid and constantly evolving. Most human resources directors welcome new ideas. Consider your family's situation, your work culture, and your management's philosophy when compiling a somewhat realistic dream list from the options on the following page. Then head to human resources to discuss your company's current offerings and the potential for new opportunities.

Alternative Work Arrangements

You got the full scoop on today's alternative work arrangements in Chapter 8. Here's a quick recap:

Full-Time Options	Schedule	Salary & Benefits	U.S. Employees with Access[8]
Flextime	Think 8:00 A.M. to 4:00 P.M. or 7:00 A.M. to 3:00 P.M. instead of 9:00 A.M. to 5:00 P.M.	Full	60%
Compressed workweek	Squeeze your full-time load into three or four longer days	Full	22%
Flexplace	Work from home	Full	30%
Reduced Hours			
Part-time	Lots of options here: three 8-hour days, four 8-hour days, five half days, or anything in between	Salary: reduced relative to schedule Benefits: often cut; try to negotiate to keep them	46%
Job sharing	Two part-time employees split one full-time position, usually overlapping Wednesdays to transition projects		27%
Part-time flexplace*	Work from home and reduce your hours		30%
Other Fun Possibilities			
Freelancing	You provide independent projects and services	Project-based fees, no benefits	Variable
Extended leave/ Flexcareer	Boomerang programs allow employees to take up to multiyear leaves with alumni status and incremental communication	On hold, potentially with subsidized continuing professional education	Not many yet, but you may have luck negotiating an informal agreement

*30 percent of employees have access to flexplace overall.

Child Care Solutions

Flexible spending accounts: As already noted, FSAs are a new parent no brainer offered by 79 percent of employers.[9] You may be using your employer's FSA already to set aside a portion of your pretax salary for health care costs. As a parent, you can apply additional pretax funds to pay for child care. If you know you won't qualify for the child care tax credit, it's especially useful to take advantage of this program.

On-site or near-site child care: Your baby shares your commute, you're accessible in case of emergency, and you can even stop by for a quick snuggle during lunch (assuming you actually get a lunch break). These employer-sponsored centers are generally offered by larger organizations with populations sizable enough to justify the cost. IBM Corporation, for example, provides care for over 1,100 employee children around the United States by sponsoring on- or near-site centers and home-based day care providers. And many state and federal agencies offer centers for children of government employees.

Resource and referral services: You don't have access to on-site care, so your search for local providers begins. Contact your employee assistance program (EAP) or human resources department; they may have already done the homework for you.

Local child care discounts: Child care is never cheap, and many employers pitch in by negotiating lower rates with local providers or national child care centers. These group discounts are common because they're easy (and free) for employers to negotiate while adding real value for working parents, according to Kathy Kacher, president of Career/Life Alliance. If your employer doesn't offer this benefit, talk to some colleagues and make a combined request to human resources. With a few phone calls, your HR director could save you 10 to 15 percent on annual child care expenses.

Child care subsidies: Some employers subsidize child care costs, although this benefit is less common because of complicated payroll logistics.

Community outreach: Some large employers work with local agencies and organizations to increase and improve the child care opportunities within their communities.

School's out programs: This year, not a problem. But when your child hits preschool, things get complicated. What do you do when she has spring break or summer vacation? Employers like Chicago-based Abbott Laboratories have set policy to head off this situation before it arises. Abbott provides facilities to care for kids when school is out and a Summer of Service volunteering program for sixth through ninth graders. If you're really lucky, your employer may step up on this one as well.

Emergency Family Accommodations

You have a child. Odds are, she's going to get sick at some point before she turns eighteen. This may not be a problem year one if you're using in-home child care. With day care centers, however, sickness is a deal breaker. What to do when you're expected at work and your little one has the stomach flu? (No, dropping her off at the day care center and making a run for it isn't recommended.)

Paid personal or sick days: These come under many names, ranging from a healthy living day off (Fannie Mae) to a balance day off (Eddie Bauer). The days are yours to use as needed.

Emergency work from home: Even if you're committed to a full-time, in-office schedule, you could request a work from home as needed emergency policy.

Backup child care: Some progressive employers, like audit, tax, and advisory services firm KPMG LLP, head off child care emergencies with guaranteed backup. Each KPMG office works with a third-party provider who offers fill-in baby-sitting and day care for sick days, snow days, and even those awkward weeks between the end of school and the beginning of camp, according to Barbara Wankoff, national director of Workplace Solutions. Employees receive an average of twenty free emergency usages each year, and they can be shared among colleagues if one doesn't need her full allocation. Ask about your employer's offerings.

Benefits That Just Make Life Easier

New parent policies: These days there's a veritable benefit buffet for new moms and dads—from lactation consulting services to designated pumping rooms, from subsidized fertility treatments to twenty-four-hour nurse hotlines. My personal favorite for full-timers? The phase back to work approach. After maternity leave, new moms work a reduced schedule at first, gradually increasing to five days over several weeks or even a few months. The timing of this process is up to you, and working from home at first is another option. Phasing back to work is often informally negotiated with individual managers—good luck with yours.

Family-friendly meeting schedules: For a working parent, those 7:00 P.M. team meetings can be a major challenge. If your manager is regularly gathering the troops when you're needed at home, repress the fear of being mistaken for a slacker, be honest, and suggest a policy of informal meetings until 5:00 P.M. And if that doesn't work, ask to phone in to meetings outside of regular business hours.

Low-stress dress: Hopefully you haven't had to pull out your power suit and heels since your last job interview, because working parenthood is a role more fit for sneakers than stilettos. Bottom line, if you can get away with informal work clothes, do it this year. As your baby's applesauce hits your shoulder for the third morning in a row, it's much less painful to grab a new sweater than to take that silk blouse to the cleaners.

Mentoring programs: Some employers, like strategy and technology consulting firm Booz Allen Hamilton, facilitate formal peer support—so employees have an ally and sounding board as they balance career and personal responsibilities. Over 5,500 of Booz Allen's female employees participate in structured mentoring and career counseling programs. Ask about formal programs or try to find a mentor on your own. Ideally, connect with a mom in a similar role who can offer advice about her challenges and strategies that have worked.

Counseling, resource, and referral services: Need a great dog walker? Someone to mow your lawn? Advice on balancing your family budget or minimizing stress? Human resources may be able to hook you up.

Convenient on-site facilities: That hour at the gym is often the first thing to go when you hit Babyville. Knowing this, lots of companies have tried to help with on-site services from fitness centers to banking, from postal delivery to dry cleaning, from minimarts to takeout food. If yours does, take advantage.

Adoption Benefits

Consultation: You've decided to adopt. You're thrilled. You're curious. And, as the impending paperwork and interviews hit you, you're probably overwhelmed. Where to go for help? Believe it or not, your best bet may be your human resources department. Some employers, like the federal government and Prudential Financial, offer consultation to help guide employees through the adoption process.

Adoption cost reimbursement: Adoption costs can make even that overpriced nursery furniture look cheap, and some employers lighten this financial load by reimbursing a portion of adoption expenses. General Mills, for example, offers up to $5,000 in adoption reimbursement, and pharmaceutical maker Eli Lilly offers up to $10,000.

Adoption leave: Adoption leave policies are often similar to parental leave programs. Talk to your human resources department for your company's specifics.

Determine Your Company's Current Work/Life Offerings

Now you know the range of work/life options currently offered by U.S. employers. Ideally, you will have easy access to many of these benefits. Pull out your employee handbook for a quick overview and then make an appointment with human resources. At that meeting, ask for a detailed explanation of all current work/life programs.

If Your Company Doesn't Offer the Supports You Need, Don't Give Up

The work/life programs at most companies are continually expanding. Human resource directors recognize it's an evolving field and often appreciate new ideas that could improve life for employees. Before submitting a formal request, build your case by talking to your most powerful allies— other working parents at the company. If you're unsatisfied with your company's work/life offerings, chances are you're not alone. Together, you can develop a request that would be hard for your human resources department to ignore. Even if your colleagues aren't interested in making a formal request, they may provide useful ideas as you write yours.

Submit a Formal Work/Life Benefit Request

You know the wide range of available work/life options, you've assessed your company's offerings, and you've gotten feedback from other employees. It's go time. Type up a request for your ideal work/life plan. Detail current benefits you'll be utilizing (no controversy there), and include suggestions for new policies you hope the company will consider. Good luck!

. . . Or Shocking Your
Colleagues and Staying
Home for a While

Today's Strategic, Temporary Stay-at-Home Moms

How to Master the Art of Sequencing

From Michelle's journal:

Finally convinced choice to stay home for eighteen months was right on. Despite maternity leave torment, greatest fears were never realized:

Fear 1: Life on one income will make daily exposure to tempting baby purchases feel like an open bar at an AA meeting.

Reality: Hello eBay! Just yesterday, sold ugly clock (wedding present from hell, no gift receipt) for $75 and bought like-new jogging stroller for $50. Drew the line at bidding on a cheap but potentially scary used toddler underwear.

Fear 2: Brain previously filled with Important Information will become unable to process anything more complicated than mixing rice cereal and applesauce.

Reality: Joined a book club, set up a family budget, figured out the digital camera, and actually started reading the newspapers that used to go straight from our doorstep to recycling. Overall, brain still alive and kicking.

Fear 3: Hermit-like existence will be highlighted by daily grocery shopping trips concocted primarily to interact with the outside world.

Reality: New moms are popping up everywhere and all seem to be looking for friends. Actually feel more popular now than prior personal best in sixth grade.

Today many women and some men choose to leave the paid workforce temporarily when entering Babyville. It's an approach called "sequencing" from Arlene Rossen Cardozo's book with that title, and full-time parenthood is considered one in a series of lifetime jobs.[1] The stage at home often lasts a year or two or, if all is going well, until the kids are in school. These full-time parents trade in career security and income not in a selfless way, but in a strategic way—choosing to balance family and work in phases.

Leaving our jobs, even for a short time, can be both liberating and daunting. You feel grateful if it's a choice you can afford to make. But you're also aware of the sacrifices: Your clear career path becomes distinctly hazy, your benefits are history, and your work colleagues are no longer down the hall. Plus, after years of making your own money, it can be an adjustment to live on your significant other's income. It takes a strong, confident person to forgo her salary and sense of financial independence even for a short time.

If you decide to take an extended leave from the paid job market, give yourself time to adjust to the new lifestyle. And don't worry, you won't have a "mommy" tattoo across your forehead when you start interviewing again. Although workforce reentry can be challenging, there are simple steps you can take to maintain your marketability.

Try these parent-tested strategies to ease your transition from the working world to full-time parenthood and back—whether your time at home lasts six months or six years. Learn about career on-ramps and off-ramps and get tips for keeping your confidence high, feeling independent while your significant other is paying the bills, staying mentally stimulated, avoiding isolation, maintaining your marketability while at home, and hitting the on-ramp at high speed.

Understand Career Off-Ramps and On-Ramps

FROM: **Allison Beckett**

TO: **Patricia Martinez**

SUBJECT: **Finally told my manager I'm staying home for a while**

Just took a flying leap off my cozy career path. Am I crazy for taking this risk? Will I ever get a job again? Will the gap on my résumé send my application to the bottom of every new hire pile? Moral support desperately needed. Tell me I'm not insane.

How prevalent is sequencing, and how do the push and pull of career factors and family coalesce as new moms weigh their options? A fascinating study recently reported in *Harvard Business Review* offers insight into the nuanced landscape surrounding career "off-ramps and on-ramps."[2] The researchers surveyed over 2,400 educated women between twenty-eight and fifty-five, and found 37 percent overall and 43 percent of mothers left their jobs voluntarily at some point. The average time at home was 2.2 years, and even less—1.2 years—for women in business. Beyond the pull of family care and the safety net of spousal income, a variety of "push" factors were also in play. Some off-rampers were eager to hit the road because of work-related negatives like being understimulated in their jobs or overwhelmed by work demands.

If you're less than thrilled with your job and have some financial flexibility, parenthood can motivate you to make a change. But the decision is rarely simple. Even if your work falls several miles short of dream job status, it's still *your* job. You earned it and you're good at it. You know how to get things done; people ask your opinions; you make your own money. In the *Harvard Business Review* study, 93 percent of off-ramped women hoped to return to the paid workforce. Yet—here's the scary part—only 74 percent of those who had tried to navigate back to their career paths were successful. Read on to make the most of your time at home and maximize your on-ramping opportunities.

Keep Your Confidence Intact

"Wow, I never pegged you for a housewife," Rhana's colleague casually replied after she explained her plan to stay home for a year.

She cringed. "Let's see. I have a degree in economics and I've been working my butt off for nine years, not to mention the part-time jobs I had during school. Now I'm going to spend twelve months with my baby before returning to work. If that makes me a housewife, I guess I am. Thanks for the support."

|•|

First, let's deal with how you feel. For years, career has been an integral part of your self-esteem, and doing your best at work has been a major focus. Now you're considering an extended leave, and this potential new lifestage may not fit neatly into your well-established self-image. If you decide to stay home for a while, how can you feel like yourself and keep your confidence in your new role?

Ignore the H Word

We really need a better title for a full-time mom. Housewife. Stay-at-home mom. The lady of the house. All anachronistic and just plain inaccurate terms for a vibrant and challenging role—but we know that, so I'll get off my semantic soapbox and cut to the chase.

Full-time moms outnumber every other female occupation in the United States, and their willingness to juggle myriad roles without pay is critical to the economy.[3] While Fortune 500 CEOs battle over seven-figure bonuses, millions of moms are doing fundamental work for free. And today many full-time moms are on temporary leave from a lifetime in the paid labor force—bringing an impressive set of skills, life experiences, and vitality to the role. June Cleaver, they aren't. If you choose to do the full-time mom thing for a while, ignore the lame titles and avoid Wisteria Lane.

Hang Out with People Who Think It's Cool to Stay Home

There will be people who get it and people who don't. If you surround yourself with those who do, staying home for a while will feel like the coolest thing going. Get lots of advice on making new mom connections in Chapter 5, "Making the Most of your Days at Home" or look into organized groups like these:

Mothers and More: The Network for Sequencing Women
- A nonprofit with lots of local chapters focused on networking, advocacy, and education. You're a sequencer; they love sequencers. Mingle.
- Mothersandmore.org

Mocha Moms
- A national nonprofit support group for moms of color who've cut back at work (beautiful website, great concept)
- Mochamoms.org

MOMS (Moms Offering Moms Support) Club
- A nonprofit organization for at-home and part-time moms
- Momsclub.org

Mommy & Me
- Despite the e-commerce angle, includes a helpful database of play groups, classes, library story times, and activities. Learn about new mom gatherings in your area.
- Mommyandme.com

Respond Proudly When You Get "The Question"

"So, what do you do?"

The Question hangs in the air, and your gut reaction tells the tale. You want to be proud of your answer; you want to be impressive. Yet in some contexts you may sense answering stay-at-home mom will peg you outside the accepted world of fifty-hour workweeks and shareholder returns.

And it's just too complicated to explain your entire career path, your years in the paid workforce followed by a temporary stint of full-time parenthood. If you experience blank stares from colleagues, friends, or random cocktail party companions after explaining your new role, just focus on the fact that you can take a hot bubble bath in the middle of the day, and they can't. Granted, you may be sharing your bath with a splashing child, but it's still fun.

Impress Yourself

Obviously you're proud of being a mom. And of course we all know that's enough. But if you want another self-esteem boost, set some goals and make them happen. I know a few moms who ran triathlons or marathons during their at-home phase. I secretly thought they were psychotic for attempting such a thing, but they seemed to get a lot out of it. Read a new book each month, hit the gym, have the will power to walk past babyGap *without* swinging by the sale rack—whatever gives you that secret thrill of personal accomplishment.

Stay Mentally Stimulated

"This morning I was so desperate for mental stimulation, I spent twenty minutes reading the exersaucer manual."

"Well, that's a good project. Did you get it set up?"

"That's the embarrassing part. Louis put it together last week; I just really needed something to read."

|•|

Our jobs, if nothing else, keep our brains busy. They keep us challenged most of the day, most of the week. The remaining hours become downtime to rest, clean the house, run errands, and on a really good day, see friends. When the mental challenge of work is removed from this equation, you don't want the activities previously allocated to downtime to fill all your time. Infant care is a fun new challenge in itself, plus these days there are lots of other opportunities to stay intellectually engaged during your at-home phase.

Exercise Your Brain

In *The Feminine Mystique,* Betty Friedan explained the unspoken malaise felt by American moms in the 1950s expected to find complete fulfillment in electric floor waxers and homemade muffins.[4] That was an era before home computers, before e-mail, before women entered motherhood with years of work and life experiences under their belts. Today, you can stay connected via IM and stay informed via MSN. You can exercise to a Pilates DVD while your seven-month-old plays with his stacking rings next to you, or you can balance the family budget while your newborn snoozes in a nursing pillow on your lap. You can even pull your creative juices out of the corporate freezer and let them thaw out a bit. Get into photography, try a do-it-yourself home project, or create a free baby website to share your early adventures. There are plenty of at-home options to stay mentally challenged and at the top of your game. Pick your favorites and have fun.

Offer Your Services to People Who Need Them

We all have skills we mastered at work—administrative, managerial, technical, financial, legal, something. Try offering your services to a nonprofit in town. You could help with a fund-raiser, review contracts, answer phone calls, work on the website—whatever utilizes your strengths. And since you're volunteering, the organization should accommodate your schedule, let you work from home, or allow you to bring your baby along to an occasional meeting. The fulfillment of work without the stress—not a bad deal.

Minimize Financial Fears and Feel Independent While Your Significant Other Is Paying the Bills

"What if you get laid off?"

"I won't get laid off."

"What if we can't afford to eat?"

"We worked out the budget last week. Eating won't be a problem."

"What if I become bitter because I don't have my own salary?"

"We have a joint account, and I won't mention the fact that it's my salary filling the account if you don't."

"Okay."

"Listen, if you want to stay home for a year, I think we can do it financially. I know your mom always felt dependent on your dad's income, but that's not us. A year without your salary won't change the whole dynamic of our relationship."

"Right. Thanks. You know, you're pretty good at this relationship thing."

"I try."

|•|

You had your own salary for years, and you liked it. You bought new shoes without hesitation; you subscribed to *Us Weekly* without guilt. Now what? Do you have to check in before every purchase? Will your beautifully balanced relationship become skewed as power shifts to the one with the paycheck? Not if you talk things out in advance and approach your one-income reality as a team.

Make a New Financial Game Plan

Decide together how you'll allocate your reduced monthly budget and where expenses may need to be trimmed. If you agree in advance to cut family clothing purchases, you'll feel a lot less bitter passing on that great new coat. For lots of ideas, check out Chapter 7, "Living for Less and Loving It."

Take Over the Family Budget and Bills

It may be his paycheck, but you're the ruler of cash flow. You'll feel informed, involved, and in charge.

Share Your Concerns

You: "If I stay home for a while, it's going to be really hard for me to sacrifice my salary and sense of financial independence. I need you to recognize that and work with me. No sarcastic comments about being the breadwinner, no double takes when I come home from shopping."

Your Significant Other: "Done."

Or something like that. Put your fears out there—you'll feel better and he'll know when to keep his mouth shut.

Get Involved in Investments

If you can actually save during your time at home, you're ahead of the game. Research 529 plans, mutual funds and bonds, or seriously motivate and join an investment club with some friends.

Avoid Isolation

"Hey babe, what's up?"

"Not much, just heading out to Target for some diapers."

"Don't we have a case in the garage?"

"Well yes, but we can always use more. And I really need to talk to someone whose vocabulary extends beyond single syllables."

|•|

Shifting to the at-home lifestyle can involve culture shock on many levels, but the most dramatic may be the sudden loss of your built-in social network. Work colleagues, for many of us, become a pseudo-family—a support system with whom we share most of our waking hours. When that support system is removed, it should be replaced before you start talking back to Katie Couric just for conversation. Check out Chapter 5 for lots of suggestions on making new mom friends.

Maintain Your Marketability While at Home

FROM:	**Erin VanEmst**
TO:	**Barbara Reynolds**
SUBJECT:	**Congrats Ms. V.P.**

Barbara,

Congratulations! Just heard about your promotion and wanted to touch base. Can I take you to lunch to celebrate? I'd love to catch up. How does your calendar look this month?

Erin

You may be officially unemployed, but keep your long-term marketability in mind. How? At the beginning of each year at home, create an annual plan of attack for the on-ramp trifecta: keeping your network strong, your résumé current, and your skills relevant.

Keep Your Network Strong

Be visible. Have lunch with former work colleagues every few months, keep in touch by e-mail, or make the occasional phone call to maintain past work relationships. And if you're really motivated, adopt an informal mentor you can meet with incrementally to stay in the loop.

Make new connections. There's no law against attending industry events when you're not exactly employed in the industry. Get a baby-sitter or wait until your significant other gets home, throw on a business suit, and hit a networking function with an old work friend. Some sequencers make business cards labeling themselves as consultants so they have something official to hand out at these events.

Keep Your Résumé Current

Volunteer smart. It's great to give back, but why not give yourself a little something at the same time? Offer your marketable skills to local nonprofits so you can repackage the experience on your résumé when you start interviewing again. They'll take any help they can get, and you'll enjoy short-term satisfaction for contributing to a worthy cause and long-term contacts and résumé filler for your period at home. Help organize an event and you've got managerial and budget allocation experience ready for your résumé.

Freelance. While you're focused on family, even one or two freelance projects a year can do wonders for those résumé black holes.

Assist family or friends for free. Maybe your uncle owns a small business or your neighbor manages a local retail shop. How could you add value without the commitment of a paying job? Consider your skill set and their needs.

Keep Your Skills Relevant

Follow the trades.   Maintain a couple of at-home subscriptions to your industry publications or sign up for free e-mail newsletters so you're ready to talk the talk the next time it's needed. You may even run across recruitment ads for freelance projects in your area.

Keep up certifications.   Sign up for annual training sessions in your field so your learning curve isn't impossibly steep when you make the return career climb.

Extend your education.   This phase could be the perfect time to start that teaching degree you always wanted or take classes in graphic design. Look for evening and weekend programs so you can attend while your significant other is on baby watch and follow a pace that fits with your lifestyle.

Hit the On-Ramp at High Speed

From Melissa's journal:

As of today, officially home for a full year. Hard to believe until I look at Riley—who's evolved from a nonspeaking, nonmoving newborn to a babbling, cruising pretoddler.

Per the family master plan, job search starts this week. Excited to work again but daunted by the reentry process. Where to begin? And more importantly, how to make twelve months singing "Three Little Monkeys" sound impressive?

Yes, the postleave job search requires motivation. But you can do it. Here's how:

Define Your Ideal Position

If you need a full-time income, you're obviously focused on full-time jobs. If you have some financial flexibility, think though your ideal schedule, responsibilities, work environment, and salary requirements. Now

YOUR ANNUAL
KEEPING-THE-ON-RAMP-IN-SIGHT PLAN

During your time at home, complete this worksheet annually to increase your odds of finding an ideal job when you're ready to on-ramp back to the career fast track.

Your Network

Make a list of key colleagues or clients and jot down the best strategy for keeping in touch with each one, from quarterly e-mails to occasional phone calls or lunches.

COLLEAGUES	PLANS TO KEEP IN TOUCH

Your Résumé

Brainstorm opportunities for volunteering, freelancing, or offering your services to family or friends. Then include timing and next steps for at least one or two projects a year. You get the résumé filler, and they benefit from your help.

POTENTIAL OPPORTUNITIES	NEXT STEPS

Your Skill Set

Make a plan for at-home trade subscriptions, e-mail newsletters, annual training sessions, certifications, and education.

TRADE MAGAZINES	E-MAIL NEWSLETTERS	TRAINING SESSIONS, CERTIFICATIONS, OR EDUCATION

that you've tasted freedom, you may not want to go all the way back. In fact, 38 percent of women in the *Harvard Business Review* report had intentionally taken jobs that they were overqualified for, despite the lower pay and reduced responsibilities, to better accommodate family life. And 16 percent had actually *turned down promotions*. (I'd like to see the stats on guys making that choice. "William, we're promoting you to director. You'll be managing the whole department!" "Wow. Thanks for the offer John, but . . . nope. I think I'll pass. Madeline is really close to crawling, and I'd rather head home earlier every day to check out her latest moves.") Even full-time, you likely won't jump right back to your old paycheck; be prepared to start at a slightly lower level and make your way up over time.

Create a Killer Résumé

Ideally, you've kept your contacts, experience, and skill set relatively fresh. Update your résumé with relevant past accomplishments and recent projects. If that volunteering work and freelancing never materialized during your time at home, you could organize your résumé using a functional (rather than chronological) format—emphasizing specific skills like managerial accomplishments or strategic planning experience and including a short job summary at the bottom. This approach may raise a red flag, but you could give it a try if you're worried about a multiyear gap.

Be Your Own Publicist

Once you've updated your resume, spread the word about your availability through your established network and new mom connections. You never know who might have a friend or relative looking for help.

Interview with Assurance

You may feel self-conscious marching into that first interview in a business suit after your extended period in casual mom mode—but you know how this game is played. Exude the confidence you may not actually have. Your potential employers will never know how much time you've recently spent scrubbing baby food out of your hair and imitating Elmo. Act like the uber-competent career gal and that's what they'll see.

Or Embrace Entrepreneurship

No need to explain a two-year hole in your résumé when you're the person hiring. Take advantage of those financial planning, time management, multitasking, and networking skills you've perfected during your time at home—and start your own business. You can set the hours, the pace, and the tone.

Cross Your Fingers and Jump

It's impossible to predict what career opportunities may open to you down the road, so leaving work requires a certain level of faith. Your lifetime career path will look different than it would have if you'd never taken time off, but what's life without a few risks, right? My sister once gave me a card that said, "Jump and the net will appear." That thought can be inspiring if you go with it.

Your Year One Guide to a Happy, Healthy Baby

The Secrets to a Happy Baby
The Feed-to-Wake Approach and
Other Strategies for Success

FROM:	Rachel Wellner
TO:	Daphne Quinlivan
SUBJECT:	Four months into parenthood and still feeling like an amateur

I've been a mom for months. Why do I still feel like I'm winging it?

Take this morning. Isabel drifted off while nursing, per the usual, so I laid her in the crib and backed out of the room. I was optimistic, but as soon as I reached the hallway the crying began. I just fed her to sleep, so I ruled out hunger. I went in and changed her diaper. Still tears. I tried to burp her. No dice. I belted out my best lullaby, rocking her with arms that felt like lead weights. Finally in desperation I tried to feed her again. She went for it, her whole body relaxing as she sucked down her fourth feeding in six hours. I was thrilled by the quiet, but had a nagging feeling something was wrong with this picture.

If there's a secret to this infant care thing, someone clearly forgot to tell me. Please send advice pronto.

The unpredictable nature of days with an infant can send even the calmest career gal into a tailspin. When to offer feedings? Naps?

Bedtime? Stimulation? Relaxed exploration? The scheduling variations are endless.

If you're not occasionally overwhelmed by infant care those first few months, you're either unbelievably good at adapting to life-altering situations, seriously medicated, or both. Most of us cycle through a sort of joy-shock-denial-confusion-fear continuum as we settle into our new roles. There are many perfect moments, but there are also perfect storms of infant care craziness—when your exhaustion, your baby's inexplicable fussiness, your significant other's attempts to "fix" things, your mother's long-distance advice, and the fact that nobody really knows what the heck is going on culminate in a wee bit of frustration.

In this chapter, you'll get a feeding and sleeping road map to Babyville, so you can better understand your baby's current needs and see where she's headed this year. And then you'll learn about the feed-to-wake approach—a simple, effective framework for infant care. Yes, newborns will throw your sense of control out the window if you let them. But you can maximize the peace. Baby chaos ends here.

Your Feeding and Sleeping Road Map to Babyville

We don't head into parenthood knowing exactly what our babies will need each day to be content. It's a gradual learning process, but here's a head start.

The Big Picture: What to Expect When

Find your baby's age on the following year one road map and review the average feeding and sleeping needs for that month. Then refer back over time so you know when to try easing your child into fewer naps, longer overnight sleep, fewer liquid feedings, and regular solid meals. (A pullout version is provided in the appendix.) Every infant is different, but you can more effectively guide your child's rest, feeding, and exploration time by mastering these fundamentals—typical needs for babies at your child's developmental stage. These basic Babyville benchmarks will help you understand her current needs and conceptualize her progress over the next several months. And that alone can do wonders for new parent confidence.

YOUR ROAD MAP TO BABYVILLE

	Birth to 4 Weeks	1 Month	2 Months	3 Months	4 Months	5 Months	6 Months	7 Months to 1st Birthday
Feeding								
Liquids (Breast Feeding or Bottle)								
Number of liquid feedings every 24 hours	8–12	5–8	5–8	4–6	4–6	4–6	4–5	4–5
Typical ounces per feeding	2–3	3–4	4–6	4–6	4–6	5–8	6–8	6–8
Total ounces recommended every 24 hours	14–20	15–26	20–32	20–32	22–32	22–32*	20–32*	20–30*
Solids								
Number of solid feedings every 24 hours	—	—	—	—	Tastings only	1: Breakfast	2: Breakfast and dinner	3: Breakfast lunch and dinner
Recommended solids by stage	—	—	—	—	Rice cereal, oatmeal and barley	Stage 1 baby food: veggies then fruits	Stage 2 baby food	Stage 3 baby food, finger foods, sippy cups
Sleep								
Number of daytime naps	5–7	3–5	3–5	3–4	3	3	2–3	2
Average length of daytime naps (in hours)	0.5–2	1–2	1–2	1–3	1–3	1–2	1–2	1.5–2
Typical number of overnight wake-ups	2–3	1–2	1–2	0–2	0–2	0–1	0–1	0
Longest stretch of sleep to expect overnight (in hours)	2–5	4–7	6–10	7–11	7–12	8–12	10–12	10–12

*Daily liquid intake may decrease slightly as solid meals are introduced.

Don't worry if your baby isn't tracking perfectly with these benchmarks—there's a wide range of infant development considered normal by pediatricians. Just use this road map as a helpful guide. Your five-month-old daughter may have a completely erratic nap schedule. Knowing that babies her age generally thrive on three naps a day, you can try putting her down consistently each morning, midday, and late afternoon. Your eight-month-old son may be waking up two or three times overnight, ready to eat and play. Babies his age should be sleeping through the night, so you can work towards putting the kibosh on the midnight play dates without guilt.

A Quick Word for Preemies

If your baby was born prematurely, expect her to develop according to her due date, not her birth date.

> **QUICK TIP FROM DR. NIED**
>
> If your child was born six weeks early, subtract six weeks from her actual age to calculate her developmental age. Use this developmental age to assess her likely sleeping and eating needs on the road map. This process is called "correcting for prematurity."

Creating Calm Out of Chaos

Five-month-old Nate was what many parents consider a dream baby—relaxed, inquisitive, and cheerful. He cried to communicate discomfort, but most of the time he was smiling and ready for anything. He loved his crib, fell asleep independently, and took three naps a day. When rice cereal was introduced, he adjusted to solids without complaint.

|•|

As new parents, we all want the same thing: happy, healthy babies. We want our infants to drift easily into naps and sleep peacefully through the night, to eat well and contentedly. We hope they'll be calm yet curious, energized yet easygoing. We've all seen babies like this—we know they exist. What's the secret? Is it luck, or can we take specific steps to help nurture contented children? Here's the good news: While basic personality traits are innate, you can significantly influence your baby's ability to sleep successfully, eat enthusiastically, and cope without crankiness.

Deconstructing the Dream Child

Nate's parents knew the first several weeks would be a time of adjustment, and they offered comfort by holding him often and minimizing unnecessary stimulation. They fed him when he woke up and over time helped him learn to self-soothe by putting him down for naps at the first sign of fatigue. As he matured, they gradually adjusted his nap times and subsequent feedings so he was well-fed and rested, and he thrived in the consistency of his days.

Nurturing Your Own Dream Child

Newborns can create chaos out of peaceful homes. Your best bet to keep the peace and meet your baby's needs? A consistent approach. You'll reclaim a feeling of control, and your child will respond. Babies hate unpredictability as much as adults, they just don't know the words for "stop the madness!"

The Feed-to-Wake Approach

Clara and Scott were stumped. Their three-month-old daughter Sydney often seemed unhappy, and they tried everything to entertain her—pulling out rattles, playing music, turning on the Baby Mozart video. "The more we try to offer her fun stimulation, the fussier she is," Scott explained.

Turns out, the play sessions often occurred just after Sydney's naps—before she had been fed. And even after feedings, playtime often lasted far too long, preventing Sydney from winding down and falling asleep. Obviously Clara and Scott had good intentions. They just needed some general guidelines so they better understood how to offer stimulation, feedings, and rest appropriately.

|•|

Your pediatrician may have warned you against feeding your baby to sleep. It's an easy habit to get into—breast-feeding or bottle-feeding your child just before naps so she'll suck herself peacefully into snoozeland. And the first six to eight weeks, when your newborn is adjusting to the world, it can be very effective. Sucking is an innate soothing strategy, and no one will complain about a little presleep snack.

So why stop? Your child will need to eat overnight the first few months, but as she matures you want her to have the comforting skills to return to sleep without your assistance when she stirs awake at night. Pediatricians call the problem an inappropriate sleep onset association. Basically, if you continue to consistently feed your baby to sleep, eating will become her cue to drift off—which is fine at first. But it becomes a problem over time when she stirs awake at 2:00 A.M. and doesn't need to eat, but can't soothe herself. She'll need the bottle or breast to resettle rather than simply shifting positions or sticking a finger or the pacifier in her mouth for comfort and drifting back to sleep on her own. And suddenly you've got yourself an overnight routine of unnecessary waking up, both for you and your baby.

But if you're not supposed to feed your baby to sleep, when should you feed her? And what's your best bet for successful naps? Use the feed-to-wake approach—your insider's guide for days in Babyville.

> **QUICK TIP FROM DR. NIED**
>
> The natural sleep cycle involves deeper and lighter phases of sleep, and it's common to briefly wake up during the lighter phases. As adults, we're able to return to sleep almost immediately, and you may not even notice these brief moments of wakefulness. Babies need to learn this skill.

> **QUICK TIP FROM DR. NIED**
>
> In the wild world of parenting, the feed-to-wake approach is a great option. It leads to babies who are appropriately rested, appropriately fed, and appropriately stimulated. Equally important, it leads to confident parents who aren't exhausted by unnecessarily frequent feedings or frustrated by an inability to decipher their infants' tears.

Feeding to Wake

Feed your baby just as she gets up in the morning and right after naps so eating becomes her bridge to happy wakefulness. Let her explore— watching for signs of fatigue. Then give her the opportunity to soothe herself to sleep using a pacifier or finger.

Here's how it works:

Feed Your Baby Just As She Gets Up in the Morning and Right After Naps So Eating Becomes Her Bridge to Happy Wakefulness

The feed-to-wake approach applies to daytime. As your baby wakes up in the morning or after naps—turn on the light, greet her enthusiastically, pull her out of the crib, and head straight to the rocking chair for a liquid feeding unless a seriously poopy diaper or urine-soaked pj's require urgent attention. Instead of transitioning her to sleep, the feeding will transition her to exploration time. After eating, she'll be energized, cheerful, and ready for action. You are literally feeding her to wake.

But what if she seems hungry again *before* her next nap? Will the two really synch up perfectly? By about two months, your baby's natural sleeping and eating cycles should generally follow the feed-to-wake framework. But always pay attention to her feedback. Feeding to wake offers a helpful foundation to guide her daily routine, but if she's extra-hungry one afternoon, an additional liquid feeding may do the trick. Even those crazy first weeks, you can still feed your newborn to wake, but don't worry if you need to offer another quick feeding soon after or if she drifts off while eating. Give yourself a break, know it's a newborn

> **QUICK TIP FROM DR. NIED**
>
> Most likely, your baby will need to eat at least once or twice overnight for the first few months. Just keep the lights off, fill her tummy, and return her quietly to the crib. As long as you don't feed her to sleep during the day, these groggy overnight feedings that lead directly back to slumber won't affect her ability to self-soothe. And over time, she won't need to eat at night, and she'll have the skills to resettle without your help.

thing, and try to offer most feedings just after sleep. Although each baby is unique, most infants respond very well to the feed-to-wake routine.

Keep in mind, you'll feed your baby to wake with breast feeding or bottles—we're talking about *liquid* feedings. Solids, which should be introduced between months four and six, are given separately during regular mealtimes, not when your baby wakes. You'll start offering one solid meal at breakfast time, and then gradually provide lunch and dinner. Think of solid meals as activities during baby's exploration times—an opportunity to grab finger foods, feel different textures, learn to use utensils, and try a variety of flavors. And feel free to offer an occasional liquid feeding with these solid meals as well.

Let Your Baby Explore—Watching for Signs of Fatigue

Infant exploration could be almost anything—being rocked, getting tummy time, watching a mobile, eating rice cereal, hanging out in the bouncy seat, or staring at your chin. It's all critical stimulation, expanding your child's understanding of the world.

How long should these exploration periods last? Between about two and six months of age, your baby will be ready to sleep within two hours of waking, so the feeding *and* exploration time shouldn't last more than a couple of hours. After six months, this awake period will gradually extend. Check the clock each time you pull your infant out of her crib and estimate her next nap time. Then watch for signs of fatigue such as a slowdown of activity, fussiness, eye rubbing, ear tugging, or yawning—and put her down sooner if she's clearly pooping out. Follow a brief, consistent prenap routine and put her in the crib tired but still awake.

Give Her the Opportunity to Soothe Herself to Sleep with a Pacifier or Finger

In a recent study, the American Academy of Pediatrics found infants who were given pacifiers just before sleep are at lower risk for SIDS. Based on those findings, the AAP now recommends giving babies pacifiers to sleep—for naps and bedtime at night—until their first birthdays. (At that point, the pacifier should be phased out because the risk of ear infection from pacifier use increases and the risk of SIDS is much lower.)

If you're breast-feeding, the AAP suggests waiting about four weeks to introduce the pacifier to avoid nipple confusion. If you're not, you can introduce it any time. Offer the binky just before placing your infant in the crib. If she takes to it, great. Continue to offer it when she's ready to sleep, and as her coordination improves she'll likely put it back in her mouth when she wakes up at night.

What if your baby rejects the pacie? You can introduce it again every week or so to see if she's interested. But some children simply never take to pacifiers. If yours doesn't, don't force it—let her soothe herself to sleep by sucking on a finger. Always comfort your child if you sense she has a real need, but after her first couple of months, start to gradually phase yourself out of her winding-down process. Get step-by-step guidance in Chapter 14: "Nurturing a Supersleeper."

> **QUICK TIP FROM DR. NIED**
>
> Sleep inducing strategies—such as consistently feeding or rocking your baby until she dozes off—are fine at first, but begin to pay attention to your pre-sleep routines after the first six to eight weeks. At this age, your child is forming sleep habits that could be hard to break. Some afternoons she'll need extra comfort, and a few minutes with you in the rocking chair may help her relax and drift off. But try not to rock her to sleep for every nap. Between two and four months she'll gradually develop the skills to fall asleep without your assistance.

The Power of Feeding to Wake

Feeding to wake works for several reasons:

It's a Consistent Approach You and Your Baby Can Learn and Anticipate

Let's start with you. Fresh from a routine of work and rational adult conversation, you may find the erratic nature of infant care disconcerting. Some days can feel like a blur of feedings, diaper changes, playtime, aborted attempts at newborn naps, and ongoing meltdown management. The feed-to-wake approach helps shape your daily schedule—so you regain a feeling of control and better understand what your baby needs each step of the way. You *know* when to feed her, how long to offer exploration time, and how to set the stage for successful naps. Instead of winging it, you're able to approach infant care with a real plan.

And then there's your baby. Consistency offers her a feeling of mastery over her environment so she can start to anticipate the next step in her day and happily go with the flow. And don't underestimate her ability to anticipate. My son knew it was feeding time as soon as he was pulled out of the crib. If anyone inadvertently altered this timing, he'd instantly communicate his frustration. When we fed him to wake, he would cheerfully transition to exploration time.

It Precludes the Walk of Terror

You know the walk I'm talking about. You just rocked or fed your infant to sleep, and she's dozing in your arms. It's cozy, but you start fantasizing about all the things you could be accomplishing (like taking a shower before noon), and you stare longingly at the crib. It's only a few steps away, but it might as well be miles. You develop a plan ("I'll rock her for three more minutes so she's *really* asleep, then I'll slowly get up and cross the room without moving my upper body in any discernible way."). All goes well until you lower her into the crib, every fiber of your being willing her eyes to remain closed. She gently touches the soft, carefully selected crib sheet and startles awake as if plopped on the bathroom counter. She looks at you with confusion and fear, you look at her with confusion and fear, and the meltdown begins. That, my friends, is the walk of terror.

With the feed-to-wake approach, you consistently put your baby down groggy but not entirely asleep so she learns to self-soothe. Once she's mastered the process, there's no drama, no fear, no need for silent, catlike steps across the nursery. You'll place her on that comfy crib sheet, and she'll suck on her pacifier, stick a finger in her mouth, or she may occasionally have a few wind-down tears that taper off as she settles herself. The message is, "Okay, Mom, I'm good. See ya later." She knows what to do when she's placed in the crib, and she isn't surprised by startling awake alone when she just dozed off in your arms. You'll walk out of the room with a bounce to your step, and that shower will feel really, really good.

It Provides Food Just When Your Infant Needs It,
So She's Energized During Playtime

A hungry baby is an unhappy baby. By feeding your little one upon waking, you're giving her the energy she needs to explore enthusiastically. It's a nice way to transition from dreamland to reality. She wakes up, snuggles, eats, and then she's ready to take on the world.

It Helps You Meet Her Needs

If you feed your baby to wake just after her morning nap, you can assume hunger is not the likely cause when she's fussy half an hour later. Instead of immediately whipping out the breast or bottle, you can check for other possible culprits such as a full diaper, boredom, overstimulation, heat, cold, the need for a burp, or the desire to change positions. (At least you ruled out one option.)

It's Easy to Execute

You're a new mom. Your life is wild and wacky in a whole new way and you don't need anything complicated to memorize or execute (as if you could memorize anything on five hours sleep).

How It Can Work for Your Baby

Every baby has her own rhythms. This is why parenting is more art than science, why our greatest challenge is creating contexts that allow our children's personalities to flourish. With that said, there are some rules for the road that simplify the infant parenting process. At four months, for example, babies generally take three naps, sleep seven to twelve hours overnight, and need four to six liquid feedings daily. With these benchmarks in mind, it's easier to respond to your baby appropriately, to identify her potential needs throughout the day.

A Typical Day

How would a typical day progress using the feed-to-wake approach? Here's an example so you can see how the continuum might flow.

6:30 A.M.	Saturday morning wake-up
6:30–7:00 A.M.	Breast feeding or bottle feeding #1
7:00–8:30 A.M.	Play on tummy, watch mobile, enjoy tasting of rice cereal
8:30–10:00 A.M.	Nap
10:00–10:30 A.M.	Breast feeding or bottle feeding #2
10:30 A.M.–12:00 P.M.	Check out the world as Mom runs errands
12:00–1:30 P.M.	Nap
1:30–2:00 P.M.	Breast feeding or bottle feeding #3
2:00–3:30 P.M.	Go for a walk in the stroller, play on a blanket in the park
3:30–5:00 P.M.	Nap
5:00–5:30 P.M.	Breast feeding or bottle feeding #4
5:30–7:00 P.M.	Hang out in bouncy seat during family dinner, take a bath, listen to books
7:00 P.M.	Bedtime (At this age she'll probably need to feed at least once overnight as well.)

Understanding Your Baby's Natural Cycles

Of course, your baby won't sleep exactly an hour and a half during every nap and take exactly thirty minutes for each liquid feeding. But you get the general idea. When your baby is between two and six months old, you can check the clock each time she awakes and put her down for her next nap a couple of hours later—including both feeding and exploration time—unless she looks tired sooner. As she develops, this awake period will gradually lengthen. Let her soothe herself to sleep and then feed her to wake. With this in mind, you can run errands, visit friends, or take a walk, and still accommodate her sleeping and feeding needs.

QUICK TIP FROM DR. NIED

Regardless of your baby's temperament, the consistency of the feed-to-wake approach should help her to thrive and you to feel more comfortable in your parenting role. Even babies considered colicky may in fact be overfed, overtired, overstimulated, or just overwhelmed. Regular feedings and appropriate naps can help calm a previously fussy baby.

It Sounds Good, But This Will Never Work for My Child

Some infants take to breast feeding and bottles without hesitation; others seem to be on a self-imposed starvation diet from day one. Some are naturally great nappers and others resist napping every step of the way. Some sleep through the night within two months; others require six. And then there are the colicky babies, whose chronic crying could drive any parent to the brink.

Whatever your child's natural tendencies may be, it's always comforting to head into new experiences with a plan. Parenthood is no different. Think of the feed-to-wake approach as your passport to happy parenting.

Nurturing a Supersleeper
Your Step-by-Step Guide to the Promised Land

Trenyce, normally a rational woman, was at a complete standoff with her five-month-old son. It was midafternoon, and Derrick desperately needed a nap. That much was clear. He'd been up for almost four hours, he was impossible to please, and he was ready to bring everyone else down with him.

She walked him in the stroller around the block. She rocked him through an entire CD of classical lullabies. Finally she laid him in the crib. Still he just fussed, turning to her as if to say, "Oh Mama, please. You insult me with your feeble nap time attempts. I may be small, but my will is mighty. Give up, kind woman, and let's never speak of naps again."

|•|

Supersleepers are the undisputed stars of Babyville. They're the infants who fall asleep happily, independently, consistently. They adore their cribs. They drift to sleep without needing to be rocked, fed, or held. Sound too good to be true? It's not. Nurture your own supersleeper, starting today.

This chapter offers a month-by-month guide, recommendations from Dr. Nied, and insights from the best-known sleeping gurus around. Learn how to set the stage for sleep, nurture a star napper, and maintain great naps during days in child care. And get the lowdown on presleep routines and reaching the promised land—a full night's sleep (for you and your little one). By implementing these strategies, you'll help promote predictable naps, happy bedtimes, and improved overnight sleep throughout year one and into the toddler years.

Year One Sleep: What to Expect Month by Month

From Sonya's journal:

Baby-sitter stopped by today for trial run and asked about the twins' typical nap schedules. (NAP SCHEDULES?) Was embarrassed to admit I had no idea a nap schedule was even possible for four-month-old infants. Took six weeks of childbirth classes, and labor was over in twelve hours. Now as actual parent feeling wildly uninformed. Just praying baby-sitter will offer tips.

In Chapter 13, you were introduced to the feeding and sleeping road map to Babyville. To review, here are monthly sleep stats so you can prepare for your impending trip through Babyville's land of nod. These are averages and there's a wide range considered completely normal by pediatricians—just use this road map directionally to help ease your baby into fewer naps and longer overnight sleep. And if your child is a preemie, base your expectations on his due date, not his birth date.

YOUR ROAD MAP TO BABYVILLE'S LAND OF NOD							
	Birth to 4 Weeks	1 Month	2 Months	3 Months	4 Months	5 Months	6 Months	7 Months to 1st Birthday
Typical number of daytime naps	5–7	3–5	3–5	3–4	3	3	2–3	2
Average length of daytime naps (in hours)	0.5–2	1–2	1–2	1–3	1–3	1–2	1–2	1.5–2
Typical number of overnight wake-ups	2–3	1–2	1–2	0–2	0–2	0–1	0–1	0
Longest stretch of sleep to expect overnight (in hours)	2–5	4–7	6–10	7–11	7–12	8–12	10–12	10–12

Now, learn what to expect month by month.

Birth Through Four Weeks: Survival Time

For the first few weeks of your newborn's life, sleep is wildly unpredictable. It may be easy one day and impossible the next. Your infant will likely sleep about sixteen to nineteen hours a day, though rarely for more than three hours at a time. He's in a state of massive transition—recovering from birth, adjusting to the world outside the womb, and learning to process sensory stimulation. Plus, his neural connections are haywire at first, creating a sense of internal chaos that manifests itself in inexplicable fussiness and sleep irregularity. When you consider everything he's grappling with, it's no wonder he's a tad moody.

Pediatricians often describe this month as survival time for parents. Expect some crazy nights, nap when your baby naps, try a variety of comforting techniques, and know the sleeping situation will improve soon.

Your One-Month-Old: Everybody's Smiling Now

Between weeks four and eight, most infants smile socially for the first time. And when your baby smiles, you should too. Not just because it's the beginning of real feedback, the sweet reward of reciprocation after all your baby talk and lullabies. The first social smile is also a sign of critical neurological development. It indicates that key neural connections have been made, and your newborn's internal chaos will soon downshift to a new sense of calm. At that point, he'll turn a corner in the attitude department. Instead of

QUICK TIP FROM DR. NIED

Newborns recognize their parents' voices from day one and they love being held closely. Sing lullabies, quietly read to your child, hold him as often as you can, and get seriously acquainted with that new rocking chair. It's a baby-bonding fest, and you will spend more time in physical contact with your newborn than with anyone in your life to date. Once he drifts off, you can put your baby down in his crib to sleep.

constant naps, he'll shift to three or four naps a day (maybe five, if you've got a serious sleep lover), and each nap will likely last an hour or more.

Your Two-Month-Old: Starting to Self-Soothe

This month, naps become less erratic, night sleep lengthens, inexplicable tears decrease, and your baby focuses increasingly on the sights and sounds around him. During the first several weeks of life, most babies can't self-soothe, so they often have trouble winding down to sleep. Between two and four months, this changes—and infants can begin to comfort themselves. Give your child the opportunity to acquire this important skill; within the next couple of months he can learn to consistently fall asleep solo. During this period, he may occasionally drift off on his own or require some TLC to settle himself. But you can start phasing out sleep crutches like feeding or rocking him until he dozes off. Familiarize yourself with his natural cycles by paying attention to his energy levels at different times of day, nap times, and overnight sleep. Feed him just after he wakes in the morning and after naps so he's energized and ready to explore.

> **QUICK TIP FROM DR. NIED**
>
> Infants this age generally cannot tolerate being awake more than two hours, some even less. Check the clock each time you pull your child out of the crib and plan to put him down for his next nap about two hours later. If you notice signs of fatigue in the meantime, you can put him down sooner so he doesn't become overtired.

Your Three-Month-Old: In the Groove

Weeks twelve to sixteen, you're reaping the benefits of your baby's maturing sleep patterns, and things seem easier. It may be the decent rest you're getting. Hopefully you're stringing a good four or five hours together at night. It may be the decrease in inexplicable baby meltdowns. It may be the daily showers you're taking for the first time since your delivery. Whatever the reason, enjoy your growing confidence as a parent and your baby's improved sleep.

Your Four-Month-Old: Supersleeping Kicks In

This month is a milestone in the world of infant slumber. Babies transition to mature sleep patterns and settle into fairly predictable nap schedules. In his book *Healthy Sleep Habits, Happy Child*, Dr. Marc Weissbluth explains:

After four months of age, an infant's sleep becomes more adultlike. Infants younger than this enter sleep with a REM sleep period, but around this age they begin to enter sleep with a non-REM sleep period, like adults. Sleep cycling, from deep to light non-REM sleep with interruptions of REM sleep, also matures into adultlike patterns around four months of age.[1]

In other words, things are looking up. You're moving beyond the chaos of newborn sleep, and the feed-to-wake approach should be working beautifully. You should be able to loosely plan your day around a morning, midday, and late afternoon nap with feedings after each one. You don't have to wait in fear for baby's next meltdown or isolate yourself at home to accommodate potential feedings every hour.

Your Five-Month-Old: Sleeping Well and Feeling Groovy

By twenty weeks, your infant is likely taking three naps a day and sleeping even longer overnight. He should be falling asleep independently without serious complaint, and his bedtime at night should be gradually moving up. At this age, an appropriate bedtime is between 6:00 P.M. and 8:00 P.M.

Your Six-Month-Old: Sleeping's a Snap, Just Drop a Nap

You and your baby should have a happy routine going. He should be sleeping through the night, perhaps occasionally waking once, and napping like a star. (If he's still waking up at night, check out "Sleeping Through the Night" later in this chapter.) You'll begin to transition your little one from three to two naps when he

> **QUICK TIP FROM DR. NIED**
>
> At six to seven months, your infant will likely start sleeping longer the first two naps of the day and resisting the third. Help things along by putting him down slightly later for the first two naps and extending the exploration time between each sleep period. And continue to feed him as he awakes from each nap.

seems ready. This shift may take several weeks, so be patient and try to gauge your child's energy level each day. Typically babies drop the late afternoon nap and the two earlier naps shift back a bit. During the transitional period, your infant may need three naps some days and only two naps other days. Every child's natural cycles vary, but here's how the schedule change might look:

NAPS	4 to 6 Months	Starting at 6 to 7 Months
Morning nap	8:30–10:00 A.M.	9:30–11:30 A.M.
Midday nap	12:00–1:30 P.M.	2:00–4:00 P.M.
Late afternoon nap	3:30–5:00 P.M.	—

QUICK TIP FROM DR. NIED

Between fourteen and nineteen months, toddlers typically drop the morning nap and move to a two- to three-hour midday nap.

Your Seven-Month-Old Through One-Year-Old: The Sleeping Road Ahead

Sleep stabilizes during the second half of year one. Your baby should continue to nap twice a day until he's beyond his first birthday. Overnight sleep should be steady at ten to twelve hours.

Why Good Sleep Matters

From Mandy's journal:

Operation Overnight Sleep still in progress. Sienna continues to wake up about every three hours 24/7. I've tried everything—cosleeping, breast feeding on demand, giving her a bottle of formula before bed. I even bought one of those white noise machines that makes sounds like ocean waves and spring rain. It may have stimulated some extra-wet diapers, but it sure didn't help her sleep any longer. Tomorrow I'm going to try keeping her up more during the day so she'll be exhausted by bedtime. We'll see if that works . . .

As a new parent, you know the importance of good sleep firsthand. Like adults, well-rested infants are happier, more energized, and more curious about the world. And though it may seem counterintuitive, your child doesn't need to be exhausted to sleep soundly.

The Ironic Effects of Exhaustion

Remember the irony of pulling all-nighters studying for finals? You'd kill yourself going through every bit of material only to find your brain had turned to mush by the time you walked into class the next morning. You were cranky. You hated the professor and everyone around you. And to top it off, your mind stopped functioning. Exhaustion has the same effect on babies. It makes them crabby. It zaps their energy. It complicates feedings. It curtails their natural curiosity. And, contrary to popular belief, it actually *prevents* them from falling asleep peacefully.

The Slippery Slope of Chronic Fatigue

Chronic fatigue can quickly become a big problem. If your baby is consistently missing naps, staying up too late, or waking throughout the night after the first few months, he may be chronically overtired. Try to implement the sleep suggestions detailed in this chapter. If he still has a bad sleep day, expect some fussiness and try to get him back on track. If he has a bad sleep month, talk to your pediatrician to get personalized help.

> **QUICK TIP FROM DR. NIED**
>
> Don't keep your baby up late or skip a nap, assuming he'll sleep better. Actually the opposite is true. Just-getting-tired babies typically fall asleep faster and with less complaint than overtired babies, and infants who nap well tend to sleep well overnight. In addition, putting babies to sleep later at night will not translate into waking up later. Morning wake-up time is determined by other factors such as circadian rhythm and daylight. As a parent, your goal is to promote a cycle of good rest.

Setting the Stage for Sleep

"Griffin can sleep anywhere," Emily proudly announced to her aunt as she pushed her stroller through the mall. "And I have so many errands to run today, I knew I couldn't hang out at home while he napped in the crib. When he's tired enough, he'll just crash in the stroller. He does it every weekend."

"That's great," her aunt replied just as seven-month-old Griffin let out a piercing scream, hurled his toy to the ground, and flung his head back in tears. "Is this what happens when he crashes?"

|●|

Let's face it, we're all busy. And it's very tempting to let our babies nap in their strollers or car seats while we're on the run. Here's the good news: The first two to three months, while many of us are on maternity leave, this is fine. Newborns truly can sleep anywhere. Take advantage of it and get out as much as you'd like. Here's the reality check: When your baby is about four months old, he'll become more distracted by outside stimulation and start to sleep best in a crib. At that point, try to schedule your days off to accommodate nap times at home whenever possible. No, you don't have to quarantine yourself until the kid hits preschool. An occasional nap on the go is no biggie. But to promote good rest, just try to make a habit of naps in the crib this year.

QUICK TIP FROM DR. NIED

Don't worry about running the dishwasher or keeping the dog quiet while your baby is sleeping; it's actually good for your infant to learn the noises of the house. By being exposed to extraneous sounds from the beginning, he'll have a better tolerance for sleeping through noise as he gets older. Similarly, twins, siblings who share a room, and babies in day care centers learn to nap through background sounds and activity.

Noise

Your baby's temperament will determine his tolerance for noise. Some infants sleep best with silence; others actually drift off better with some background noise like quiet music.

Light

To state the obvious, babies sleep best in the dark. The room doesn't have to be pitch-dark; a nightlight is fine. During daytime naps, close the shades and turn off the lights. At night, close the door to the nursery to keep the environment dark while your baby is falling asleep. Once you head back to work, your child care provider may not have a darkened room for infant naps. Don't worry, your child will adapt at day care, but it never hurts to maintain the stimulation-free environment during his naps at home.

Swaddling

Full details on swaddling—snugly wrapping your newborn in a receiving blanket cocoon—are provided in Chapter 2. It works best for babies one month and younger, although some infants continue to find comfort in swaddling after the first month.

Temperature

Your baby should be warm—not hot, not cool—when you put him down to sleep and throughout the night. If you find his nursery hot, he probably does too. If you can't control the temperature of the room, adjust his clothing as necessary.

Sleepwear and Bedding

As already mentioned, blankets, quilts, pillows, and stuffed animals should be kept out of your child's crib during year one to minimize the risk of sudden infant death syndrome (SIDS). So, do you leave your baby on a bare crib sheet when you're seconds away from diving under your cozy down comforter? Basically. Crib bumpers should be the only other items in the crib, and these are optional and essentially decorative. For the first few weeks, use a knit cap unless it's particularly warm and swaddle your baby each time you put him down to sleep. Under the swaddling, your newborn can wear a cotton T-shirt or pajamas depending on the temperature. Pajamas should fit snugly and be labeled flame resistant.

> **QUICK TIP FROM DR. NIED**
>
> Once your baby becomes too active to stay in his swaddling, I recommend using a sleeveless sleep sack if he needs an extra layer for warmth. These handy little sacks are endorsed by the SIDS Alliance because they zip over your baby's pajamas and ensure warmth without using blankets. If your baby perspires while sleeping, try removing a layer to prevent overheating.

Our mothers were told to put us to sleep on our stomachs when we were infants to prevent choking on spit-up, and some parents today still have this concern. Don't worry; newborns can easily move their heads from side to side while on their backs, and newer research has shown the choking risk does not increase. Since the promotion of the Back to Sleep campaign, the number of U.S. SIDS deaths has decreased dramatically.

Sleep Positioning

Since 1992, the American Academy of Pediatrics has recommended putting infants to sleep on their backs to minimize the risk of SIDS. This is usually easy—newborns can't even roll over so they'll typically sleep in any position you choose. However, some newborns are born tummy lovers and they fuss whenever they're placed on their backs. If this sounds like your child, stay strong. Your infant will eventually adjust to sleeping on his back, and his safety is worth living through some crabbiness. The AAP now also recommends offering a pacifier to sleep.

The Family Bed and Other Close-at-Hand Sleeping Options

The Family Bed Philosophy

Dr. William Sears is the pediatrician generally credited with bringing the concept of cosleeping into the American mainstream. (Of course, most of the world's population had known about this little secret for centuries.) Here's the idea in a nutshell: Baby sleeps in the "family bed" from day one. Mom and dad's snuggly warmth, familiar smells, and reassuring sounds throughout the night create a sense of security, facilitating confidence, healthy development, and—let's not forget—good sleep.

Cosleeping is tempting. You're exhausted. You're feeding your baby around the clock. You're desperate. You think having your newborn in bed will allow for easier night feedings. You imagine pulling your little snuggler to your chest for a relaxing 2:00 A.M. feed instead of trudging down the hall for a groggy half hour in the rocking chair. It sounds like new parent nirvana. If the family bed appeals to you, check out Dr. Sears's books. Some parents swear by his approach.

The Family Bed Reality: At Least in My Wacky World

In the interest of full disclosure, I'll share my personal experience with the family bed. By day six with my son, I was dead tired. My labor had lasted twenty-nine hours, so I started parenthood fresh off an all-nighter. I was up every couple of hours breast-feeding. I was rarely taking showers. I was barely finding time to eat. I was living the life of every new mom. My sister, who happens to be a midwife, suggested cosleeping. She said I could breast-feed easily in bed and swore I'd feel twice as rested. She explained a friend of hers, a doctor, had been cosleeping with her own baby for months with great success. This persuaded me. I figured if a doctor was doing it, the family bed approach couldn't be completely crazy.

So I psyched myself up and tried it. At 8:00 P.M. that night my son was ready to go to sleep, and so was I. My husband wasn't the least bit tired, but I convinced him to come with us in the interest of an authentic family bed experiment. We all snuggled into bed, and sure enough my son drifted off like an angel. I was ecstatic. Five minutes later I heard my "not-in-the-least-bit-tired" husband breathing the deep, long breaths of real sleep. I smiled to myself. It was all coming together. My guys were sleeping beside me; I was going to have an unbelievably restful night. Less than a week in Babyville, and we had this parenting thing mastered.

About half an hour later, I pinpointed the downside of the family bed—fear. Sleep-preventing, mind-numbing, impossible-to-ignore fear that I would roll onto my infant son in my sleep, that he'd inadvertently suffocate under the covers, or that my husband would forget the baby was in bed and groggily attempt a midnight spooning session, crushing our child under his massive man-size body. As I lay there willing myself to fall asleep, these things swirled in my head, warding away slumber more effectively than a super-size espresso. I eventually drifted to sleep and had a horrible nightmare about my son slipping through my fingers into a weird, infant-eating sinkhole. I started awake in a panic, grabbed my sleeping child, and marched him into his crib. And that was the end of our family bed.

(And maybe my instincts were good. The AAP recently strengthened their recommendation against cosleeping.)

Not Quite the Family Bed: Other Close-at-Hand Sleeping Options

Not interested in the family bed but looking for ways to cut down the commute to your baby's mouth when nighttime feedings hit? Let your little one snooze beside your bed, and you're ready for action. You can hear those cute little sleep sounds without fear of inadvertently creating a baby pancake.

There are several close-at-hand sleeping options for your infant:

- Bassinet
- Cradle
- Moses basket
- Cosleeper
- Portable crib (also known as a pack 'n' play or play yard)

Bassinets, cradles, Moses baskets, and cosleepers can be fine for infant sleeping needs. However, they're not cheap, and newborns outgrow them before you know it. I recommend portable cribs because they grow with your child and serve multiple purposes. At first, you can keep yours bedside with your newborn sleeping in the removable bassinet on top. As he grows, the portable crib can move to the family room, allowing him to hang out in the removable bassinet while watching the attached toy bar or playing with his toes. A few months later, remove the bassinet component and utilize the actual play yard if your baby is up for playing in a contained area (mine never was). And they're lifesavers during trips, providing a safe, portable sleeping spot well into the toddler stage.

Nine Steps to Creating a Supernapper

FROM:	**Diane Kim**
TO:	**Cassie Myers**
SUBJECT:	**HELP!**

I can calm overwrought clients, but I'm in way over my head with Dennis. Every time I put him down to nap he screams like I've just left him in the wild to be raised by wolves. I'm heading back to work in two weeks, and I'd love to get a handle on this nap thing before I take him into day care. (Or maybe they can figure it out and tell me what to do.) Any tips from your new mom days?

Thanks!

What's a supernapper? It's a baby who drifts to sleep independently, following a relatively predictable nap schedule, without serious complaint. By about four months of age, babies can gradually learn to fall asleep without assistance. The transitional period is tricky; some naps your child might drift off in the car seat, and some mornings he'll need extra help to relax. During this stage, offer your baby presleep comfort as needed, but start to slowly phase yourself out of his required winding-down process.

How can you help him learn to drift off independently? Use this step-by-step guide. It's based on recommendations from the most respected sleep gurus in the field, and it's been road-tested by parents just like you. If you follow this approach consistently, your baby should learn to doze off without major tears or assistance, and nap time will be a pleasure for both of you. You can apply this same philosophy to establishing great bedtimes at night as well.

Step 1: Timing Is Everything

All great infant nappers have one thing in common: caretakers who know when to put them down to sleep. Put your baby down too soon and he'll quickly let you know. (Who wants to be left in a crib when you're wide awake and ready to explore?) Wait too long and your baby's exhaustion will make it even harder for him to peacefully drift off. Do your best to put your baby in his crib just as he's starting to wind down—so he's not energized for exploration or overtired. But how do you pinpoint the perfect nap time?

Know nap needs by age.   Use the Road Map to Babyville's Land of Nod to understand infant nap needs at every stage. The chart below can help you to anticipate typical nap starting times between the ages of four and twelve months, and then simply gauge you child's energy level each day.

TYPICAL NAP STARTING TIMES	
4 to 6 months	**Put your baby down to nap sometime between:**
Morning nap	8:00 A.M. and 9:00 A.M.
Midday nap	12:00 P.M. and 1:00 P.M.
Late afternoon nap	3:00 P.M. and 4:30 P.M.
Starting at 6 or 7 months	
Late morning nap	9:00 A.M. and 10:00 A.M.
Afternoon nap	1:00 P.M. and 3:00 P.M.

These are averages and your baby's natural nap cycle may not fall perfectly into these ranges. Just use this as a directional guide and pay close attention to his cues. You'll know it's time to try shifting him from three to two naps when he seems ready to stay awake longer in the morning or isn't settling into the midday nap as easily.

Track your baby's naps.   You can't control how long your infant will sleep during each nap. For a better sense of his natural sleep cycles, track his schedule for a few days. Your child may take longer naps the first half of the day and a quickie late afternoon. He may consistently nap for two hours or never break one hour. He may be raring to go in the morning or find his best energy in the early evening. Pay attention to these patterns, and it'll be much easier to predict ideal daily nap times.

Keep your eye on the clock.   Each time your baby wakes up, check the clock and loosely plan when he should be ready for his next nap. Try not to keep him up for too long. Unless he seems particularly tired, you can generally put your baby down when the next nap time hits.

Look for nap readiness cues.   There will be times when your baby is ready for a nap sooner than usual. Like all of us, he may have blah days or I'm-just-not-at-the-peak-of-my-little-baby-self afternoons. You can say, "I feel like crap and need a nap," but your baby can't. However, he does have his ways of communicating nap readiness. When you notice one or more of these cues, you may need to put your baby down even if it's earlier than his typical nap time:

- Slowdown of activity
- Glassy eyes, appearing somewhat dazed
- Fussiness, from simple irritability to inconsolable crying
- Impatience with any new stimulation
- Rubbing eyes
- Pulling an ear
- Avoiding extended eye contact

Step 2: Presleep Routine

When you've decided it's nap time, start with a consistent presnooze routine. The routine cues your baby that sleep is approaching, giving him time to transition. For naps, this routine can be brief. It may involve going

QUICK TIP FROM DR. NIED

I recommend a more extensive routine before overnight sleep when babies are particularly tired. For more details, check out "Nighttime Routines—And the Secret of the Six Bs" later in this chapter.

into his room, changing his diaper, and quietly reading a short board book. This relaxing period should help your baby wind down.

Step 3: Full Baby Check

Before placing your child in the crib, rule out potential sources of impending tears such as hunger, body temperature, a full diaper, or discomfort. If you notice he seems too hot, for example, remove a layer and then settle him down.

Step 4: Crib Time

Offer your baby a pacifier and place him in the crib relaxed but still awake. Quietly tell him it's time for his nap and use consistent language when saying good-bye. Remember how you felt as a child when you were tucked in with parting words like, "Sleep tight, don't let the bed bugs bite"? These little presleep rituals may seem silly at first, but children love them. Babies understand your words sooner than you think, and even short routines offer a sense of calm and comfort. Don't drag out your departure; walk out of the nursery and close the door.

Step 5: The Moment of Truth

Once your baby is in his crib and you've left the room, there are two possible scenarios. In the first, he's mastered self-soothing and your job is now complete. He'll drift off, and you won't hear from him again until his nap is over. The second scenario goes something like this: Initially there is quiet within. You hold your breath, leaning against the nursery door and willing your baby to sleep. Still nothing. You celebrate silently and turn to walk away just as a high-pitched screech explodes from the general direction of the crib. Or it may happen instantaneously. You lean down to place your baby in the crib and—as if you just flipped some internal switch—the meltdown hits. In either case, what should you do next? Pull him out of bed and try to rock him to sleep? Pat him on the back? Put the pacifier back in his mouth—and hope this time it works? Leave him to cry it out?

Step 6: When Your Baby Fights Sleep with Tears

This is a highly controversial and personal issue. I'm convinced mothers are biologically incapable of hearing their children cry without instantly adopting a fierce, predator-like aggression toward the source of those tears. And if *you* are essentially to blame for the drama by putting your child in the crib, forget about it. Rationally, you know you're trying to do the right thing. But the voice of rationality is a feeble whisper behind the clanging drum of maternal instinct.

It's like conception includes a branch development—a mini–child protection agency housed somewhere above your uterus, that officially opens during childbirth and subsequently detects baby tears at a hundred yards. Then watch out. It immediately overrides all other bodily functions—your spine goes stiff, you hear nothing but the sounds of sobbing, your head throbs, and you're closer to throwing up than in those first trimester days of morning sickness. Your only hope for regaining some semblance of physical control? Heed the warnings churning through your bloodstream like a bad virus: "STOP THE CRYING. REPEAT. STOP THE CRYING." To ignore this maternal reaction is about as easy as ignoring second stage labor.

QUICK TIP FROM DR. NIED

You could try putting the pacifier back in your baby's mouth, but she may not take to it—and don't force it. Although this is an extremely difficult process for parents, most sleep experts believe some winding-down crying is to be expected as babies learn to comfort themselves. Ideally the presleep fussing lasts only a few days until self-soothing is mastered. At that point, your baby should learn the routine and become comfortable settling himself independently. From then on, when you place him in his crib for naps—he should start to suck contentedly on his pacifier or stick a finger in his mouth and quietly drift off to sleep. Other babies may consistently wind down with a few tears as they doze off. You'll learn your child's approach to settling himself, and just step in if you think he has a real need.

QUICK TIP FROM DR. NIED

If your child's fussing continues, you could try checking on him after a few minutes and then, if necessary, after incrementally longer periods. You may be able to calm him down by briefly patting him and reassuring him in a calm, quiet tone. And then head back out. Ideally, this will provide the needed comfort as he learns to fall asleep in his crib. Progressive check-ins were popularized by Dr. Richard Ferber's book, *Solve Your Child's Sleep Problems*,[2] and they're often effective. Many parents, however, feel their babies actually become more upset by incremental check-ins. If you encounter this reaction from your child, try peeking in the room from a cracked door without letting him see you. You'll be able to visually assess the situation without creating further anxiety for you or your little one.

Don't assume all crying is the same. By now, you've likely learned to differentiate normal winding-down tears from true· discomfort. Utilize your newfound baby translation skills to decipher your child's crying. I'm-just-plain-tired tears are common as babies settle themselves. These often begin with intensity and then gradually diminish. More forceful no-I'm-actually-starving-and-I-can't-believe-you-just-put-me-in-this-crib-when-I'm-wasting-away tears will typically sound different and often increase in intensity. You want to teach your baby you're available if needed, just not as an essential bridge to sleep.

Step 7: The Waiting Game

Let's assume your baby is having some good ol' fashioned winding-down fussiness. You could wait for a few minutes in the hall or the kitchen—somewhere he can't see you.

Step 8: Stepping In

If the fussing continues, when should you step in and take your baby out of the crib? It's your call. (Don't you hate it when I say that?) If he's quietly whimpering for an extended period, he may simply be taking the slow road to snoozeland. If he's getting increasingly agitated over time, you may want to step in.

When you're starting the process, consider your infant's temperament, listen to his reactions, and try to determine the amount of time he generally requires to settle himself. Be relatively consistent in your approach unless you sense he has a real need. (I know this is tough; just do your best!) By sending mixed signals, you could confuse him and delay the process. When you've determined he isn't going to settle himself, pick him up and see how he's doing. You may be able to comfort him so he can try sleeping again, or you may need to feed him and move on with exploration time.

Listen to your baby, go with your gut, and good luck! When my son's sleeping patterns were becoming more predictable, the timing seemed right to help him learn to self-soothe. I tried to keep my eye on the clock and watch his cues each day—so I could follow a fairly consistent nap schedule and put him down just as he was getting tired. And within a few days, he learned being put in the crib meant it was time to sleep. Nap times became a relatively predictable, drama-free routine. Granted, he's naturally a good sleeper (one upside of a child who never stops moving while awake), and some babies take a bit longer to feel comfortable with self-soothing. Each child is different; trust your instincts and gauge the timing and approach that feel right for you and your baby.

> **QUICK TIP FROM DR. NIED**
>
> If your baby usually wakes from his naps cheerfully, that's a great sign he's getting the rest he needs. If you hear him waking up before he's taken what you consider an appropriate nap, don't run in to get him right away. Give him a little time, and he may drift back to sleep.

Maintaining Great Naps During Days in Child Care

"So, you know how Lucy's been napping better in day care than she does at home?"

"Yep. You were ready to start hiding in the bushes outside the center to learn their secret."

"Well, the secret is out. I just heard they give the babies bottles at nap times every day. They basically feed them to sleep every nap. No wonder she's been so fussy when I've put her down for naps on the weekends. She's hooked on a sleep crutch."

|•|

Your baby's naps are just coming into focus as your maternity leave ends, and suddenly you have to share the daytime sleeping reins with your child care provider. How to ensure your infant will be put down for naps appropriately while you're at work?

Discuss Naps in Advance

Take the team approach from the beginning. Your little solo sleeper should continue to thrive, and the predictability of the feed-to-wake approach should ease her transition to child care. Before you return to work, talk to your caregiver about your baby's nap schedule and presleep routine. Explain your preference for putting him in the crib with a pacifier just as he's getting tired so he falls asleep independently. Your efforts to promote self-soothing can backfire if your daytime caregiver starts feeding your child to sleep or using another type of sleep crutch before every nap. To maintain the feed-to-wake approach, simply request liquid feedings immediately after each nap. (Some larger day care centers may have established feeding and sleeping schedules for infants, so ask for details.) If you're still working on the nap schedule and presleep routine, don't worry; you and your caregiver can focus on these things together. Day care centers and baby-sitters often have their own useful tips.

Be Proactive About Safe Back-to-Sleep Practices

Close to 20 percent of SIDS deaths occur in child care. Less than half the states have licensing regulations that require child care providers to follow safe back-to-sleep practices, and some caregivers still put babies to sleep on their stomachs. This is extremely risky for your child. Back sleepers who are put to sleep on their fronts in child care are significantly more likely to suffer from SIDS. These infants are unaccustomed to tummy sleeping, and they often don't have the neck strength to shift their heads well from that position. Many SIDS-related deaths occur during the first few days in child care.

If you're using a day care center, talk to the supervisors and every adult who may put your child down for a nap. Some may argue babies sleep better on their tummies. This philosophy puts your child at risk. Be tactful but clear: You expect everyone to follow safe back-to-sleep practices.

Ask for Daily Nap Updates

When you head back to work, ask your caregiver to keep a daily log of your infant's naps plus feedings and exploration time. Baby-sitters and small day care centers should provide this; larger centers may simply offer verbal summaries of your child's day. Each evening, make time for a nap debriefing. Don't hesitate to ask detailed questions. The more you know about your baby's sleep patterns during your workdays, the more effectively you can facilitate his naps during your days off. If you're uncomfortable with your caregiver's nap scheduling or use of sleep crutches, be honest.

> ### QUICK TIP FROM DR. NIED
>
> The American Academy of Pediatrics launched the Healthy Child Care America Back to Sleep campaign in 2003 to educate caregivers and families about this issue. Go to healthychildcare.org, print out some of the free safe-sleep materials for child care providers, and share them with your caregiver. Discuss the recommendations in detail before your baby's first day in child care.

Follow the Same Nap Schedule As Your Child Care Provider

Create a seamless sleep flow between your baby's days in child care and with you. Day care centers often have set times for infant naps, so know he'll probably follow this schedule and try to offer the same nap times during your days off. And if you're using in-home care, simply coordinate nap times with your baby-sitter.

Transition Naps Together

Infants typically nap three times a day when they're four to five months old, and start to transition down to two naps at about six or seven months. When your baby seems ready to start dropping his third nap, discuss your plan for the transition. You can start pushing his morning nap back a bit during your days at home and your caregiver should do the same during your days at work. (Again, some day care centers may offer less nap time flexibility. For example, some centers put all babies down to nap twice a day, so your child may simply drop his third nap as soon as he enters day care. You could even help this transition by moving him toward a two-nap routine before you return to work.) By using a consistent approach and maintaining open communication, you and your caregiver should be an effective napping tag team.

Nighttime Routines—And the Secret of the Six Bs

"I just put Emma to bed, and—as usual—it wasn't pretty. She's five months old now and she still hates going to sleep."

"What's her bedtime routine?"

"Her what?"

"What do you guys do before putting her down?"

"Well, I guess it's different every night. Sometimes she gets a bath right before bed. Sometimes dinner. Sometimes we play. Or, if I have to run an errand, I might put her down as soon as we get home. And I'm not sure what David does when I'm running late at work. Why?"

"I think I may have a suggestion that could help."

|•|

QUICK TIP FROM DR. NIED

Your baby's bedtime routine should include the same events each night, but should not always be done by the same person, if possible. You want your child to be comfortable following the routine regardless of the adult involved, so you can leave him with a caregiver or relative in the evening without disrupting the process.

A nighttime routine offers your baby the necessary cues to wind down from the day and emotionally prepare for sleep. He'll love the predictability, and you'll quickly notice a decrease in bedtime fussiness. It's simple but mysteriously powerful stuff.

And establishing a nighttime routine is easy. Just do it. Starting tonight. Any routine could work as long as it's relatively consistent every evening and ultimately gets your child fed and in bed.

The Secret of the Six Bs

Here's a road-tested, parent-approved evening routine to get you started:

Big meal: By about six months, your baby will be eating a real dinner each evening. Make that meal the beginning of his nighttime routine. (And before that age, just skip this step.)

Brush: Once your infant's teeth come in, clean them with water and a soft brush or washcloth. Don't use toothpaste until at least two years; fluoride can lead to fluorosis in babies.

> **QUICK TIP FROM DR. NIED**
>
> As your child gets older, give him a small toothbrush and let him try to brush his teeth while you brush your teeth beside him. Young children typically love this activity, and it's great to establish the habit early. For effective cleaning, however, finish the job yourself until your child is at least five years old.

Bath: Babies generally adore bath time with Mom or Dad. Introduce bath toys or books, teach your infant to splash, and play water games. This is his last playtime of the day.

Bed clothes: After the bath, wrap your baby in a towel and carry him to his room. Give him a fresh diaper and put on his pj's. He'll be clean, damp, and snugglicious.

Books: The American Academy of Pediatrics recommends reading to your child for at least fifteen minutes daily from the age of six months. But it can't hurt to start even earlier. Build reading into your child's life by making books part of your nighttime routine from the beginning.

Bed: Your baby is now clean, full, and relaxed. It's the big B: bedtime. If you're still in the swaddling stage, you can swaddle your baby and place him on his back in the crib. If he's older, zip him into his sleep sack or simply place him on his back in his pajamas or onesie. Babies close to one year may sleep with attachment objects like small stuffed animals.

Sleeping Through the Night: The Promised Land

It's 4:30 A.M. You just fed your newborn for the third time since any rational being went to bed, and your brain is filled with a thick fog. The previous feeding was only an hour before, and the sleep you experienced in between doesn't count because you were dozing in a state of wired anticipation—certain you'd hear your baby's cry any second. Like some freakish miracle, he now snoozes in the nursery.

You dive under your comforter (was it always this warm? this soft?), staring through glazed eyes at the digital clock on your bedside table. You begin a compulsive mental monologue, making calculations as fast as your sleep-deprived mind can function. If he sleeps for two hours, you figure, we'll make it to daybreak. The natural light will be my salvation. Sure, I'll be tired—but the sun will be out. Please, just let him sleep for two hours or more. Maybe three. Whoa, three hours. That would be 7:30 A.M. Too much to hope for, perhaps, but please—when I next open my eyes let it be 7:30 A.M. Even 7:15 would be really, really good. Okay, I'll take anything in the sevens. You finally drift off with the glowing numbers still in your head.

|•|

The likelihood of multiple night waking depends on two things: your baby's age and dumb luck.

The Age Factor

As we've already discussed, the beginning of your child's life is a sleeping free-for-all, and he may still need to feed at least once overnight until he's about six months old. And then one day, it'll happen. You'll put your child down to sleep at 7:30 P.M., and you won't hear from him again until 6:00 A.M. You'll do a double take as the digital numbers on your clock come into vision. You did it. You reached the promised land.

The Dumb Luck Factor

Then there's the dumb luck factor. Despite the averages, some sleep-gifted babies start snoozing six or more consecutive hours overnight after just a few weeks. This is one of those things like eye color or sense of humor that seems innate in children. I wish you good luck getting an early overnight sleeper and patience if you don't. Whatever you do, don't blame yourself or your child. In twenty years, you'd probably love to relive some of those sweet moments at dawn with your newborn. Okay, maybe not. Just go with me here, and know you've got the rest of your life to catch up on sleep.

Managing Overnight Waking: The Early Months

For the first few months, when overnight waking is part of your infant's eating cycle, respond with a quiet feeding session in the dark. Don't greet your child enthusiastically, don't play This Little Piggy, don't even turn on the light. Go directly to the rocking chair, try for a full feeding to minimize future waking, snuggle quietly for a couple of minutes, and then return him to the crib. Most infants take the hint at this point and drift back to sleep.

QUICK TIP FROM DR. NIED

Ideally, after six months of age your child should sleep ten to twelve hours nightly without interruption. If your baby is consistently eating overnight at this age, he's probably waking up out of habit, not necessity, and you should chat with your pediatrician. She'll likely suggest phasing out these nighttime sessions by gradually reducing the feeding times over a few nights and then letting your child fuss himself back to sleep. If your seven-month-old is consistently waking up around midnight and 3:00 A.M., for example, you could phase out the midnight feeding over a week or so and then gradually phase out the 3:00 A.M. feeding. Both you and your child need a full night's sleep at this point.

When Your Super Overnight Sleeper Regresses

Even if your baby has been consistently sleeping through the night for months, don't be surprised if he occasionally regresses. Your ten-month-old super overnight sleeper may suddenly wake in tears at 2:00 A.M. Why?

There are lots of potential causes:

- Teething discomfort
- Sickness
- Growth spurt
- Scary dreams (Yes, even infants can have nightmares that startle them awake.)
- Separation anxiety (When it peaks, usually starting at about nine or ten months, your baby may inadvertently wake up and then cry for your company.)

Usually a few minutes with Mom or Dad is all it takes to ease the pain of teething or calm a baby who had a bad dream.

Creating an Enthusiastic Eater
Making the Goopy Stuff Look Good and More

"Granted, I wouldn't eat this goop if you paid me," Courtney muttered, staring in frustration at the soupy bowl of barley in her lap. "And Nicholas couldn't agree more."

Her brother smiled at his nephew, who looked like he was enjoying some kind of deep cleansing barley face mask. His cheeks were covered in the stuff. And his forehead. And his chin. He pulled a clump out of his hair, glared at it in disgust, and let it drop to the floor.

|•|

I know, I know. You are, at this point, a baby feeding goddess. You've mastered the perfect latch-on. You prepare bottles in fifteen seconds flat. Your little one has grown cheeks like the Gerber baby and zipped through several dozen diaper genie refills. Just as your parenting pride reaches an all-time high, just as you start *offering advice* about breast feeding or bottles to novice moms, just as you round the corner of month four—the goopy games begin. And it's a whole new learning curve in the shape of a bright green plastic baby bowl.

This chapter gives you the inside scoop, so to speak. It offers a monthly guide, advice on introducing solids for the first time, tips for encouraging happy eating, and a year one grocery shopping hit list. Get the details now to establish healthy eating habits and enthusiastic mealtimes from the beginning.

Year One Eating: What to Expect Month by Month

From Audrey's journal:

Ventured into the baby food aisle today and eventually walked away completely confused. No idea where to begin. Possible next steps:

1. Call pediatrician and admit incompetence. (Subsequent note on our file: "Parent can't even figure out baby food. Watch for continued signs of neglect.")

2. Call Mom and risk hour-long monologue about how she grew organic vegetables and pureed them by hand for all our infant meals. (So not worth it.)

3. Call new mom friends and nonchalantly ask how baby mealtimes are going. Try to pick up tips without directly admitting irrational fear of seemingly infinite baby food options. (Bingo.)

QUICK TIP FROM DR. NIED

You know your infant is eating (or more accurately, drinking) enough the first few months if she gains about four to seven ounces a week, has about six wet diapers a day, and is generally following the eating guidelines in "Your Feeding Road Map to Babyville." Regular dirty diapers are another good sign, but their frequency may vary from many times a day to once every few days.

For first-time parents, the feeding road ahead is always elusive. When exactly do you qualify for the baby food aisle? Is there a right way to start solids? And what's the deal with sippy cups, anyway? Use the feeding road map on the next page to see where your baby is headed this year.

Now, the monthly details.

Birth Through Three Months: Living on Liquids

Your baby will literally live on liquids until she's four months old. Breast milk is nature's most perfect food, and formula is the next best thing—so she'll receive all the nutrients she needs without a single fruit or veggie.

YOUR FEEDING ROAD MAP TO BABYVILLE

	Birth to 4 Weeks	1 Month	2 Months	3 Months	4 Months	5 Months	6 Months	7 Months to 1st Birthday
Feeding								
Liquids (Breast Feeding or Bottle)								
Number of liquid feedings every 24 hours	8–12	5–8	5–8	4–6	4–6	4–6	4–5	4–5
Typical ounces per feeding	2–3	3–4	4–6	4–6	4–6	5–8	6–8	6–8
Total ounces recommended every 24 hours	14–20	15–26	20–32	20–32	22–32	22–32*	20–32*	20–30*
Solids								
Number of solid feedings every 24 hours	—	—	—	—	Tastings only	1: Breakfast	2: Breakfast and dinner	3: Breakfast lunch and dinner
Recommended solids by stage	—	—	—	—	Rice cereal, oatmeal and barley	Stage 1 baby food: veggies then fruits	Stage 2 baby food	Stage 3 baby food, finger foods, sippy cups

*Daily liquid intake may decrease slightly as solid meals are introduced.

In fact, introducing solids too early has been associated with an increased risk of food allergies and atopic dermatitis (eczema). No need for water at this point either.

Your Four-Month-Old: Getting Used to the Goop

The American Academy of Pediatrics recommends gradually introducing solid foods between months four and six (starting at month six for exclusively breast-fed babies), so think of this month as your child's training period. The goal: Teach her how to eat from a spoon and expose her to a few basic flavors. Start with rice cereal, which is easiest to digest and least likely to cause an allergic reaction. (For help, check out "Introducing Solids for the First Time" later in this chapter.) Then introduce oatmeal and other grains such as barley. Gradually decrease the ratio of water, formula, or breast milk in your mixes, and try to offer the tastings before her morning nap so she can smoothly transition to a regular breakfast next month. Don't worry about how much she actually eats—she's still getting all the nutrients and energy she needs from breast milk or formula.

QUICK TIP FROM DR. NIED

Although we offer feeding advice starting at four months in this chapter, if you are exclusively breast-feeding, you can introduce solids at six months and simply shift our guidelines back by two months.

Your Five-Month-Old: Hit the Baby Food Aisle or Pull Out the Food Processor

Your baby is now a spoon-eating pro. Your goal this month is exposing her to additional flavors and establishing a regular breakfast routine. Continue to offer rice cereal, oatmeal, and other grains, which are high in iron, and start to add veggies and fruits. You have two options here: serve stage 1 baby food from jars (look for brands without unnecessary additives like sugar or salt) or make the mushy stuff yourself. There are a variety of books and websites that offer baby food recipes, but the basic process can be summarized as follows:

1. Locate nutritious food item.

2. Stick said item in the steamer, microwave, or blender and press go.
3. Mush into a gooey, gummable consistency.
4. Serve. And pretend the goop on your spoon is irresistible. Good luck.

Time-saver for do-it-yourselfers: Make large portions and freeze the extra servings in a plastic ice cube tray. Then thaw each serving as needed.

Wait three or four days each time you introduce a new food, and look for negative reactions like a rash, diarrhea, vomiting, or painful indigestion. (Hard things to miss.) If your baby has a bad reaction to a new item, don't serve it to her again until you've talked to your pediatrician. If she simply doesn't like the taste of a certain food, try again in a few days. Many babies don't like certain tastes the first time they try them but change their tune on try three or four. Or you may have just hit her on an anti-peaches morning. And next time, you could mask the flavor by mixing in a neutral-tasting grain or a food she likes.

Ideally, introduce new foods in this order:

> **QUICK TIP FROM DR. NIED**
>
> Don't serve baby food directly from the jar; saliva can lead to bacterial growth when refrigerating unused food. Instead, pour a portion into a plastic bowl, gradually adding more as necessary. Any uneaten food in the bowl should be thrown away, and unused food in the jar can be refrigerated about twenty-four hours.

1. Orange veggies like carrots and squash, which are particularly easy to digest
2. Other veggies such as peas and green beans
3. Fruits like peaches, bananas, and pears

Your Six-Month-Old: Baby Food, the Sequel— Starting Stage 2 Foods

Your infant should be ready for stage 2 baby food jars or slightly denser foods in larger portions. When the stage 1 jar isn't filling her up, you're ready to make the shift.

Don't worry; you'll know. Your infant will offer a subtle clue along the lines of an expression of pure horror immediately followed by frantic screeching as you walk away with the empty plastic bowl. "Noooooooooo!" she would be saying if her mouth could form the words. "What are you doing, lady? I used to think you actually cared about my well-being! Now you offer me that measly, pathetic excuse for a breakfast and walk away? But I'm STARVING OVER HERE!" Fortunately babies aren't shy when they're hungry.

Try to offer two meals a day—ideally breakfast and dinner. Continue to provide your tried-and-true grains, veggies, and fruits, and introduce some new items. Soft foods like applesauce, yogurt, cottage cheese, mashed potatoes, and avocado are perfect for six-monthers. A baby this age might have rice cereal and fruit for breakfast, oatmeal and a veggie for dinner, and if needed, some full-fat plain yogurt plus fruit for a midday snack. Rice cereal and other grains are important sources of iron and should be given once or twice each day.

Seven Months Through First Birthday: Finally, the Good Stuff

Between seven and nine months, you can shift to stage 3 baby food, which is thicker and chunkier, and over the following few months you should gradually move to a real food diet. To time this transition, gauge your child's interest in different foods and your tolerance for preparation. Vitamin-fortified baby food is great because it's easy to transport and serve. Real food takes more prep time, but eventually you'll need to make the switch. You've likely identified any food allergies at this point and know which items to avoid.

Your baby's meals should now parallel yours—breakfast, lunch, and dinner—and you could offer light snacks between meals if her energy is getting low. Try to provide a combination of dairy products, fruits, veggies, carbohydrates, and proteins, and you can offer water, breast milk, or formula with some meals.

How much to serve? Let your child set the feeding pace. You'll notice a gradual increase in food intake, although some days she may be particularly hungry or disinterested. This is normal, but talk to your pediatrician with any concerns.

Baby meal ideas:

Breakfast
- Full-fat yogurt or cottage cheese
- Oatmeal or tiny pieces of soft whole wheat bagel
- Small pieces of banana or cantaloupe

Lunch
- Bite-size chunks of turkey, chicken, or tofu
- Strips of string cheese (Full string cheese can get lodged in little throats.)
- Small pieces of watermelon or grapes cut into quarters

Dinner
- Whole wheat pasta, macaroni and cheese, or veggie soup
- Cooked peas, green beans, sweet potatoes, or carrots
- Applesauce

Finger foods: Between seven and nine months, your baby will start picking up small objects with her thumb and forefinger—an important milestone called the pincer grasp. When this kicks in, you can introduce finger foods. Put them directly on the high chair tray or in a baby bowl with suction cups to minimize spills.

Popular starting finger foods:

- Toasted oat cereal that dissolves easily (like Cheerios)
- Toddler wagon wheels or teething crackers (available in the baby food aisle)
- Small pieces of rice cake
- Tiny cubes of cheese
- Grapes cut into quarters
- Small bite-size pieces of banana or pear
- Tiny pieces of cooked veggies like sweet potatoes, peas, or carrots
- Cooked pasta or rice

My finger foods disclaimer: These cheerful snacks practically scream *choking hazard* the first time you consider offering them to your child. The soupy stuff was one thing, but finger foods are the real deal, and that infant CPR class suddenly seems decades past. I'll never forget the first time I gave my son a wagon wheel. I was with some new mom friends, and a particularly savvy mother in the group discovered none of us had made the leap to finger foods. "You're kidding!" she said, "Lily's been eating wagon wheels for weeks!" The rest of us eyed her like she was offering crack and shook our heads.

"He'll choke," one mom murmured quietly, looking at her son.

"No, seriously—he'll be fine. Let's do it together." She pulled out the plastic baggie of wagon wheels and knowingly handed them to us like a high school senior passing out cigarettes. We sat there, palms up, quietly looking at each other as the wagon wheels taunted us. Then Savvy Mom broke the tension. "Here you go Lily," she said to her daughter, placing the disc of doom in her child's open mouth. A hush fell over the room as Lily casually gummed the wagon wheel into bits and swallowed it without so much as raising her eyes from the toy cell phone in her hands. It was possible. We had to admit that. So we all tried it, one by one, and the kids were fine. Yours will be too.

Mushy meat: If you plan on serving meat and poultry, you can introduce it now. Given the ick factor with baby food beef and chicken, however, some infants aren't interested until the real stuff is offered. If your child rejects the mushy meat, just wait and provide small bites of real chicken, beef, and turkey as she seems ready. For nonmeat eaters, offer other sources of protein such as egg yolks, tofu, or soft beans ground into a mushy consistency to prevent choking.

Utensils: By about ten or eleven months, your child should try eating with a baby spoon and fork. This leads to a whole new level of food chaos, but it does help with eye-hand coordination and independent eating. Plus, most babies love it.

Sippy cups: During this stage, sippy cups also hit the scene. Don't let this transition stress you out; just offer them when your baby seems strong enough and let her take the lead. When she has the strength, coordination, and desire, she'll take to the cups. She should make the full transition from bottles to sippy cups around her first birthday.

Introducing Solids for the First Time

FROM:	**Lori Svoboda**
TO:	**Tanya Brackett**
SUBJECT:	**Weekend plans**

Tomorrow morning: Big breakfast date with the little dude. Just me, him, his first bowl of rice cereal, and a few dozen wet wipes. Tonight: Locating that infant CPR brochure just in case. Wish me luck.

Giving your baby solid food for the first time can be scary. You imagine the worst—crazy allergic reactions, choking, and horror movie–like spitting up. You put it off for weeks and then finally gather your supplies like a chef preparing for a gourmet meal. Then the moment of truth arrives, and it's wildly anticlimactic (in a good way). Your baby takes a few bites of soupy rice cereal, and you snap some cute shots for the baby book. No drama and no need for infant CPR. This step-by-step guide walks you through the process to take the mystery out of your infant's first solid meal.

Step 1: At Four Months, Start Watching for Signs of Solid Food Readiness

Before you serve rice cereal for the first time, your baby should:

- Be able to sit in a high chair or booster seat with an infant-appropriate setting (Have you ever tried eating cereal on your back? Me neither, but it can't be easy.)
- Show an interest in your food (This is hard to imagine until one day you realize your baby has become a mini–food stalker, obsessively staring at your mouth as you eat.)

- Seem hungry, as if liquid feedings aren't quite enough anymore (Or you may notice an increase in liquid intake, indicating maturing energy needs.)
- Be at least twice her birth weight and weigh twelve pounds or more

Step 2: Pick the Right Moment to Start

When your baby is at least four months old and showing food readiness signs, it's go time. Pick a day when she seems well rested and content. Morning is often a good time for the big moment because babies are generally energized and ready to explore. Plus, you can gradually extend your morning tasting sessions to a breakfast routine. Offer a liquid feeding first, so she isn't famished during your first attempt at solids.

Step 3: Dig Out the Bibs, Itty Bitty Spoons, and a Camera

Those cute bibs you received as baby gifts have probably been gathering dust in the closet. Go find them now; the beginning of solids is the beginning of major food messes in your life. Pick your favorite, attach it around your baby's neck, and enthusiastically explain what's happening. Your child will love being the center of attention in this new activity. Use a rubber-tipped or plastic baby spoon to protect her gums and grab your camera—this is a definite moment for the baby album.

Step 4: Prepare the Goop

Your baby's first solid food isn't much of a solid at all. In fact, it should have the consistency of thick soup. Start with one tablespoon of iron-fortified rice cereal, which is bland enough to agree with evolving taste buds and sensitive tummies, and add water, formula, or breast milk according to the ratio on the box. You'll be lucky if your baby successfully swallows even that amount.

Step 5: Put Your Baby in Feeding Position

Your infant should be upright, either in her bouncy seat or the high chair. Pull a seat up so you're directly facing each other to minimize distractions.

Step 6: Serve with a Smile

Fill about half your baby spoon with the rice cereal, channel that high school drama class, and try to make it seem like the most enticing thing on earth. When your child's interest is piqued, offer her some food. Slowly place the spoon on her tongue and let her have a taste. Ideally, she'll suck the rice cereal off the spoon. If she goes for it, great. Keep the food fiesta going as long as she wants. If she spits it out, gags, cries, pulls away, or looks at you with complete disgust, just stop and try again every couple of days until she shows more interest. Don't rush things; your infant will take to eating when she's ready, and she's getting all the nutrients she needs from breast milk or formula at this point anyway.

> **QUICK TIP FROM DR. NIED**
>
> If your baby pushes the spoon out of her mouth with her tongue, this is called the extrusion reflex and it means she's not yet ready for solids. Try again in a week.

Encouraging Enthusiastic Eating

Alena imitated every baby food commercial she could remember, gamely attempting the baby-food-as-airplane move, the mushy chicken peek-a-boo, and even faking a bite herself. Her daughter Lia was completely unimpressed.

"Honestly, I can't blame you," she finally said, giving up. "Pureed chicken? Not one of my favorite foods either."

|•|

Convinced your baby is the world's fussiest eater? You're not alone. Many parents find themselves on the losing end of daily food battles, but the war ends here. Try these parent-tested, pediatrician-approved strategies for helping your child approach eating with enthusiasm.

Kiss Matt Lauer Good-Bye (Sorry, I Know He's Cute)

We've all mastered morning multitasking—dressing and feeding ourselves and our bundles of joy in less time than it takes Diane Sawyer to interview the latest reality show cast-off. And it's always fun to fit in a little mindless entertainment—I mean news—as we grab breakfast before work. However, mealtime distractions can lead to antsy eaters, so multitask right up to your baby's breakfast, and then stop. Just for a few minutes.

Turn off the morning news. Don't check your voice mail, straighten the kitchen, or iron your shirt. Just sit with your baby and help her eat. I realize this is a radical suggestion, but your child is guaranteed to focus more on breakfast when you do. And don't worry—once she's mastered mealtimes, you can always reconnect with Matt.

Let Your Little One Take the Lead

Offer a balanced assortment of nutritious foods, and then allow your child to take the lead in terms of pace, portions, and preferences. She may gobble down her meals in five minutes; she may be a leisurely luncher. Try to follow her natural timing and offer food as long as she seems hungry. And don't engage in unnecessary food battles. Let's say your infant starts spitting out her peas. Then her green beans go airborne. Finally she adopts a sudden disdain for anything green. You could obsessively offer the dreaded green items and spend endless hours trying to get a few peas down her throat, or you could accept her green boycott at face value and move on.

If your baby won't eat her peas, offer a nutritious alternative or two she normally likes. If those also get the veto, consider the meal over. She may be feeling sick, which often diminishes appetite, or she may be full even if she ate less than usual. Keep a pleasant and relaxed tone; you want exclusively positive associations with mealtime. And if she seems hungry forty-five minutes later, you could provide a healthy snack. As long as you make a good-faith effort to offer your baby nutritious foods, she'll eat what her body needs. Expect some atypical days, when she eats more or less than usual, and consult your pediatrician with any concerns.

> **QUICK TIP FROM DR. NIED**
>
> Young children, including older babies and toddlers, may reject food to gain a feeling of control. They don't often have the opportunity to make choices, and the thrill of refusing food can be exhilarating. As the adult, you can end the battle before it begins by calmly accepting food refusals. Give your child control over her food intake now, and you'll set the stage for a lifetime of healthy eating and actually lessen the likelihood of obesity and eating disorders.

Become Really, Really Boring;
Follow a Regular Mealtime Routine

It's 6:30 P.M., and you're running through the grocery store on your way home from work, popping bites of banana in your baby's mouth. It's not exactly dinner at the Cleavers, but who has the time?

If you're trying to manage a fussy eater, a mealtime routine could be your secret to success. Consistent timing, placement of objects, and processes make children feel confident and secure. To create an enthusiastic eater, coordinate with your child care provider and try to offer meals in a highchair or booster seat at about the same time each day. Establish a consistent mealtime routine and stick to it.

QUICK TIP FROM DR. NIED

The occasional meal on the run is inevitable, and if your baby has mastered eating this might not pose a problem. But if you're struggling with food battles, stick to a mealtime routine as much as possible.

Adopt a Lunch Date Attitude

Enthusiastic eaters look forward to mealtimes with their parents or caregivers. They know what to expect, they know they'll get food they want, and they enjoy the quality time with their favorite people. Don't confuse meals with playtime—the toys and books should be kept away—but always engage your baby verbally, try to stay upbeat and patient even if she's having a bad food day, and eat your meal as she eats hers. She'll be more likely to try grapes or avocado if she sees you eating them.

Don't Go Ballistic Over Bagels (Or Any Other Food Obsession)

Your baby may take to a few favorite foods and subsequently rule out any other options. Some crave dairy products, some want fruit, and some practically live on whole wheat bagels. You name it and there's a child out there obsessing about it. These intense food preferences may start out of the blue after months of normal eating, or they may emerge as soon as you introduce solids. Either way, don't panic if your baby's diet isn't a perfect balance of the four food groups. During her first year, you've got a great nutritional safety net: breast milk or formula. Her liquid feedings are like superpowered energy shakes pumping her with a broad range of nutrients.

QUICK TIP FROM DR. NIED

Keep offering a variety of nutritious options and talk to your pediatrician if the food fixations continue. Generally babies outgrow them within a few weeks.

Coordinate with Child Care

After maternity leave, your caregiver will set the tone for your child's daytime liquid feedings, lunch, and snacks.

In-home care: If you're using in-home care, you have the feeding trump card—you supply the food. Simply ask your sitter to offer liquid feedings immediately after naps and let her know what's available for daily lunches and snacks. Talk to her about a consistent mealtime routine and schedule you can both follow, and ask her to offer all meals in the high chair or booster seat.

Day care: Day care providers often expect parents to supply rice cereal, oatmeal, and other grains starting about month four. Once your child moves on to gummable veggies, fruits, finger foods, meat, and poultry, these items should be offered for lunch and snacks, so make sure you're comfortable with their selections. Before your baby starts day care, ask about their approach to liquid feedings, mealtimes, and snacks, and discuss any specific food requests. Try to provide a similar feeding schedule on your days at home.

Your Year One Grocery Shopping Hit List

These are your archenemies in the world of baby nutrition—edibles and drinkables that can cause allergic reactions, pose choking hazards, or upset little tummies. Don't serve them this year.

Common Food Allergens

- Peanut butter or nuts

- Fish and shellfish
- Chocolate
- Egg whites (Stick to the yolks year one.)

Choking Hazards

- Popcorn and nuts
- Hard candies or lollipops
- Berries or raisins
- Olives
- Whole string cheese (Only offer thin strips.)
- Whole grapes (Cut into quarters.)
- Whole hot dogs (Cut lengthwise first and then into bite-size pieces.)

Tummy Troublers

- Honey (Can cause botulism in infants.)
- Beets, turnips, broccoli, and kale (Too high in nitrates for babies.)

Bad Beverages

- Juice (High in sugar, can cause allergic reactions, and less nutritious than formula or breast milk.)
- Whole milk (Should replace formula at one year. Introducing it earlier can cause iron deficiency anemia.)

Ideal Toys and Activities
for Every Infant Stage

To Keep Your Baby
Entertained and Amazed

"Finally, this morning, the moment arrived," Naomi said to her friend Sasha as they pushed their strollers to their favorite coffee shop. "I wasn't feeding, burping, rocking, carrying, consoling, or cleaning Noah. He was bright-eyed and ready for action. 'Okay, Mommy,' he seemed to be saying, 'What's the plan?'"

"Great!" Sasha responded, knowing parenthood was a major transition for Naomi, an advertising manager more comfortable caring for clients than infants.

"And suddenly," Naomi continued, "I was at a complete loss. I finally mastered feedings and baths, and now I'm stumped by playtime."

|•|

It may have been years since you tried to remember a children's song. Or you may have a closet full of baby toys but no idea when to pull out the stacking rings versus the wooden blocks, the dollhouse versus the foot rattles. Never fear. Check out these recommended toys and do-it-yourself activities so you can appropriately stimulate, entertain, and amaze your child at any age.

Birth to Three Months

Susie and Blake sat quietly watching their three-week-old daughter lying between them on the couch. Claire had been staring at the back cushion for five minutes and showed no signs of shifting her gaze. As far as they could tell, she was enraptured by the shadows playing across the beige upholstery.

"I never realized this couch could be so fascinating," Susie finally commented.

"Apparently, for a newborn it's better than MTV," Blake replied. "And remind me again why we bought all those toys?"

Terrific Toys and Ideas to Engage Your Newborn

You have a new baby—time to hit the toy store, right? Not yet. For the first several weeks, your infant is primarily adjusting to life outside the womb, and he's as happy to stare at shadows on a wall as a shiny developmental toy. This initial period is all about comforting your newborn as he transitions from the coziness of the womb to the craziness of the world. Let him relax on your chest, keep his tummy full, swaddle him, wear him in a sling as you make dinner—whatever works.

Over the first three months, he'll stay awake longer, smile, and become more engaged in his environment, but even then his idea of playing will involve watching his mobile in the comfort of his crib. You'll begin to see his distinct little personality—mellow, energetic, chatty, quiet, intense, easygoing, or anything in between. He'll start laughing, pushing up during tummy time, and paying close attention to your voice. (Remember this when he hits puberty. He really did listen to you at one point.)

During this stage, a bouncy seat can free your arms, and a newborn play mat is better than Disney World. Look for one with a colorful, padded mat and objects dangling from above; it doesn't get any better than this when you can't move around and your vision is best at twelve inches. Snuggle, tickle him, make funny faces—anything to provoke that little smile.

Keep the toys simple for now and pick up or borrow these basic items:

- Colorful (ideally musical) battery-operated mobile
- Bouncy seat
- Play mat with objects hanging from above

Age-Appropriate Activities for Newborns

Mad About Music

Even before iPods, some expert figured this out: Music gets to people. In a good way. And like the latest pop hit wafting over a stadium full of pre-teen girls in hormone-induced rapture, music offers a variety of benefits for your baby. It can relax him, engage him, and stimulate him. So let the music play from day one:

Play upbeat tunes in the car.   There's a huge variety of children's music with simple lyrics and melodies designed to engage the little people. Don't miss Justin Roberts, Ralph's World, Dan Zanes, and Laurie Berkner.

Play calming music before bedtime.   Anything relaxing is appropriate. Pull out your old Joni Mitchell CD or play classical lullabies.

Sing, sing a song.   Your baby really doesn't care if you can carry a tune. He'll love your enthusiasm, and in his (admittedly limited) world, you have perfect pitch. Can't remember a single song from childhood? The lyrics are probably back there behind the periodic table you memorized in high school, the details of your job, and critical current news like the dating status of every Hollywood celebrity. Do a quick online search for "children's song lyrics," and you'll find dozens of websites that can refresh your memory. Here's one children's classic to get you started:

The wheels on the bus go round and round
Round and round, round and round

The wheels on the bus go round and round, all around the town
Following verses:
The doors on the bus go open, close
The horn on the bus goes beep, beep, beep
The windows on the bus go up and down
The children on the bus say, "I love you"
The parents on the bus say, "I love you, too"

Tummy Time

The current back-to-sleep approach can result in a slightly flattened infant head and underdeveloped neck muscles. To ensure a round noggin and strong upper body, there's tummy time—awake periods each day when your baby hangs out on his front. Some infants take to tummy time from the beginning without complaint; they're probably just thrilled to finally change positions. Others fight these stomach sessions. Welcome to the world of parenthood, where creative solutions are required:

Introduce the position gradually.   Sit on the couch with your back propped against a pillow and hold your baby belly-down on your chest so he's at a slight incline. Over time, lower yourself until he adjusts to lying flat on your body. Once he's content with this position, lay him on a blanket on the floor.

Place a rolled towel or nursing pillow under his chest.   That way, he's able to look around and more easily lift his head.

Put a mirror in front of him on the floor.   Encourage him to "find the baby" and point out his reflection to keep him distracted.

Lie down face-to-face and make funny noises.   Stick out your tongue or sing a song—anything to keep his focus on you rather than his position.

Avoid tummy time just after feedings.   Some babies are happier on their stomachs when they're not full.

Window Watching

Crawling around the room? Not yet. Stacking rings? Nope. Perusing the world from the safety of his bouncy seat? Absolutely. At this age, your newborn can't explore through physical manipulation, but his visual, auditory, and cognitive development is in overdrive. Don't be deterred by his inability to respond; help him understand the visual world by holding him or placing his bouncy seat in front of a window and describing everything you see. Name the objects outside. Identify different colors. Explain the sounds you hear from the road. This activity can become a happy morning ritual, and as your child gets older he'll start pointing out the trees and mailbox himself.

Flying the Newborn Skies

Once your baby can support his head, lie back on the floor with your knees up, letting him rest tummy down on your shins so you can see each other. Gently raise and lower your feet, holding him securely in place with your hands. A good stretch for you and extra time off his back in a supported "airplane flight" for him.

Family Face Time

Fortunately for everyone, babies love looking at faces. (We just carried these kids inside our bodies for nine months; the least they can do is look at us, right?) Capitalize on the infant face fetish and give your child a head start on her family tree. Buy a small vinyl photo album that holds about a dozen pictures ($5 or so at your local drugstore) and fill it with family face shots, inserting your child's picture as the cover. As he becomes increasingly curious about his environment, show him the photos and tell him stories about each relative. Yes, it'll be a while until the stories sink in, but in the meantime he'll love the interaction and Aunt Lynn will be thrilled to see her picture included when she comes to visit.

Variation for the crafty: Glue family pictures to a magnetic sheet (available at most craft stores). Cut around the faces, and you've got yourself personalized family magnets. Keep them on the fridge and point out each one when that relative calls or sends a gift.

Four to Six Months

"I'm no expert on infant fashion, but those shoes look a little impractical," Blake said to Susie as he walked into the nursery. Claire, now five months old, was lying in her crib examining the two googly-eyed frogs attached to her feet. She held her legs up, her toes just a few inches above her face, to get the best possible view of her entertaining new friends.

"They're foot rattles," Susie replied. "And they really work. You know how Claire has been into her hands lately? Well, I figured I'd give these a try. Now she realizes she has feet as well."

Blake nodded, watching his daughter in the crib. "That, or she's wondering when she grew amphibians on the end of her legs."

Terrific Toys and Ideas to Engage Your High Roller

Your infant will start rolling over around four months, usually front to back first and not always on purpose. (He's pushing up from his tummy, proudly beaming. "Look at me!" he would be saying if he could, "I'm so strong! I'm so high! I'm so . . . huh? On my back again? This upper body stuff is harder than it looks.") Encourage his new rolling skills by lying on the floor next to him with your arms outstretched, calling him toward you, and offering enthusiastic applause to build his confidence during early attempts. (And you thought NBA cheerleaders looked funny.)

He'll discover his hands and feet, start reaching for things, stick objects of interest into his mouth for further exploration, and possibly sit up and begin squirming around by month six. Teeth may start to emerge. And expect lots of new sounds, possibly including mama and dada, although your baby's babbling is essentially random at this point.

Offer toys that assist in these developmental milestones like foot rattles that engage an infant on the verge of discovering his toes and colorful teethers that can be held or chewed when gums are sore. The exersaucer will replace the bouncy seat as your child's favorite spot to play, and he'll enjoy holding or chewing on soft toys and small stuffed animals. Help your early sitter build balance and core strength by placing him often in a sitting position either in your lap or solo with pillows behind him and a basket of small, engaging items at his side. And break out the board books, if you haven't already. The American Academy of Pediatrics recommends reading to your child at least fifteen minutes a day from six months on. Offer any of the following:

- Discovery cubes
- Teethers
- Hand and foot rattles
- Stuffed animals or soft dolls
- Board books
- Exersaucer

Age-Appropriate Activities for Four- to Six-Month-Olds

Life Before Brio

There are a few givens in this world: The sun rises in the east, bell-bottoms come back into style every couple of decades despite all hopes to the contrary, and kids love trains. Know this now and get ready for a little choo-choo in your near future. Enjoy these days before your soon-to-be-toddler becomes obsessed with the $300 Brio set, and create your own baby train using household items. Pull out a laundry basket or inflatable baby tub, line it with towels, and place your child gently inside. Throw in a couple of stuffed animals as additional "passengers" and pull the basket slowly around the living room doing your best Thomas impersonation. (Yes, this is where the choo-choos come in). Enjoy the resulting baby bliss and be glad your boss can't see you now.

Crazy Fun with Object Permanence

Sometimes it's the simplest activities that most effectively educate and entertain. If you haven't been playing peek-a-boo with your baby, start now. Put your hands over your face, cover his eyes with a cloth, pull a bear from under a cushion—all variations will be appreciated. While it's beyond basic for us, your infant will be amazed. Plus, the game helps him begin to understand things continue to exist when out of sight—a cognitive milestone pediatricians call object permanence. For more crazy fun with object permanence, try "Open, Shut Them":

Open, shut them.
On "open," hold your hands up, palms facing your baby.
On "shut them," close your hands into fists.

Open, shut them. Repeat motions.
Give a little clap. Clap your hands.

Open, shut them. Open, shut them. Repeat motions.
Put them in your lap. Hide your hands in your lap.

Creep them, creep them, slowly creep them . . . right up to your chin.
Starting at baby's belly, slowly "creep" fingers up toward his face, then tickle his chin.

Open up your little mouth . . . Place your fingers on your baby's mouth.
. . . but do not let them in. Run fingers down baby's body and hide them in your lap.

Even Really Little Can Feel Big

By the age of six months, your baby may be starting to mimic simple arm and hand movements. Reinforce this newfound skill with a classic infant game. Ask your little one, "How big is [fill in his name]?" Then guide his hands over his head and answer, "So big!" He'll enjoy the interaction now, and over time he'll respond with raised hands and a sly grin every time you pose the question.

Piggy Toes

Babies discover their hands and feet during this stage; reinforce this discovery with another blast from your childhood past. Continue to ignore the irony of a pig going to the market to buy roast beef and give it a go, wiggling each scrumptious little toe along the way:

> *This little piggy went to market.*
> *This little piggy stayed home.*
> *This little piggy had roast beef.*
> *This little piggy had none.*
> *And this little piggy cried, "Wee, wee, wee," all the way home.* (Tickle your baby.)

Clappingpalooza

Here's another back-to-basics suggestion: clapping. It's one of the first meaningful actions most babies mimic. When your child rolls over, finishes his oatmeal, or actually completes a diaper change without peeing on you or himself—give him some applause. And include "If You're Happy and You Know It" in your daily repertoire. Within the next few months he'll start clapping as soon as you begin the song:

> *If you're happy and you know it, clap your hands.*
> *If you're happy and you know it, clap your hands.*
> *If you're happy and you know it, then your face will surely show it.*
> *If you're happy and you know it, clap your hands.*
> (Then stomp your feet, shout "Hurray!"; do all three—you know the drill.)

Seven to Nine Months

"I'm telling you, Claire is going to be an architect just like her dad!" Blake called to Susie, who was working on the computer in the next room. "I've been stacking her soft blocks into little houses, and she can't take her eyes off them! The kid has an innate appreciation for good design!"

"Right," Susie called back, unfazed. "Or she's just waiting for you to get out of the way so she can knock them down."

Terrific Toys and Ideas to Engage Your Little Explorer

During this stage, your baby will be sitting independently, showing an increased attention span, and enjoying a new array of toys from his upright vantage point. He'll begin to knock down soft blocks, roll balls back and forth, manipulate the stacking rings, and play with small drums or shakers.

Expect him to be increasingly mobile—wriggling, scootching, squirming, and eventually crawling. He'll probably begin with a commando crawl. (Picture a soldier trying to stay out of view by dragging himself low to the ground across a field of battle. Then omit the fatigues. And the gunfire. And the field. And substitute your living room. It's kinda like that.) Then one day, your baby will unwittingly find himself up on his hands and knees in a real precrawl stance. Over time, he'll coordinate his upper and lower body movements—with a variety of cute little face plants along the way—and eventually you'll realize he just crawled from one end of the room to the other. And from that point on, nothing is ever the same.

He'll also be vocalizing a variety of new sounds, probably start clapping and waving, and begin holding small objects between his forefinger and thumb—an important developmental milestone called the pincer grasp. Reply to your baby's babble as if you're in a real conversation. (Him: "dadadadadada dadada da!" You: "Yes sweetie, I love that plastic frog too."). Engaging him verbally will encourage additional expression and help him learn the nuances of dialogue. You'll feel silly at first, but then you'll realize it's not that different from many conversations you've had at work. You're *so* in your element on this one.

Create an accessible kitchen drawer of plastic bowls and baby-safe utensils. Let your mini explorer "discover" the contents whenever he wants, and just throw the items back in the drawer at the end of the day. (Or if you're having a dinner party. Whichever comes first.) And offer any of the following:

- Soft stacking, sorting, and nesting toys
- Colorful interactive toys

- Simple musical instruments
- Puppets
- Balls
- Soft blocks

Age-Appropriate Activities for Seven- to Nine-Month-Olds

Sensorama

Remember when everything in the world was new to you? When a dew-drop or a shadow on the wall could keep you riveted for twenty minutes? When each new texture and taste was like a little universe revealing itself for the first time? Neither do I, but that's what's so fun about babies. We can marvel at their Zen-like ability to be in the moment, enjoying their fascination vicariously, and then put them down for naps so we can catch up on e-mail while listening to voice mail and pulling up our latest prerecorded shows on Tivo. Give your little Zen master food for thought—offer unique stimuli for all five senses. Rub his hands against objects with different textures. Look around your house for sources of unique sounds. Let him smell your shampoo, lick a cracker, and check out different shapes and colors. He'll love the stimulation and quality mom time.

Singsational Spider

Don't ask me how a water-logged spider became the hero of a children's song. There were some freaky folks penning children's tunes back in the day—let's just be thankful this one doesn't involve a cradle falling from a tree. You probably remember it from your childhood, and even in today's world of celebrity-voiced, computer-animated characters, kids continue to love our soggy little arachnid:

> *Itsy, bitsy spider went up the water spout.*
> Use your hands to make the climbing spider.
> *Down came the rain and washed the spider out*
> Move your fingers down and up to represent the rain,
> then throw them to the side to wash the spider away.
> *Up came the sun and dried out all the rain.*

Hold your hands above your head, making a circle to represent
the sun.
And the itsy bitsy spider went up the spout again.
Do that wacky hand spider one more time.

Here's a Game to Keep Your Baby in Stitches:
A Scavenger Hunt for Buttons and Switches

This is another one for the why-buy-toys-when-random-household-
items-are-just-as-riveting-to-your-child category. Babies and men have
one thing in common: an obsession with remote controls. For babies, this
obsession extends to anything with buttons to push: calculators, door-
bells, telephones, and elevators. Light switches have the same allure. Unless you're living in a high-rise, you probably don't have easy access to an
elevator, but you'll be amazed by how many buttons and switches there
are in your home. Carry your baby around and find them all. Let him
play with the remote control, press your doorbell, and flick the light
switches on and off in every room. Infants this age generally understand
cause-and-effect relationships, so this activity contributes to cognitive development as well. Your little one will be entertained, and you may find
that old calculator you haven't seen in years.

Shake It Up, Baby

Make your own shakers and then make some music. Pour uncooked rice
or Cheerios into a couple of sippy cups or small plastic containers with
lids. Give one to your baby and keep one yourself. Put on some music,
make sure your drapes are safely closed (no need to establish oneself as
an oddball neighbor), and start shaking your groove thang. The crazier
you get, the more your child will love it.

A Sign of the Times

If you're motivated, you can begin to introduce simple sign language
toward the end of this stage to help your baby communicate even before his verbal skills develop. This is not a busy parent requirement. I
never tried it myself, but I have some mom friends who found it fun,

so I wanted to give you the basics. Feel no pressure, but enjoy if you want to try.

Start by consistently using a few basic signs when interacting with your child. Those that can help him make requests are a great first step. Over time, he'll start to mimic the signs and then use them independently. This process often takes a few months, so don't be discouraged by his blank stares the first few weeks. And explain the signs you're using to your child care provider so she won't be stumped when your baby starts "asking" for things.

If you're intrigued, there are plenty of books, classes, websites, and DVDs on this topic. Signingbaby.com offers comprehensive guidance, and if you have a high-speed Internet connection, the video dictionary of signs at babyhandsproductions.com is very helpful. Here are a few baby-friendly signs to get you started:

More	close the fingertips of both hands and tap them together
All done	hold up closed fists, then open both hands outward to show nothing is there
Eat	close the fingertips of one hand and tap your lips
Drink	make a C shape with one hand and mimic raising a cup to your lips
All gone	blow across your open palm, as if it's now empty
Hat	tap your head
Ball	your hands mimic holding an imaginary ball
Hurt	tap the ends of your index fingers together
Book	your hands mimic a book being opened
Mommy	tap the thumb of one open hand against your chin
Daddy	tap the thumb of one open hand against your temple

Ten to Twelve Months

"Now, you *have* to admit she's an architectural prodigy," Blake exclaimed with pride. Claire, eleven months, was holding on to the edge of her activity table, assembling Legos along the top. "If you squint your eyes, those Legos almost look like buildings in a primary-colored urban landscape."

Terrific Toys and Ideas to Engage Your Supercruiser

Watch out, world, your baby is ready for action. He's on the move, most likely crawling, cruising, ascending stairs, standing independently, and possibly even walking by his first birthday. Introduce toys that make the most of his strength and mobility like pull-alongs, crawling tunnels, and activity tables. He's also manipulating increasingly complex objects—dropping balls into holes, fitting shapes into one another, and stacking blocks.

Your soon-to-be-toddler is probably pointing to things he wants and making funny faces and noises to elicit laughter from his favorite people. He's also able to understand easy requests. And after months of nonsensical babbling, he's likely using mama and dada intentionally and experimenting with specific sounds as early "words." (He earnestly looks at you from the high chair and says, "buh." You nod, smiling. Then he says it again. And again, with gusto. Finally you realize he's looking at the ball in the toy basket, and it all becomes clear. This time it isn't just random babble. "The ball!" you respond, having an actual conversation with this child who entered the world only months before. "You want the ball!" You hand it to him, his eyes light up, and there's no going back.)

This is a great stage for playtime. Enjoy it and remember to narrate your baby's activities aloud—he's soaking up every word you say like a two-foot-tall linguistic sponge. Sing goofy songs, crawl next to him on the floor, or put in your favorite CD, hold your baby's hands, and make like John Travolta circa *Saturday Night Fever*. All the hip jiggling without the white suit. Help build your little cruiser's balance and strength by supporting his hands and guiding him around the house. Your back may start to feel like it did when you were eight months pregnant, but remind yourself your baby's about to take his first steps away from you. Enjoy the finger-gripping phase while it lasts.

Your cruiser will love any of the following:

- Shape sorter
- Wooden blocks
- Action and response toys (e.g., jack-in-the-box)
- More complex interactive toys (dollhouses, toddler-size basketball hoops)
- Activity table
- Pull-along toys
- Crawling tunnels

Age-Appropriate Activities for Ten- to Twelve-Month-Olds

Tub O' Fun

There's nothing more exciting for the pretoddler set than putting small objects into containers and then pulling them out. There are lots of toys that capitalize on this skill, but you can create a free homemade version that's guaranteed to keep your child entertained. Pull out that inflatable infant tub your baby has outgrown and fill it with things from around your house—bath toys, board books, plastic spoons and bowls, a calculator, an old remote control with the batteries removed, measuring cups, or stuffed animals. If your child likes it, throw it in. He'll love pulling the objects out, crawling around with them, putting them back in and climbing into the tub himself. I put a tub of toys next to an activity center we had just gotten as a gift, and despite the activity center's groovy colors, bells, and whistles—my son spent twice as much time playing with the tub.

A Homemade Fort for the Cuddly and Short

The next time you open an oversize baby item in a box bigger than your child, try this one. Cut doorways in two opposite sides of the cardboard box to create a tunnel. On the inside, tape a large rectangle of aluminum foil so your baby can check himself out when he crawls inside. Add a few of his favorite toys or board books, and you're good to go. If you're one of those people who watches *Trading Spaces* for the do-it-yourself ideas rather than the hot carpenter, feel free to decorate the box more extensively and explain the whole process to your intrigued child. And just ignore your significant other when he walks in and offers, "So, you had a little too much time on your hands today, eh?"

No box on hand? Make a fort out of pillows from your couch. All the thrill from your baby's perspective, with no cardboard required.

Rice Up Your Life

Here's an easy one. Fill a big plastic bowl with uncooked rice, then dig into it with a small paper or plastic cup. Show your baby as you pour the rice into another cup, and then pass it on so he can play. He'll be fascinated by transferring the rice, sticking his hands in the bowl, and shaking the cups for added sound effects.

Foreign Language Fingers

Our babies benefit from listening to us talk. That much we know. And early exposure to foreign languages can't hurt—some even say it has lasting benefits. You could run out and invest in multilingual toys and DVDs or take the old-school approach: a little uno, dos, tres on your own. Just say, "Let's count to ten in [English, Spanish, or French]" and hold up your fingers while counting. Your child will have fun grabbing your fingers and listening to the sounds. If he actually learns something over time, that's always a bonus.

	Spanish		French	
	Word	Pronunciation	Word	Pronunciation
one	uno	sounds like it looks	un	uh
two	dos	dose	deux	dur
three	tres	trayz	trois	twa
four	cuatro	qua-tro	quatre	catra
five	cinco	sink-o	cinq	sank
six	seis	sayz	six	seez
seven	siete	see-eh-tay	sept	set
eight	ocho	sounds like it looks	huit	wheat
nine	nueve	new-eh-vay	neuf	sounds like it looks
ten	diez	dee-ez	dix	deese

Monkey Mania

First, a soggy spider and now bed-bouncing chimps. Go figure. At this stage, your baby can mimic and remember increasingly complex motions. Challenge him with this classic interactive poem:

Three little monkeys jumping on the bed
Bounce three fingers on your palm to represent the jumping monkeys.
One fell off and bumped her head
Gently pat your hand on your head.
Mama called the doctor
Talk into a pretend phone.
And the doctor said, "No more monkeys jumping on the bed!"
Shake finger and talk in deep voice.
Repeat for two monkeys and one monkey.

Babyville Basics: What Every New Parent Needs to Know

Year One Milestones, Infant Health, Childproofing, and Traveling with Your Tot

I recently attended a baby shower for some friends, Elizabeth and Michael—two attorneys expecting their first child the following month. During the shower we played a game. The expecting couple had to guess when most babies reach the major year one milestones—the first smile, the first word, the first rollover, the first step. We would see how much this highly educated twosome knew about typical infant development, how prepared they were for their impending trip to Babyville.

"Okay, Elizabeth," the host began, "When do babies usually sleep through the night?"

"Oh, I should know this," Elizabeth responded, realizing she had no idea. "Well, this may be optimistic, but I'll guess six weeks."

The new moms in the room exchanged knowing smiles. Another sucker. She had no idea what she was in for.

|•|

After years of focusing on school and career, you may be surprised by the steep learning curve in Babyville. If early parenthood feels strangely like freshman year, think of the baby basics in this chapter as the prerequisite courses. Learn when to expect those year one milestones—from the first smile to the first step. Get the lowdown on infant health, from well-baby visits to signs of sickness. Child-proof your home before your little one is mobile. And prepare to travel with baby in tow. Yes, it is possible.

Year One Milestones: The First Smile to the First Step

FROM:	Teresa Hernandez
TO:	Ellen Finnerty
SUBJECT:	**Impending motherhood panic setting in**

Due date two weeks away and starting to think recent obsession with perfectly color-coordinated nursery may be masking underlying fears about actual infant care. Paint and cute window treatments I can control, but what do I really know about babies?

P.S. Don't answer that question.

|•|

At some point before your child's arrival, your mad scramble for infant info begins. When should you expect that first real word? The first roll from back to front? The first giggle? Well, scramble no further.

Typical Year One Timing

Here are the major milestones in one handy chart. Preemies' development tracks with their due dates, not their birth dates.

Smiles	1 to 2 months
Makes cooing sounds	1 to 2 months
Laughs	2 to 3 months
Discovers hands	2 to 4 months
Sleeps through the night	3 to 6 months
Rolls over	4 to 5 months

Begins baby babbling with consonants	5 to 6 months
Sits up	6 to 7 months
Squirms around on tummy	6 to 8 months
Crawls	7 to 9 months
Stands with some support	7 to 9 months
Waves and claps	8 to 10 months
Pulls up	8 to 10 months
Cruises	9 to 11 months
Climbs stairs on hand and knees	9 to 11 months
Calls parents mama and dada	10 to 11 months
Uses specific sounds as early "words"	10 to 11 months
Stands independently	10 to 11 months
Says a few real words	12 to 15 months
Walks	12 to 15 months

Really Official Disclaimer: Milestones, Shmilestones

While it can be helpful to see the year one big picture, please don't take this timing too literally. Every baby follows her own developmental schedule, and charts like this are always based on averages. There is a wide range of normal for every milestone.

I realize that rational explanation flies out the window when your fifteen-month-old has yet to take a step and you're convinced she never will. But trust me on this one. It really doesn't matter if your child starts to walk "early" or "late" or right smack as expected. Same deal with rolling over and crawling and saying mama. It's a fun mystery unfolding before you, a miraculous series of tiny advancements. Your baby develops in barely recognizable increments, and one day you've got a toddler on your hands—walking and talking and

QUICK TIP FROM DR. NIED

Some perfectly healthy babies start crawling at eleven months and walking at fifteen or sixteen months. Some skip crawling altogether and one day just stand up and walk. And babies today often roll over later than babies in previous generations because they sleep on their backs. If you have any concerns about your child's development, however, just consult your pediatrician.

communicating very clear opinions. And at that point, you won't even re-member if she was an early roller or late crawler.

Well-Baby Visits, Vaccines, and Signs of Sickness Every Mom Should Know

From Shauna's journal:

New day care center is Germapalooza. Should start outfitting Jordan in a surgical mask. Probably wouldn't help his rep with the big kids, but if he stayed well for a few months I could actually return to the pediatrician's office without getting those snarky sidelong glances from the nursing staff. So worth it.

There are three health-related givens during your baby's first year: she will occasionally have weird tummy troubles; she will probably get at least one ear infection; and she will have a runny nose—many times. Plus, there are the inexplicable coughs, the inevitable tumbles, and the seven well-baby visits required during year one. I tell you this not to scare you but to prepare you. So when that first runny nose hits, you won't beat yourself up for taking your baby to the park without her hat or letting the cousins give her kisses. It's not your fault—just par for the course in Babyville.

QUICK TIP FROM DR. NIED

Try to keep your infant away from other children for the first six weeks and ask friends and family to wash their hands before holding her for at least the first two months. Then just do your best. The occasional sniffles are an inevitable part of childhood, and they're not entirely bad. Exposure to viruses actually helps strengthen your child's immune system by creating disease-fighting antibodies.

Well-Baby Visits

Well-baby visits are the fun part of year one health care. You arrive at the doctor's office with confidence, knowing your child is perfectly healthy (along with being perfect in general, but no need to flaunt the obvious). The nurses smile and your baby smiles back. The doctor whips out the measuring tape and gives you the stats—your child's ranking on the developmental bell curve. The immunizations are a clear low point from your infant's perspective, but she survives and you emerge from the examination room filled with pride. "This is my child! How great is she?" you would be announcing to everyone in earshot if it were socially acceptable. "Sure, she cried during the shots, but look at her now! What a comeback!" You head out the door feeling confirmed as parent. All is well in the world.

Schedule year one well-baby visits for:

- 1 to 2 weeks
- 4 weeks
- 2 months
- 4 months
- 6 months
- 9 months
- 12 months

At each of these visits, your pediatrician will:

- Provide an overall assessment of your baby's development
- Measure her length, weight, and head circumference
- Offer vaccines appropriate to that stage
- Allow you to ask questions

Sick Baby Visits

In addition to the well-baby visits, you may hit the pediatrician's office for the inevitable ear infections and

QUICK TIP FROM DR. NIED

The average child gets seven colds a year, and the average cold lasts two weeks. There is no way to prevent colds, although hand washing and avoiding secondhand smoke (either directly or on a caregiver's clothing or hair) will reduce the frequency. There is no cure for the common cold, and although there are many over-the-counter cold medications, I don't recommend them for children under one year. Most colds can be managed at home, although you should contact your pediatrician if your child is also experiencing high fever, difficulty breathing, ear tugging, or excessive coughing.

colds babies love to give one another. (At least they're learning to share, right?)

Recommended Year One Vaccines

Vaccines, while painful for your baby and you, are a fundamental part of year one health. The Academy of Pediatrics revises its recommended vaccine schedule annually, and we've included their guidelines at the time of publication. For updates, check with your pediatrician or the American Academy of Pediatrics' website at aap.org.

Recommended Vaccines:	Protects Against:	Recommended Month for Vaccine											
		1	2	3	4	5	6	7	8	9	10	11	12
Hepatitis B (HBV) There are two possible schedules:	Hepatitis B	x		x						x			
			x		x					x			
Haemophilus influenzae type B (Hib)	Pneumonia, meningitis, epiglottitis	x		x		x*							x (month 12–15)
Polio (IPV)	Polio	x		x					x				
Pneumococcal (PCV)	Pneumonia, meningitis, ear infections	x		x		x							x (month 12–15)
Diptheria, tetanus, and acellular pertussis (DTaP)	Diphtheria, whooping cough, tetanus	x		x		x							x (month 12–18)
Influenza, (the flu shot)	The flu						during flu season						

After twelve months of age, your child will also require vaccines to protect her from varicella (chicken pox), measles/mumps/rubella, and hepatitis A.

*A 6 month shot may or may not be needed, depending on the brand of vaccine.

How do vaccines protect your child? A pediatric nurse (or, in some practices, the physician herself) injects part of or an inactivated version of potentially threatening bacteria or viruses—like those that cause polio or chicken pox—into her thigh. Your child's immune system then goes to work, creating disease-fighting antibodies that will fight the actual disease if she's ever exposed.

When to Call the Pediatrician

Odds are, your baby won't suffer from anything worse than a cold. You should still be on the lookout, however, for symptoms that indicate serious illness. Call your pediatrician if your child has any of the following signs of sickness.

- A fever of 100.4°F or higher
- A significant reduction in appetite
- Persistent vomiting
- Tugging at her ears or experiencing a discharge from her ears
- Coughing and wheezing or breathing rapidly
- Unusual crabbiness, fatigue, or extended, inconsolable crying
- A runny nose that lasts more than two weeks
- Diarrhea with signs of dehydration (dry mouth, sunken eyes, decreased urination)
- A skin rash beyond a typical diaper rash

When to Quarantine Your Baby

Yes, I admit it. I have wiped my son's runny nose just as we were entering a play date with friends because I really needed to get out of the house. Am I proud of this? No. Am I the only one to bring a potentially

QUICK TIP FROM DR. NIED

Some parents worry about the association between the MMR vaccine and autism. Although one physician in the United Kingdom claimed there was a relationship, various studies since then have completely disproven his theory. In addition, there used to be concerns about thimerisol, a preservative containing mercury that prevented bacteria growth. But it's no longer used in these recommended vaccines. Although we rarely see vaccine-preventable diseases in the United States today, I strongly recommend following the full AAP vaccination schedule.

QUICK TIP FROM DR. NIED

If your child has *any fever* when she's less than two months old, call your pediatrician.

sick baby into public? I really doubt it. In my defense, he was cutting a new tooth at the time and I convinced myself teething was the benign cause of the runny nose. But I didn't know *for sure*.

The inevitable new mom question—when to keep your child home sick—is a highly personal one. Some parents keep their babies in for days if a single cough is detected; others tote their children around until they're too weak to emerge from the car seat. Once your maternity leave is over, child care complications can make that first sneeze even scarier. Using a baby-sitter? Simply ask her to keep your infant away from other children until she's cough-free. Using day care? Go with your gut and keep your baby home if she's clearly contagious. Hopefully you have a backup plan for days like these so you don't have to stealthily drop your little sniffler at the center door and high-tail it to your 9:00 A.M. meeting. Find an approach that feels comfortable for you, your child care provider, and the people with whom you'll be interacting.

QUICK TIP FROM DR. NIED

As a general rule, you should keep your child at home until speaking to your pediatrician if she has:

- A fever
- Vomited more than once in twenty-four hours
- Significant respiratory symptoms such as a consistent cough, wheezing, or difficulty breathing
- Severe diarrhea
- A pink or red eye associated with an eye discharge (which is likely conjunctivitis)

Childproofing: Scary Stairs, Wobbly Chairs, Renegade Dog Hairs, and More

"Kaiya? Where are you?" Migene walked down the hall, looking for her eleven-month-old daughter. She heard splashing around the corner. Then giggles. Not a good sign. She opened the bathroom door just in time to see her bundle of joy stuff a third roll of toilet paper into the overflowing toilet. Kaiya paused, looked up at her mother, and smiled.

|•|

Before you know it, your infant will be rolling, squirming, crawling, cruising, and toddling around your house. Make sure you've child-proofed before she's mobile.

Top 10 Childproofing Strategies for Your Home

1. If it can tip, attach it to the wall. Do a quick tour of your house and identify all freestanding bookshelves, dressers, and floor lamps. Any item your child could pull over should be fastened to a wall before the crawling stage hits. You can buy fasteners at most baby stores.

2. Look for potential poisons. Cleaning fluids, detergents, medicines, sunscreen, nail polish, lotions, paint—anything potentially hazardous to your child should be placed in a secure spot before she's on the move. Even childproof containers are actually just child resistant and should be stored in an unreachable cabinet.

3. Declutter. Your baby will soon be grabbing anything in reach—from picture frames to magazines. Plus, dozens of plants are toxic or poisonous if ingested by infants (including hydrangea, mistletoe, and holly), and dangling vines can be pulled down in an instant. Sadly, much of the cute stuff has to go. Move your favorite accessories and plants to visible but unreachable spots.

QUICK TIP FROM DR. NIED

Don't store products containing lye like liquid drain openers around the house. If you need to unclog a drain, purchase the liquid drain opener and then immediately dispose of any unused portion.

4. Install covers over all electrical outlets. Your child's little fingers will be reaching for these in no time. Cover them now and hide electrical cords behind the furniture or using hide-a-cord devices.

5. Secure curtains and miniblind cords. Babies love to play with dangling cords, but they're a serious strangulation hazard. You can buy cord pulls at any baby store.

6. Create a pet-only area.   Infants are inevitably drawn to pet food bowls, litter boxes, and fur-covered dog beds. Move pet stuff into a baby-free zone.

7. Install stair gates and window guards.   Stair gates need to be installed by the time your baby can crawl. They come in myriad varieties—from relatively cheap to seriously pricey, from permanent to pressure-mounted, from white to wood. And window guards are essential if you plan to open your windows during warmer months. Even with these guards, keep chairs and tables away from your windows—some children can climb before they can walk. Check your local baby store for options that meet your needs.

> **QUICK TIP FROM DR. NIED**
>
> If you live in an apartment above the first floor and have children under ten, you are legally required to have window guards.

8. Type out a list of emergency contact information.   Include your pediatrician, poison control (800-222-1222), police, fire department, health department, hospitals, gas company, and even helpful neighbors. Post one by all your phones.

9. Replace the batteries in your smoke alarms and carbon monoxide detectors. Batteries should be checked and potentially changed every three months, although most of us are lucky if we remember once a year. Do it now to create a safe environment for your child. Make sure you have smoke alarms and carbon monoxide detectors in every bedroom and purchase a fire extinguisher.

10. Know your home.   Make sure you know how to shut off the gas and water in case of emergency. Devise an escape route in the event of a fire. Look for lead-based paint. Check your water heater; it should be set so the maximum temperature is below 120°F. Do a thorough review so your home is safe and you're ready for anything.

The Kitchen

- When cooking, try to use the back burners. If this isn't possible, turn the pot handles toward the wall so little fingers are less likely to grab them.
- Use appliance latches on your refrigerator and oven, place knob covers on your stove, and plug in small appliances like blenders and food processors only when in use.
- Put child locks on all kitchen cabinets and secure sharp items like knives, forks, and cheese graters; breakables like glasses, ceramic cookware and china; kitchen cleaners and dishwashing detergent.
- Put your trash can in a cupboard or use a child-resistant lid.
- Don't use a tablecloth or runner that can be pulled down.
- Don't place containers of hot beverages on counter or table edges and never pick one up while holding your baby. Her little arms can flail into your coffee mug in a millisecond.

The Bathrooms

- Baby-proof your tub. Put a soft cover over the faucet, use a baby mat during baths, put a cover on the knobs, and make sure your water temperature isn't too hot.
- Put a child lock on all cabinets to secure hair dryers, toiletries, razors, makeup, nail polish, and cleaning supplies.
- Install a baby lock on your toilet and keep the lid down.
- Plug in hair dryers, flat irons, and other electrical items only during use.
- You may need to keep toilet paper rolls on a shelf instead of the dispenser. Many babies are convinced these are their personal rolls-o'-fun and pull the paper out, stuffing it into the toilet or even their mouths.
- Gather all necessary supplies before baths, and don't leave your baby in the bathtub even for a split second to grab a towel.
- Keep the bathroom door closed to prevent your baby from exploring this hazardous area.

The Living Room

- Babyproof your fireplace using a hearth pad or gate and avoid making fires while your baby is in the room.
- Cover the edges of your coffee table.
- Make sure curtains and miniblinds are out of your baby's reach.
- Secure any standing lamps or furniture that could be pulled over.
- Put away accessories.

The Nursery

- Make sure your crib is baby-safe. Crib slats should be two and a quarter inches apart or less. The mattress should be firm and fit tightly in the crib to prevent little fingers from getting wedged in the gap. Never put soft bedding, pillows, or blankets in the crib with your infant. Remove the mobile when your baby can pull it or when she's on her hands and knees. Remember to drop the mattress to the lowest setting and remove the crib bumper as soon as your child pulls to a stand. And check for dangling cords or heavy objects your little one could grab from the crib.
- Create a safe diaper-changing space. If you're using a changing table, the pad should be secure and you should always use the strap. Never leave your child on the table, even for a moment to grab a new diaper. Keep sharp objects out of your baby's reach and consider putting a thick rug under the table in case she falls.
- Secure any standing lamps or furniture that could be pulled over.
- Make sure your toy chest lid can be opened and closed without pinching your child's fingers.
- Use a doorstop to protect little fingers.
- Don't put out toys with buttons, eyes, or beads that can be pulled off and swallowed.
- Install a smoke alarm in the nursery.

And If You're Lucky Enough to Have a Pool or Pond

Consider enclosing it with a fence. (Not the most scenic addition to your family oasis, but beautifully baby-safe.)

Flying the Not-So-Baby-Friendly Skies

From Evelyn's journal:

> *Tomorrow: Flight home. By myself. With Jack and a couple hundred*
> *unsuspecting passengers. The kid won't sit still for five minutes—how is he*
> *going to last on an airplane for five hours? And I used to think business*
> *travel was stressful.*

Considering a plane trip with your tot? Follow these parent-tested tips for relatively painless flights, even with baby-on-board.

Try to Wait Until Your Infant Is At Least Three Months Old

When your little one hits three months, you're ready for the runway. Why wait? Because crowded environments like planes increase your infant's exposure to germs. Between months three and six, there are a few things on your side: Your car seat is part of your stroller (easier to lug around); your baby doesn't require lunch; and if you're still breast-feeding, you don't even have to shlep bottles. Keep in mind, your child should be at least six months old before international travel requiring immunizations. (So much for that family safari you were planning two months after giving birth.)

Play That New Parent Game of Chicken; Buy a Seat for Your Baby or Gamble for a Free, Open Seat When You Check In

Here's the good news: Children under two fly free if you hold them during the flight. That's right, the new parent budget at last gets a break. Here's the less good news: Although you're not required to secure a seat for your baby, you should anyway. Airline turbulence has done serious harm to children being held on parents' laps. A car seat strapped into the seat next to you is your baby's safest bet. In fact, given the risks to babies and toddlers flying car seat-free, the Federal Aviation Commission considered *requiring* a restraint system for children under two. However, in a fascinating study, researchers predicted this would lead to increased child fatalities because more families would choose to drive if required to buy the extra plane seat, and driving continues to be more dangerous than flying.[1]

Most major airlines will offer half-price tickets for children under two so you can buy a seat in advance. Or ask about the likelihood of unsold seats when booking your flight. If there are open seats, the flight attendants will generally let you nab one for baby's car seat during check-in. And at that point there's no charge. Increase your chances for a free open seat by flying off-peak days and times.

Enjoy the VIP Treatment

What to expect once you get to the gate for your baby's first flight? Initially, after a lifetime of waiting in tedious airport lines, you realize you finally qualify for preboarding. Forget going into politics or winning an Oscar—you get the VIP treatment just because you're a mom. You stand proudly in the preboarding area next to that equally lucky retired school-teacher in the wheelchair and try not to gloat.

Channel Your Inner Pack Mule

Then the flight attendant calls for preboarding to begin, and it hits you. Entering first is only a luxury when you can actually *enter*. You have a baby, a car seat, a stroller, a diaper bag bursting at the seams and a second carry-on you packed in a moment of insanity. If you're traveling with another adult, you can split the load, channel your inner pack mule, and drag your belongings slowly onto the plane—leaving your stroller with the flight attendant just as you board. Or one of you can head in first, claim a baby-friendly row, set up the car seat, and fill the seat back pockets with entertainment essentials while the other stays at the gate so your baby can bounce, squirm, crawl, or toddle around until the last minute.

If you're traveling solo, immediately make eye contact with the most sympathetic-looking flight attendant at your gate. She may try to look away or stare desperately at her computer screen, but you've gotten this far with your infant and her assorted gear—will power streams through your veins like iron-fortified formula through a plastic stage 4 nipple. She has no chance. Eventually she will give in, acknowledge your plight, and offer assistance.

Let the Games Begin

You're on the plane. Your baby is safely strapped into a car seat beside you and if it's a particularly good day, that seat was even free. All your infant paraphernalia is jammed into the various required spots, and the stroller is safely below deck. You wipe the sweat from your forehead, lean back, and close your eyes with a sigh of relief. You did it.

Then a siren-like wail emerges from your left. You instinctively cop a who's-letting-her-kid-cry-on-an-airplane attitude, until you realize that kid is yours. In a nanosecond, you open your eyes, lunge for the screaming baby, and apologize to the fifty-year-old businessman on your right. And this is when things really get fun.

To survive a flight with an infant, you need the essentials. These vary in specifics depending on your baby's age, but generally include:

1. Small, but highly engaging toys
2. Small, but highly engaging board books
3. Small, but really delicious age-appropriate snacks (if your baby is eating solids)
4. Lots of liquid (i.e., breast, bottles, or sippy cup)

Your goal during the next few hours is to use these items to entertain, distract, occupy, hydrate, and feed your baby.

Ideally your child will drift off at some point, or if you've got a crawler or cruiser who's fighting the seat, you could try a lap or two down the aisle. No, crawling down an airplane aisle isn't the most sanitary thing your baby's ever done, but desperate measures

> **QUICK TIP FROM DR. NIED**
>
> If you've introduced bottles, offer one during takeoff and descent. Swallowing will minimize your baby's ear pressure and subsequent fussiness. Although I recommend using a car seat, you could also breast-feed during these times if your child is not restrained. And while I normally don't recommend TV or videos for children under two, extreme situations require creative parental solutions. If you have a portable DVD player, you could give it a try. Good luck!

are justified. When she's strapped back in her seat, douse her hands and face with antibacterial baby wipes, and she's good to go. If her fussiness continues despite your best efforts, just ignore the dirty looks coming your way and focus on your destination. And keep your eye on that sympathetic flight attendant. You'll need her again when you hit the ground.

Road Trips

FROM:	**Nirali Kella**
TO:	**Kim Gillespie**
SUBJECT:	**What I did on my Memorial Day vacation**

Let me set the scene. It was midnight. And pouring down rain. And we were pulled over at a rest stop in the middle of nowhere. I'm not talking about one of those shiny new rest stops with varied global cuisine, family bathrooms, and a Starbucks. This was an old-school rest stop—the type where beef jerky is the featured food and tiny ceramic cats are considered viable merchandise. There I sat in the dark backseat of our car—wedged between the car seat and piled high suitcases, attempting to breast-feed my overtired child as the rain poured down around us. And I just kept thinking: Remember when a road trip sounded fun?

Given the hassles of flying with an infant, many new parents opt for the somewhat simpler road trip approach. Try these tips to minimize bumps on the road with a baby.

Give Your Baby a Backseat Buddy

You're twelve weeks old, and you're strapped into a car seat facing backward. You can't see Mom or Dad; you can't access a food source; you can't even roll over. Understandably, you're not psyched. Make your baby's travel experience more tolerable by giving her a companion. If you're traveling solo, this is obviously not an option. Belt out your best rendition of "Itsy Bitsy Spider" from the front seat (minus the hand movements unless you're a professional stunt driver), bring a few baby-friendly CDs, and plan for lots of stops.

If you're lucky enough to have an unwitting adult travel companion, send him to the backseat. It's time for zone defense. A playmate will extend the time between required breaks and dramatically improve your baby's travel attitude. Equip the guy in the back with several bags full of toys, books, snacks, and bottles. And when the toys get old, he should be ready to sing your baby's favorite songs, play "This Little Piggy," make funny faces—whatever it takes. And incrementally switch places. A bitter backseat buddy is never a good thing.

Take a Red-Eye Drive

Consider driving overnight so your baby sleeps the whole way. This approach requires planning—there's no time for delay or you'll have a crabby, overtired infant on your hands. Your car should be packed and gassed up in advance. Then follow your baby's typical nighttime routine, place her in the car seat instead of the crib, recite a silent prayer to the gods of travel, and hope for the best. Your little one may slide into a sweet slumber as you pull away, or she may be stimulated by the unexpected night drive. Consider your child's personality and make the call.

Leverage Naps

If you prefer daytime drives, try taking off just before your baby's nap. She should drift off quickly, and there's nothing better than an hour or two of complete silence to start your trip. Plan on making a stop when she wakes up for a diaper change and snack.

Build in Time for Breaks

Unless you're opting for the red-eye approach, road trips take longer with kids. While you can tolerate five hours on the road without any real breaks, your baby can't. Newborns need time out of the seat to snuggle, get a diaper change, take a liquid feeding, and stretch. Older babies need breaks to squirm, snack, and let off steam. Plan to stop at least every two hours and watch for signs of earlier burnout.

Baby Geniuses

The Hype, the Mozart Effect, and Real Strategies
for Nurturing Your Baby's Intellectual Curiosity

FROM:	**Kirsten McDermott**
TO:	**Shelby Coe**
SUBJECT:	**Update from Steve's Learning Land**

I knew Steve would want the twins to go to Brown, but this is ridiculous. He came home a few weeks ago with the entire line of Baby Einstein videos, muttering something about offering the best visual and auditory stimulation possible. Like the world suffers from a real lack of visual stimulation otherwise. He has Madeline completely hooked on Baby Beethoven, and he actually said these words last night: "I can tell she has a real ear for classical music. How early do you think we can start piano lessons?" And the kid can't even drink out of a sippy cup.

Visit soon. And help me bring some sanity to this loony bin.

How about your own baby Einstein? Sounds pretty good, right? Of course we all want clever kids, but today's educational toy, CD, and DVD manufacturers have flooded the market with baby genius hype. Get the facts on early brain development, educational toys, and the Mozart Effect—plus ten strategies for nurturing your baby's intellectual curiosity.

Your Baby's Mind Boggling Brain and
Why the First Three Years Are Critical

"She definitely has your eyes."

"I know, but let's hope she got your math mind. I'd hate to pass on my fear of fractions."

|•|

The debate used to be nature versus nurture. Do genetics or environmental factors, researchers asked, shape personality and intellect? Today, child development experts consider that question obsolete; we now know these two elements are the yin and yang of parental influence.[1] Your child is born with a predisposition for personality traits—from calmness to volatility, from optimism to depression, from independence to shyness. Even musical and artistic abilities begin with good genes. But these traits and intelligence can be significantly influenced by nurturing relationships. Your child may have inherited your temper, but you can help him learn to manage it. He may have a natural gift for language, and you can inspire his intellectual enthusiasm. Genetics lays the foundation, but from the day your baby is born, you help to shape his personality and mind.

This is powerful stuff. When we were born, common wisdom held education begins with school. Our parents were expected to feed us, bathe us, and treat us kindly, but boosting baby brain power wasn't even on the radar screen of cultural consciousness. There was no Baby Einstein then. But over the past few

QUICK TIP FROM DR. NIED

During the first three years of life, your baby's brain develops at an astounding pace—growing from 25 percent to 90 percent of the average adult brain size. This growth is driven by expanding brain cells and miles of neural circuits being established based on sensory stimuli. You may think your infant is staring blankly at your face, but this visual experience is creating fundamental neural connections. Everything he sees, hears, touches, smells, or tastes adds structure to his evolving brain.

decades, breakthroughs in neuroscience have changed the way we think about the brain. Now we know real education essentially begins at birth. Your child's relationships and stimulation during the first three years of life largely define his brain's potential—hardwiring his mind for a lifetime of learning. And here's the good news: It's easy.

The drive to explore and understand is innate; you can see that in any infant learning to roll over or crawl. Your baby's need to satisfy his curiosity is as real as his need for food and sleep. He's years away from dreaded homework and boring classes; at this stage, everything is new, fascinating, and an exciting opportunity to know more. Engage your child with enthusiasm and lots of unstructured, imaginative playtime. By creating an environment of loving support and allowing his personality to evolve naturally, you're doing everything right. And while the first thirty-six months are important, don't hang up the proverbial teaching towel the day your child hits four. Share his passion for discovery at every age, and you'll set the stage for a lifetime of happy learning.

Baby Genius Hype: Developmental Toys, the Mozart Effect, and More

"A Learning Friends phonics bus?" Andrew read aloud, standing in the toy store aisle. "Is this supposed to be a toy?"

"I was going to ask you the same thing about this geometric sorting board. And the Alphabet Pal. And the PowerTouch Learning System."

"This stuff sounds about as fun as playtime in physics class."

"Wait, here's the Laugh and Learn Learning Phone. That could be entertaining."

"They actually put both 'learn' *and* 'learning' in the name? Sounds like a real blast."

The Wild World of Developmental Toys

At the foundation is a perfect storm of social pressure and scientific progress. Colleges and universities are riding a decade-long wave of increasing applications, driving up the standards for new applicants across the country.² But rising to the challenge is at the heart of American culture, and the academic game is on. Not just in high school; in light of our newfound respect for early brain development, it seems it's never too soon to seek an educational edge for your child. Brand-new parents scramble to buy houses in the better school districts. Preschool acceptances feel like the NFL draft. And foreign language classes are offered for toddlers at $30 an hour. This hyperemphasis on structured early education has a natural next step: baby toys that teach not passively, but dynamically with classical bells and multilingual whistles so everyone in the room knows Junior is Learning Something Important. We all want the best for our kids, and a little knowledge about infant cognitive development can be a dangerous thing in a culture that sells high-tech solutions for every human need.

Conveniently, today's science makes developmental toys possible. As speech synthesis technology sharpens and microchips shrink, manufacturers can build increasingly sophisticated electronic playthings. Rather than just looking at alphabet blocks, your ten-month-old can press buttons on an alphabet bus and hear each letter pronounced by a computer-generated voice. But does that mean he's learning more? And, more importantly, what happened to toys just being fun?

It's not just a ball anymore—it's a Discovery Ball and it plays twenty-six melodies, flashes lights to the beat, and says the alphabet on demand. Forget baby bongos. You can now give your child a Learning Drum that utters numbers, letters, or "a traditional drum sound." Even toys that promise actual entertainment also come with a cognitive slant—from Elmo's Sing & Teach Table to the Laugh & Learn Learning Puppy. Many of today's toy brands sound like they're straight out of a required curriculum—from Learning Curve to IQ Baby—and whether you're picking up a Multisensory Clutch Cube or a Learning Friend Lily, the message is clear: Toys, even for infants, are not just for kicks anymore.

Deciphering Baby Genius Speak

Baby Counting Pal Plush by LeapFrog, manufacturer's description: "This soft learning pal is truly a multi-sensory learning experience with tons of activities for baby to touch, hear and see! With four modes of play, this pal musically introduces counting and colors, while offering a variety of different classical tunes. The Baby Counting Pal also offers an assortment of tactile activities." For ages three months and up.[3]

Translation: Your three-month-old is about as likely to understand counting as he is to stand up and speak fluent Swahili. But if you're lucky, the dangling attachments will keep him distracted long enough for you to fit in a four-minute shower.

Toy manufacturers have mastered the language to close the deal with parents looking for early intellectual stimulation. Even infant playthings are often categorized by learning values from math and language skills to logic, and the most basic baby items are marketed to feel like essential stimulation for any child on the pre-pre-pre-college track. The key: to read between the developmental lines and assess a product for what it truly offers you and your baby.

Do Developmental Toys Really Work?

Today's educational toys are the shiny, loud overachievers in the world of childhood playthings. Do they engage children? You bet. They capitalize on innate behaviors (kids love buttons, they got buttons!), require inter-action, and stimulate multiple senses—all important elements in the learning process. But is there evidence they facilitate infants' cognitive growth better than board books and soft blocks? No, says Dr. Judy French, chair of early childhood studies at Boise State University and former pres-ident of the state's Association for the Education of Young Children.

According to Dr. French, toy makers have exploited the interest in early brain research, flooding the market with "educational" products while the real child development applications are commonsense interpersonal strate-gies: Hold and talk to your baby as often as possible. Build on his natural cu-riosity. Make him feel safe and comfortable exploring the world. The major headline at a recent early learning conference session on brain research? It's the relationship, stupid. A compelling reminder in an environment of high-tech gadgetry promising to stimulate your little guy out the wazoo.

Some small-scale studies have demonstrated improvements in early literacy among school-age children using interactive learning tools in the classroom environment.[4] And additional large-scale research, partly funded by the U.S. Department of Education, is being conducted.[5] But does that alphabet-singing pull-along caterpillar warrant the supersize price tag for your twelve-month-old? It's your call. If the beeping antennas crack him up, go for it. Just know as you applaud his attempts to drag it along, your enthusiasm is more valuable than the synthesized ABCs.

QUICK TIP FROM DR. NIED

A caregiver sitting on the floor playing "Itsy Bitsy Spider" is more stimulating than any educational product, and simple wooden toys or household items like plastic bowls can be just as effective to teach motor skills, spatial relationships, and independent play. Developmental toys can be a fun supplement to your baby's playtime, but don't overemphasize these products or expect them to give your child an intellectual inside track.

Demystifying the Mozart Effect

The Mozart Effect. Catchy, isn't it? Could be the sequel to *The Da Vinci Code* or the next Tom Cruise flick. Actually, it's an urban myth of motherhood. The real Mozart Effect originated with a 1993 study at the University of California–Irvine. The researchers gave college students, not babies, spatial reasoning problems from a standard IQ test after (1) ten minutes listening to Mozart's Sonata for Two Pianos in D Major, (2) ten minutes with a nonmusical relaxation tape, and (3) ten minutes waiting in silence. The students performed best after listening to Mozart.[6] And that's what the hoopla's all about.

Even the researchers acknowledged that the positive effect on spatial reasoning didn't last past fifteen minutes, and the findings have been hotly debated ever since. Academics have tested Mozart and other forms of music in various contexts, with mixed results. The original Mozart Effect has not been consistently replicated; a team from Appalachian State University attempted to replicate the initial study and found Mozart music had no statistically significant effect.[7] And some researchers believe the original test score improvements could be attributed to arousal or improved mood rather than enhanced reasoning.[8]

Despite the short-term and limited positive effect in the original study and the ongoing controversy within the scientific community, news of a potential IQ optimizer spread through the generation of parents burdened with baby brain boosting like a bad Internet virus. A cottage industry evolved around media coverage and marketing hype, and the governor of Georgia proclaimed all newborns in his state would receive classical CDs. Many parents now honestly believe classical music ranks up there with rice cereal as a year one essential. Mozart music makes babies smarter, the myth goes, despite the lack of conclusive evidence.

But now you know the facts, so don't feel guilty if you haven't been playing classical CDs since your child was able to hear in utero.

We all know music can be stimulating, relaxing, joyful, and inspiring—and a home filled with beautiful sound is enriching for everyone. Play music whenever you're in the mood, but don't expect it to be your baby's golden key to the Ivy League.

Ten Real Strategies for Nurturing Your Baby's Intellectual Curiosity

From Hallie's journal:

> There I stood in the grocery store, talking to Justin about the broccoli in sing-songy falsetto, when my old client Chuck tapped me on the shoulder. The man once trusted me with critical business decisions, and now he catches me waving broccoli around like Emeril Lagasse and trying to engage a three-month-old with a titillating ode to produce. Not my coolest moment, but at least Justin was learning something.

How to nurture a clever kid? Get back to the basics:

Come On, Get Chatty

Yes, at first it seems a little weird spending days on end talking to a non-speaking child. You may feel self-conscious. You may feel silly. You may occasionally feel like that crazy guy at the bus stop who's always chatting with himself. But it's all worth it. Your child's verbal development is directly related to the *quantity* and *quality* of what you and your caregiver say to him. Janellen Huttenlocher, Ph.D., a psychologist at the University of Chicago, found compelling relationships between (1) the *amount* of parent speech and children's early vocabulary growth[9] and (2) the *complexity* of parent speech and children's mastery of multiclause sentences.[10] In other words, talk to your child a lot and don't always dumb it down just because he can't respond.

> **QUICK TIP FROM DR. NIED**
>
> Feel free to use the enthusiastic, sing-songy tone parents often employ naturally with babies. Studies have shown this animated vocal style engages infants more effectively than a typical adult speaking tone.

Pay attention to your interactions with your baby over the next few days. He can't start a conversation with you, and it's easy to let your mind wander as you change his diaper, make breakfast, or drive to day care. But these are perfect moments to engage him. Get in the habit of verbalizing your thoughts, no matter how random. Your baby will benefit even from listening to you chat about your plans for the day during your morning drive.

Stop, Look, and Listen

It's easy to write off your baby's babble as nonsensical ramblings, but responding with respect can help build confidence, encourage communication, and expand his vocabulary. When he "speaks," try to stop what you're doing, turn to him, and really listen. Nod, make eye contact, and act as you would in a conversation with an adult. When he's finished, respond to extend the dialogue.

> **QUICK TIP FROM DR. NIED**
>
> If your eleven-month-old is pointing to his bottle and saying "ba-ba," you could either make a game out of mimicking his sounds back to him or respond by explaining, "So, you want your bottle. You must be thirsty. Let me fill it up and you can have a drink." Your baby's comprehension will far outpace his verbal skills, and your words will sink in before you realize it.

Don't Let Squirming Squelch Storytime

Your nine-month-old won't sit still long enough to get through a single book. What do you do? Wrestle him to the ground, maniacally shouting Dr. Seuss rhymes across the nursery? Be patient, don't force it, and continue to introduce stories before naps and bedtime. Sometimes he'll be interested, sometimes not. You might need to get creative. I learned if I let my supersquirmer stand, hold on to my legs, and bounce while I was reading, I could actually keep his attention (at least for a few extra minutes). Grabbers can often be neutralized by letting them hold one book while you read another, and you could always read aloud while your baby plays next to you on the floor. Start with cloth or board books that can withstand baby tugs and mouthing, and keep the story time going as long as your child remains (at least partially) engaged.

Don't Be a Tube Boob

Like Haagen-Daaz and overpriced shoes, TV sucks us in despite all rational arguments against it. We know prime-time reality shows make even soap operas look like high drama, yet somehow we can't look away as Random Successful Beefcake We'll Never Meet In Our Lives deliberates among potential mates. But that's us. With our children, we can take the high road.

The American Academy of Pediatrics recommends no screen time for kids under two.[11] Zilch. Zippo. So much for that Baby Einstein video. And that's part of the challenge—the AAP's thoughtful guidelines have essentially been trampled beneath the stampede of DVD, video, and television producers marketing electronic media for infants and toddlers. What's a parent to think? Every baby store on the planet has dozens of "educational" offerings, and PBS's *Teletubbies* clearly isn't for third graders. You almost feel guilty if you *don't* buy that Brainy Baby DVD, like you're keeping your child from reaching his true genius potential to save $19.99. We live in a world where the marketplace has trumped the AAP's message—the sheer magnitude of electronic options for infants implies it must be right. But it's not.

Which brings us to the million dollar question: Is the AAP recommendation realistic? That depends on your version of reality. My sister hasn't owned a TV in years, so it's very realistic for her and the three people like her in the civilized world. For the rest of us, there is temptation. And it's very tempting temptation. It's Sunday afternoon, you spent the morning with your eleven-month-old child, and now you really need to pay the bills. Or run downstairs and do the laundry. Or assemble and sign several dozen holiday cards. Something that's a lot easier to accomplish when your baby is occupied. You look at the stack of bills; you look at your child, and you look at that Baby Da Vinci DVD on the shelf. "It's educational!" you say to yourself, slipping it in and running to the bills before that nagging guilt in the back of your mind starts to get annoying.

Bottom line, an occasional Baby Da Vinci DVD will not turn your child into an electronics junkie. But while he's watching television, he's not using his imagination, manipulating objects, or making choices, and these are all integral elements of childhood learning. In a perfect world, you should sit there and chat with your child about that freaky dragon puppet and the bouncing shapes on the screen—incorporating the DVD within the context of dynamic interaction. (So much for those bills.) And like everything tempting, TV should only be used in moderation. Despite the AAP guideline, kids under two in our country spend an average of *two hours daily* in front of a screen, and 26 percent have TVs *in their bedrooms*.[12] And that's just sad. This year, try to use the tube only as an occasional last resort, not as a regular habit, and give your baby all the attention in the world. Just please don't give him a private media center.

> **QUICK TIP FROM DR. NIED**
>
> Don't allow inappropriate TV content to air while your baby is in the room, even if he seems to be otherwise engaged. Your child absorbs everything he sees and hears, and these days prime-time programming, news coverage, and even commercials offer far too much violence and confusing imagery for little brains to process.

Have Realistic Expectations

Learn about infant development now, so you can introduce appropriate activities, build your child's confidence, and save yourself some frustration.

I remember my relief when I learned babies drop things from their high chairs out of curiosity, not rebellion. Because I promise you, it'll seem like warfare until you know the truth. Similarly, no matter how hard you try, your ten-month-old will never grasp the concept of sharing. Don't sweat it and don't waste time disciplining him when he nonchalantly rips a teddy bear out of another child's hands. Gently return the bear and redirect his behavior. You can explain, "We don't take toys, sweetie; we share." But don't expect your words to sink in, and don't lose it when he heads right back for the bear. He's simply too young to get it. Get the scoop on age-appropriate activities in Chapter 16.

Encourage Repetition

I can tell you now, you will probably grow to hate *Pat the Bunny*. And as a mature adult, you will stifle your urge to scream "Nooooo!" as your eleven-month-old eagerly points to it for the hundredth time. But what seems boring to you is ideal intellectual stimulation for your baby. Children thrive on repetition. It gives them the opportunity to establish mastery over objects and information. Each time your child repeats an activity, he's building fundamental neural connections. So, rotate between six or seven favorite books, repeat the same silly games every day, and enjoy your child's expanding confidence.

Get Down Tonight (And Tomorrow and the Next Day)

One of the most common mistakes new parents make? Failing to get down on the floor and play like a kid, according to pediatric speech language pathologist Karen Pieters. Many of her clients feel self-conscious or just plain silly crawling around with their babies or lying on the rug building soft blocks. But this interaction is fundamental to infant learning and verbal development. To truly engage your child, join him at floor level, inspire him with multisensory fun, and explore the world through his eyes.

Pull Out the Pom-Poms

Infants are pure, unrestrained emotion. There's no harbored resentment, no embarrassment at Dad's dorky taste in shoes, no complex sibling rivalries to muddy the emotional waters. The need for enthusiastic parental support is obvious. Your baby will beam with pride as he stacks his rings or crawls across the room for the first time. But the effects of your praise go beyond his immediate happiness. Your enthusiasm reinforces the neural connections that motivate your child to try new things. And by trying new things, he expands his knowledge base. Be your child's cheerleader now, and you'll have even more to cheer about as he gets older.

> **QUICK TIP FROM DR. NIED**
>
> Your positive feedback will motivate your child to explore and show off his skills. Clap your hands and say, "Yeah!" even for his smallest accomplishments.

Get Great Care

A consistent, loving caregiver creates a context of security that allows your child to seek out and process new experiences. And, believe it or not, it's also good for his brain. The infant–caregiver bond facilitates healthy neural connections, literally shaping his brain structure. Find a child care provider who seems genuinely engaged with your infant—a day care center staff or baby-sitter who will talk to him consistently, introduce stimulating activities, and offer enthusiastic support for his explorations. Ask about center turnover or potential babysitters' long-term plans. Look for a child care environment, if not your home, that's stimulating and comfortable. Day care

> **QUICK TIP FROM DR. NIED**
>
> While it's always difficult to leave your child in someone else's care, take solace in the fact that your caregiver will have different techniques for stimulating your baby—introducing her own favorite songs, games, and activities and ultimately broadening his early experience.

centers with enriching environments and a trained staff that consistently focuses on early learning can offer excellent stimulation for babies and toddlers. The key is finding one that meets this high standard.

Follow the Pint-Size Leader

Offer guidance when your baby tries to crawl head-first down the stairs. During playtime, let him set the ground rules. Introduce activities or toys if you like, but always be open to rejection. Your child's curiosity is boundless. He may become transfixed by the remote control one minute and obsessed with the pile of clean socks the next. Assuming the objects of his attention are safe, simply help him explore the world.

QUICK TIP FROM DR. NIED

Even as an infant, your baby will tell you what interests him and what doesn't. Smiles, laughter, and direct eye contact give you the go-ahead. Darting eyes and squirming indicate boredom. Once your child is mobile, there's no question about his preferences. He'll roll, crawl, cruise, or walk over to objects of interest. And before you know it, he'll be carrying toys to you and waiting eagerly to play.

Conclusion

Next Step Toddlerville
(And You Thought This Year Was Wacky)

That's it! I wish you all the best as you make your way through Babyville. And I hope this book has helped you feel even more confident and supported as a mom. Feel free to send me your thoughts about the book, your life parenting experience, or anything else you feel like sharing (in care of Da Capo Press, 11 Cambridge Center, Cambridge, MA 02142).

Enjoy this year and get ready for Toddlerville—the land of walking, talking little people whose emotional range make postpartum moms look freakishly even-keeled. Yes, the fun has only begun . . .

Appendix A

Your New Baby Shopping List:
The Stuff You Really Need

How to wade through the baby gear ads and options to pinpoint what you actually need? Here's a quick guide. It's designed to be pulled out and kept in your purse while you're shopping so you can check things off as you go.

NURSERY

Essential:
- ☐ Crib (no more than 2¼ inches between slats)
- ☐ Fitted crib sheets (2—between spit-up and leaky diapers, you'll use both)
- ☐ Waterproof crib mattress (tight enough so two fingers can't fit between the mattress and crib)
- ☐ Storage for baby clothes and gear (closet, dresser, or armoire)
- ☐ Receiving blankets (3 to 5, great for swaddling at first and then as blankies)
- ☐ Baby monitor (not needed in small apartments or homes where you can hear your baby from every room)

Nice to have:
- ☐ Changing table (money-saving alternative: change your baby on your bed)
- ☐ Changing pad and cover (for your changing table or secured on top of a dresser)
- ☐ Colorful mobile (the more engaging, the better)
- ☐ Supportive rocker or chair for feedings

CLOTHES FOR YEAR ONE

Essential:
Items needed for each stage: birth to three months, three to six months, six to nine months, and nine to twelve months

- ☐ Pajamas/sleepers—ideally, footed pj's during cooler seasons to minimize wrestling with baby socks that always pop off (3 to 6 per stage)
- ☐ Onesies—to wear alone or layer for extra warmth, short-sleeve or long-sleeve depending on the season (3 to 6 per stage)
- ☐ Soft tops and bottoms for daytime (4 to 6 per stage after the first few months—initially, pj's and/or onesies are fine all day)
- ☐ Cotton hats (1 to 2 for stage one—birth to three months—and during cooler seasons)
- ☐ Socks (3 to 6 pairs per stage)
- ☐ Sleep sack; highly recommended once your infant outgrows swaddling, a sleeveless zip-front sack that's zipped over his pajamas or onesie to keep him cozy while sleeping without putting him at risk for SIDS

For winter months, depending on your climate:
- ☐ Sweaters (1 to 3)
- ☐ Fleece bunting or snowsuit (a fleece, zip-up lining for the infant carrier is also handy)
- ☐ Warm hat

For summer months:
- ☐ Bathing suit, baby sunglasses, and sun hat

Nice to have:
- ☐ So-cute-you-could-die baby outfits (but keep in mind, dresses get seriously tangled up in babies' knees during the squirming and crawling stage, usually between seven and eleven months)

DIAPERING
Essential:
- ☐ Disposable diapers (45 to 60+ per week—no, I'm not kidding) or cloth diapers (24 to 36+ total, depending on your tolerance for washing them)
- ☐ Diaper wipes
- ☐ Petroleum jelly or A+D ointment (to apply during each diaper change)
- ☐ Diaper rash cream with zinc oxide (to use if your child gets a rash)
- ☐ For cloth diapering, diaper covers to prevent soaking through to clothes

Nice to have:
- ☐ Odor-preventing diaper pail and refills

HEALTH AND GENERAL CARE
Essential:
- ☐ Thermometer

- ❒ Infant pain reliever (don't use before two months without consulting your pediatrician)
- ❒ Bulb syringe (for suctioning out stuffy noses)
- ❒ Brush or comb (even if you have a baby baldie, you'll use these eventually)
- ❒ Baby lotion (for dry skin after the first few months)
- ❒ Prepackaged first aid kit

Nice to have:
- ❒ Humidifier (to help with decongestion during colds)

BATHING

Essential:
- ❒ Plastic infant tub with supportive sling or baby-size sponge to prevent slipping (used until your baby can sit up)
- ❒ Inflatable baby tub (provides support in the real tub when your baby first sits up)
- ❒ Baby shampoo
- ❒ Washcloths (2 to 4)

Nice to have:
- ❒ Bath toys (from about six months on)
- ❒ Hooded towel (otherwise a regular towel will work)
- ❒ Soft cover for bathtub spout (once your baby is in the big tub at about seven to eight months)

BABY ON THE GO

Essential:
- ❒ Car seat (to be secured facing backward until your child is one year and twenty pounds)
- ❒ Stroller (recommended options: a travel system, which works for all ages, or a universal frame stroller to use with your infant car seat and then a toddler stroller starting at about six months)

Nice to have:
- ❒ Front carrier, sling, or baby backpack (a front carrier can be used when your infant is eight pounds, and a backpack can be used at six months)
- ❒ Portable crib (great for travel, and the removable bassinet is a perfect play space or bedside sleeping option for your infant during those first few months at home)

NURSING MOMS

Essential:

- ☐ Nursing pillow (to keep your baby in position and save your back)
- ☐ Breast pads (to prevent leakage)
- ☐ Lanolin cream (to prevent chafing)
- ☐ Cloth diapers or burp cloths (3 to 5 for catching baby spit-up while burping after feedings)
- ☐ Breast pump (electric or manual, only essential if you want to continue breast feeding after maternity leave)
- ☐ Pump carrying case, plastic bags for storing milk in the freezer, and supplies
- ☐ Bottles (2 to 3 for serving pumped milk)

Nice to have:

- ☐ Bottle warmer (for warming refrigerated breast milk if your baby prefers the warm stuff)

BOTTLE FEEDING

Essential:

- ☐ Bottles (5 to 8)
- ☐ Nipples of different sizes as baby ages (stage 1 for infants, moving up to stage 4)
- ☐ Dishwasher caddy (to wash the plastic nipples)
- ☐ Cloth diapers or burp cloths (4 to 6)
- ☐ Formula (ask your pediatrician for a personalized recommendation)

Nice to have:

- ☐ Bottle warmer

FEEDING SOLIDS

Essential:

- ☐ High chair or booster seat with an infant-appropriate seating position
- ☐ Baby food (grains like rice cereal at four months, stage 1 food at five months, stage 2 at six months, and stage 3 at seven to nine months—or you can make your own)
- ☐ Baby spoons (3 to 5)
- ☐ Plastic baby bowls (4 to 6)
- ☐ Sippy cups (starting at about eight to ten months, 4 to 6 needed)

CHILDPROOFING

Essential:

- ☐ Safety gates (if you have stairs)
- ☐ Toilet locks
- ☐ Cabinet locks
- ☐ Electric outlet plugs
- ☐ Furniture fasteners (to secure bookshelves, dressers, and precarious items to the wall)
- ☐ Miniblind cord pulls (to wind up long cords, preventing the risk of strangulation)
- ☐ Soft pads (for coffee table edges and fireplace hearths)

BABY PLAYTIME

No, you don't need all of these toys; pick your favorites.

Birth to Three Months

- ☐ Colorful mobile
- ☐ Bouncy seat
- ☐ Swing
- ☐ Play mat with dangling objects hanging from above

Four to Six Months

- ☐ Discovery cubes
- ☐ Teethers
- ☐ Hand and foot rattles
- ☐ Stuffed animals or soft dolls
- ☐ Exersaucer
- ☐ Board books (read daily from now on)

Seven to Nine Months

- ☐ Stacking, sorting, and nesting toys or simple interactive playthings
- ☐ Basic musical instruments like shakers or small drums
- ☐ Puppets
- ☐ Balls
- ☐ Soft blocks

Ten to Twelve Months

- ☐ Activity table
- ☐ Action-and-response toys like a jack-in-the-box
- ☐ More complex interactive toys like doll houses and toddler-size basketball hoops
- ☐ Pull-along toys
- ☐ Wooden blocks

PRESERVING THE MEMORIES

Nice to have:

- ☐ Digital camera (to snap tons of baby shots without worrying about film, and e-mailing family)
- ☐ Video camera (the only way to really capture baby laughs, crawling, and early steps)
- ☐ Photo albums

DIAPER BAG CONTENTS

Essential:

- ☐ Diapers (2 to 3 in your bag at all times)
- ☐ Diaper wipes (in small travel case)
- ☐ Diaper rash ointment (travel size)
- ☐ Thin, portable changing pad (just a little extra protection from the germfest in public restrooms and other on-the-run diaper changing spots)
- ☐ Cloth diaper (for burping or runny noses)
- ☐ Snacks (appropriate to age)
- ☐ Bottle or sippy cup (unless exclusively breast-feeding)

Nice to have:

- ☐ Small toys (2 to 3, appropriate to age)
- ☐ Board books
- ☐ Change of clothes (in case of unexpected spit-up or leaky diaper)

Appendix B

Final Countdown to Baby To-Do List

For additional details and guidance on each step, refer to the full to-do list in Chapter 1, page 25.

WORK

Ideally, two to four months before your due date:

- ☐ Meet with someone in human resources and confirm your company's approach to maternity leave.

> **Questions for Human Resources:**
> 1. How many paid and unpaid days do I receive under our parental leave policy?
> 2. Do I qualify for short-term disability (STD) coverage (either from your employer or the state)? If so, how many weeks and what portion of my salary is covered?
> 3. Do I qualify for any supplemental coverage if I need to go on bed rest or experience childbirth complications that require extended recovery time?
> 4. How many vacation, sick, and personal days have I accrued? Can I borrow from future vacation days?
> 5. Will my insurance benefits continue during my time at home? Will my child be covered at birth, or do I need to fill in some forms to add the baby to our health care plan?

- ☐ If your employer doesn't offer fully paid leave (and few do), calculate how many unpaid days off you can afford to take. If needed, consider a gradual return to work to extend your time at home.

☐ Begin exploring your postmaternity leave work options, such as flextime or part-time, by talking to your manager and colleagues.

☐ Start researching child care options.

Ideally, two to three months before your due date:

☐ Submit a maternity leave request (and plan for returning to work).

☐ Remind dad to request paternity leave or, if nothing else, schedule vacation or personal days so he can be home for a while after the baby's birth.

Ideally, at least one month before your due date:

☐ Plan for your impending departure.
- Remind your boss of your timing and explain your plan for the transition.
- Start meeting regularly with the people who will be taking over your responsibilities while you're at home.
- Begin documenting everything so you can hand projects over at any point.
- Leave a clear list of tasks to be covered while you're at home.
- Set up a plan for checking in if necessary.

The remaining to-do items can be accomplished within the last month or so of your pregnancy, except for ordering nursery furniture, which often requires three months lead time.

BABY GEAR

☐ Stock up on basic baby supplies and nursery furniture using your new baby shopping list.

☐ Wash your stage 1 clothes and baby linens using a mild, baby-friendly detergent like Dreft.

☐ Install your car seat. Find a certified child passenger safety technician in your area on the National Highway Traffic Safety Administration; website: nhtsa.gov.

YOUR BABY'S HEALTH

☐ Select a pediatrician.

☐ Make a decision about circumcision.

NESTING

☐ Get organized.

☐ Catch up on home projects.

CHILDBIRTH PREP

- ❐ Take a childbirth class.
- ❐ Write your birth plan and share it with your doctor or midwife.

INFANT CARE AND BREAST FEEDING PREP

- ❐ If you plan to breast-feed, take a class now.
- ❐ Take infant care and CPR classes.
- ❐ Lose the pregnancy books; prepare for parenting.

FINANCES, WILL, AND GUARDIANSHIP

- ❐ Start to think about a life-with-baby budget and college savings plan.
- ❐ Create a will and choose a guardian for your child.

FRIENDS AND FAMILY

- ❐ Plan now for visitors.
- ❐ Catch up with friends before the time warp of new parenthood hits.

WHAT'S IN A NAME?

- ❐ Pick a name.
- ❐ Pick out baby announcements.

PREMOM PAMPERING

- ❐ Get a haircut.
- ❐ Get a pedicure.

Appendix C

Baby-Sitter/Nanny Interview Questions

What to ask when your candidates arrive? Here are some expert-recommended questions to get you started. Feel free to remove these pages and use them during your interviews.

TRAINING AND CHILD CARE PHILOSOPHY

1. Do you have training in early childhood education? Infant CPR? First aid?
2. Are you familiar with safe back-to-sleep practices?

   Babies should always be put to sleep on their backs, and the risk of SIDS is particularly high when infants begin child care. If a caregiver starts putting a back sleeper down on his tummy, he may not have the neck strength to shift his head well from that position and he'll be at much higher risk for SIDS. Make sure your baby-sitter consistently follows safe back-to-sleep practices.

3. Why do you enjoy working with children? How would you describe your style of care?
4. What activities would you introduce to our child at this age? At six months? Nine months? A year?
5. How do you comfort a crying baby?
6. What would you do if our baby starting choking?
7. When would you normally put a baby this age down for naps? How do you feel about making sure naps are always taken at home? When would you provide bottles?

   This is a great time to discuss the feed-to-wake approach described in Chapter 13. Make sure she's comfortable following a consistent routine and putting your baby down to sleep independently so he learns to self-soothe. Some experienced caregivers have strong opinions about how feedings and naps should be provided; you should make sure her approach is compatible with yours.

8. How do you discipline older children? Please offer specific examples from past positions.

JOB SPECIFICS

1. What hours are you available?

   If you have occasional late nights or weird hours, make sure she can accommodate your needs.

2. What is your hourly rate?

   Or you could research the going rate in advance and tell her what you'd like to pay.

3. How long will you be able to keep this position? Do you have any plans or commitments that might take you away in the next year or two?

4. Would you be willing to take our child to activities and the park as he gets older?

5. We provide two weeks paid vacation. (This is standard.) Would you mind taking your vacations when we take ours?

   If you're lucky, she'll agree so you're not forced to find alternate care during her weeks off and committed to pay her for nothing when you're on vacation. Some families suggest a compromise arrangement: They pick one vacation week and their baby-sitter requests one week.

6. How will you get here every day? Do you have a driver's license?

7. Would you like to baby-sit occasionally on weekend evenings? Overnights? On vacation with us? (If you're interested in any of these things.)

   Some would like the extra cash; others prefer the free time.

8. What type of housekeeping will you do during the day?

   As I mentioned, don't expect much. But do make specific requests now so she's committed to some regular tasks like emptying the diaper pail or changing the crib sheets as necessary.

EXPERIENCE

1. Describe your past child care positions. How much experience do you have you caring for babies this age?

2. What did you enjoy most about each position?

3. Describe your typical day at a previous job. What did you do with the children? What did you do during their naps?

4. Can you think of any books the children particularly enjoyed? How often did you read to them?

5. Why did you leave those jobs?

6. Have you ever dealt with a medical emergency or sick child on the job? If so, what did you do?

7. How many days were you sick or unable to make it to work while at those positions?
8. Can you provide a list of references?

   Call her past employers and ask for their impressions of her performance, reliability, child care style, and personality. Even if the first two are glowing, call all her references for comprehensive feedback. Also, ask them for tips on working with her. Normally, you'll pick up some useful advice.
9. Do you have children?

Appendix D

Day Care Center and

Home-Based Day Care Interview Questions

What to ask as you visit potential providers? Here are some expert-recommended questions to get you started. Feel free to remove these pages and use them during your interviews.

BACKGROUND

1. How long have you been in business?
2. What type of licensing do you have?

    Review your state's licensing requirements in advance using either of these sources (both have free online listings):

    - Child Care Aware—Phone: 800-424-2246; website: childcareaware.org
    - The National Resource Center for Health and Safety in Child Care— Phone: 800-598-KIDS; website: nrc.uchsc.edu

    The facility should meet these minimum state requirements.

3. Are you accredited?

    Accredited facilities generally have training and provide structured activities that surpass minimum state licensing requirements. Ask for details about their training and approach.

4. Do you accept infants? Toddlers?
5. How many children do you care for at any given time? What are the typical ages?
6. Do you have an opening?
7. What is the monthly cost? How do you bill parents? Are there any other fees we may incur?
8. What are your hours? What happens if I'm running late from work one evening?

9. Do you have written policies we can review?
10. Do you have a list of references?

Call these parents and ask about their experience with the provider and any issues of particular concern. If the management can't provide a formal reference list, just talk to a few of the current families. (In fact, it never hurts to do that anyway.)

STAFF

1. How many adults do you have on staff? What's your adult-to-child ratio?
2. What kind of child care experience do the caregivers have? Experience with infants?
3. Are they all trained in infant CPR? First aid? Have they all passed background checks?
4. Are all caregivers trained in safe back-to-sleep practices?

Babies should always be put to sleep on their backs, and the risk of SIDS is particularly high when infants begin child care. If a caregiver starts putting a back sleeper down on his tummy, he may not have the neck strength to shift his head well from that position and he'll be at much higher risk for SIDS. Make sure all staff consistently follow safe back-to-sleep practices.

5. What is your turnover rate among staff members?
6. Will one person be focused on our child? If so, describe her background and training.

HEALTH AND SAFETY

1. How often are the toys disinfected? How often is the center fully cleaned?
2. How do you deal with children who seem sick?
3. What's your plan for handling emergencies?
4. How have you childproofed the facilities? Where are the cleaning supplies and other hazardous materials kept? Do you have first aid kits on hand?
5. Do the caregivers wash their hands after every diaper change?

SCHEDULE AND ACTIVITIES

1. What is the daily schedule? When are naps given? Bottles? Diaper changes?

To follow the feed-to-wake approach described in Chapter 13, ask if they can offer bottles right after naps and put your baby down to sleep with a pacifier groggy but still awake so he can soothe himself. Some facilities have specific schedules for infant naps and feedings; make sure you're comfortable with their timing.

2. Once my baby starts eating solids, what will you typically feed him for lunch? What snacks are offered?
3. What activities do you generally plan for the kids? How will our child be involved?

CHILD CARE APPROACH

1. How do you soothe crying babies?
2. How do you discipline older children?
3. How do you facilitate interaction and socialization? What kind of one-on-one time can we expect our child to receive?
4. How can parents become involved?

Appendix E

Baby-Sitter/Nanny Contract

For explanations, check out the detailed sample baby-sitter/nanny contract on page 232. Feel free to remove this version and use it, blacking out irrelevant points. Or create your own contract, using this as a guide.

SAMPLE BABY-SITTER/NANNY CONTRACT

Employer

Names of parents: _____

Names of children: _____

Address: _____ Home phone: _____

Mom's work phone number: _____ Cell phone number: _____

Dad's work phone number: _____ Cell phone number: _____

Emergency contact information: _____

Baby-Sitter/Nanny

Name: _____

Address: _____

Home phone number: _____ Cell phone number: _____

Social Security number: _____ Driver's license number: _____

Emergency contact information: _____

Start date: _____

Job Description

CHILD CARE RESPONSIBILITIES:

HOUSEHOLD CONTRIBUTIONS:

DAILY UPDATES:

TRANSPORTATION:

ADDITIONAL POLICIES:

Weekly Schedule

Days: _____

Overtime policy: _____

Salary and Benefits

Employer will provide $____ gross per hour, to be paid at the end of each week.

Employer will pay one-half of Social Security and Medicare taxes (7.65% of employee's gross salary), and all unemployment insurance and Worker's Compensation insurance. Employee's half of Social Security and Medicare taxes will be withheld each pay period and, if desired, employer will also withhold federal and state income taxes.

Other benefits:

Performance Reviews and Termination Notice

Performance reviews will be provided ____ times a year, and salary increases will be provided annually if warranted by performance.

Baby-sitter should provide at least four weeks notice before leaving position.

Paid Days Off

Employer will provide ____ paid holidays: _____

_____

____ paid sick days, and ____ paid vacation days.

Baby-sitter must provide ____ weeks notice prior to vacation days.

Confidentiality

The baby-sitter may become aware of personal, financial, legal, health, or work-related information about the employer's family. All family information is confidential and should not be shared without the employer's written consent. If this confidentiality is breached, the baby-sitter may be discharged.

Signatures

Employer: _____ Date: _____

Baby-sitter: _____ Date: _____

APPENDIX F: FEEDING AND SLEEPING ROAD MAP TO BABYVILLE

	Birth to 4 Weeks	1 Month	2 Months	3 Months	4 Months	5 Months	6 Months	7 Months to 1st Birthday
Feeding								
Liquids (Breast Feeding or Bottle)								
Number of liquid feedings every 24 hours	8–12	5–8	5–8	4–6	4–6	4–6	4–5	4–5
Typical ounces per feeding	2–3	3–4	4–6	4–6	4–6	5–8	6–8	6–8
Total ounces recommended every 24 hours	14–20	15–26	20–32	20–32	22–32	22–32*	20–32*	20–30*
Solids								
Number of solid feedings every 24 hours	—	—	—	—	Tastings only	1: Breakfast	2: Breakfast and dinner	3: Breakfast lunch and dinner
Recommended solids by stage	—	—	—	—	Rice cereal, oatmeal and barley	Stage 1 baby food: veggies then fruits	Stage 2 baby food	Stage 3 baby food, finger foods, sippy cups
Sleep								
Number of daytime naps	5–7	3–5	3–5	3–4	3	3	2–3	2
Average length of daytime naps (in hours)	0.5–2	1–2	1–2	1–3	1–3	1–2	1–2	1.5–2
Typical number of overnight wake-ups	2–3	1–2	1–2	0–2	0–2	0–1	0–1	0
Longest stretch of sleep to expect overnight (in hours)	2–5	4–7	6–10	7–11	7–12	8–12	10–12	10–12

*Daily liquid intake may decrease slightly as solid meals are introduced.

Notes

CHAPTER 1

1. U.S. Bureau of the Census, "Estimated Median Age at First Marriage, by Sex: 1890 to Present," 2004.
2. National Center for Health Statistics, "Births: Final Data for 2002," *National Vital Statistics Reports* 52, no. 10 (2003): 1–114.
3. Kristin Smith, Barbara Downs, and Martin O'Connell, "Maternity Leave and Employment Patterns: 1961–1995," *Current Population Reports*, 2001, 70–79.
4. Families and Work Institute, *Highlights of the National Study of the Changing Workforce*, 2002.
5. Bureau of Labor Statistics, "Employment Characteristics of Families in 2004," 2005.
6. Denise Fields and Alan Fields, *Baby Bargains: Secrets to Saving 20 Percent to 50 Percent on Baby Furniture, Equipment, Clothes, Toys, Maternity Wear, and Much, Much More* (Boulder: Windsor Peak, 2005), 2.
7. Projected private university costs based on results from the college cost projector at FinAid.org, a website designed to assist students with financial aid. Current costs listed on the site: "According to the College Board, the 2002–2003 average costs were $12,841 for students attending public colleges and universities, and $27,677 for students at private colleges and universities. Out of state students attending public colleges and universities pay an average total cost of $19,188." www.finaid.org/calculators/costprojector.phtml (accessed June 5, 2005). In the finaid.org college cost projector on that page, $27,677 was used for current private college costs; it assumed 7 percent annual tuition inflation rate, and 17.5 years until matriculation. First year projected cost was $76,731.14; second year, $81,335.01; third year, $86,215.11; fourth year, $91,388.02.

CHAPTER 6

1. Benjamin Spock, M.D., and Robert Needleman, M.D., *Dr. Spock's Baby and Child Care*, 8th ed. (New York: Simon & Schuster, 2004), 1.

CHAPTER 7

1. Denise Fields and Alan Fields, *Baby Bargains: Secrets to Saving 20 Percent to 50 Percent on Baby Furniture, Equipment, Clothes, Toys, Maternity Wear, and Much, Much More* (Boulder: Windsor Peak, 2005), 2.

CHAPTER 8

1. Women Employed, *Facts about Working Women,* 2004.
2. Hewitt Associates, *SpecSummary: United States Salaried Work/Life Benefits, 2003–2004.*
3. Hewitt Associates, *SpecSummary.*
4. Hewitt Associates, *SpecSummary.*
5. Hewitt Associates, *SpecSummary.*
6. *A New Approach to Flexibility: Managing the Work/Time Equation* (New York: Catalyst, 1997), 25–26.
7. Hewitt Associates, *SpecSummary.*
8. Families and Work Institute, *Highlights of the National Study of the Changing Workforce,* 2002.
9. Center for Women's Business Research, *Privately Held, 50 Percent or More Women-Owned Businesses in the United States, 2004: A Fact Sheet.*
10. Center for Women's Business Research, *Privately Held.*
11. Denise Fields and Alan Fields, *Baby Bargains: Secrets to Saving 20 Percent to 50 Percent on Baby Furniture, Equipment, Clothes, Toys, Maternity Wear, and Much, Much More* (Boulder: Windsor Peak, 2005), 2.
12. Mercer Human Resources Consulting, *Worldwide Study Exposes Wide Variations in Parental Benefits,* 2003.
13. Families and Work Institute, *When Work Works,* 2004.
14. Fields and Fields, *Baby Bargains,* 2.

CHAPTER 9

1. Hewitt Associates, *SpecSummary: United States Salaried Work/Life Benefits, 2003–2004.*
2. Families and Work Institute, *When Work Works,* 2004.

CHAPTER 10

1. Committee on Family and Work Policies, *Working Families and Growing Kids: Caring for Children and Adolescents* (Washington, D.C.: National Research Council, Institute of Medicine of the National Academies, 2003). Cited in *Child Care in America Fact Sheet* supplied by NACCRRA, the Nation's Network of Child Care Resource and Referral.
2. Committee on Family and Work Policies, *Working Families and Growing Kids.*

3. Committee on Family and Work Policies, *Working Families and Growing Kids.*
4. Society for Human Resource Management, *2005 Benefits Survey Report,* 2005.

CHAPTER 11

1. Families and Work Institute, Catalyst, and Boston College Center for Work and Family, *Leaders in a Global Economy: A Study of Executive Women and Men,* 2003.
2. Ann Crittenden, *The Price of Motherhood: Why the Most Important Job in the World Is Still the Least Valued* (New York: Holt, 2001), 22.
3. Douglas E. Bowers, "A Century of Change in America's Eating Patterns: Cooking Trends Echo Changing Roles of Women," *FoodReview* 23, no. 1 (2000): 23–29.
4. Business and Professional Women's Association, *101 Facts on the Status of Working Women,* 2004.
5. Bureau of Labor Statistics, *Employment Status of the Civilian Population by Sex and Age,* 2003.
6. Business and Professional Women's Association, *101 Facts on the Status of Working Women,* 2004.
7. Women Employed, *Facts about Working Women,* 2004.
8. Hewitt Associates, *SpecSummary: United States Salaried Work/Life Benefits, 2003–2004.*
9. Society for Human Resource Management, *2005 Benefits Survey Report,* 2005.

CHAPTER 12

1. Arlene Rossen Cardozo, *Sequencing* (New York: Collier, 1986).
2. Sylvia A. Hewlett and Carolyn Buck Luce, "Off-Ramps and On-Ramps: Keeping Talented Women on the Road to Success," *Harvard Business Review,* March 2005.
3. Ann Crittenden, *The Price of Motherhood: Why the Most Important Job in the World Is Still the Least Valued* (New York: Holt, 2001.), 17.
4. Betty Friedan, *The Feminine Mystique* (New York: Norton, 2001).

CHAPTER 14

1. Marc Weissbluth, M.D., *Healthy Sleep Habits, Happy Child* (New York: Ballantine, 1999), 129.
2. Richard Ferber, M.D., *Solve Your Child's Sleep Problems* (New York: Simon & Schuster, 1985).

CHAPTER 17

1. Thomas B. Newman, Brian D. Johnston, and David C. Grossman, "Effects and Costs of Requiring Child Restraint Systems for Young Children Traveling On Commercial Airplanes," *Archives of Pediatrics & Adolescent Medicine* 157 (2003).

CHAPTER 18

1. Jack P. Shonkoff, "'Neurons to Neighborhoods' Offers Insight on Early Development," *AAP News* 19, no. 2 (2001): 81.
2. David A. Hawkins and Jessica Lautz, *State of College Admission* (National Association for College Admissions Counseling, 2005).
3. Baby Counting Pal Plush by LeapFrog, Manufacturer's description retrieved from LeapFrog corporate website May 30, 2005, www.leapfrog.com/do/findproduct?ageGroupKey=infant&key=babypal.
4. "The LeapFrog SchoolHouse Ready, Set, Leap! Program Shows Critical Gains in Early Literacy," press release, May 30, 2005.
5. "U.S. Department of Education Selects LeapFrog SchoolHouse to Participate in Multi-Million-Dollar Early Literacy Studies," press release, May 30, 2005.
6. Frances H. Rauscher, Gordon L. Shaw, and K. N. Ky, "Music and Spatial Task Performance," *Nature* 365 (1993): 661.
7. Kenneth M. Steele, Karen E. Bass, and Melissa D. Crook, "The Mystery of the Mozart Effect: Failure to Replicate," *Psychological Science* 10, no. 4 (1999): 366–369.
8. William F. Thompson, E. Glenn Schellenberg, and Gabriela Husain, "Arousal, Mood, and the Mozart Effect," *Psychological Science* 12, no. 3 (2001): 248–251.
9. Janellen Huttenlocher, "Language Input and Language Growth," *Preventive Medicine* 27, no. 2 (1998): 195–199.
10. Janellen Huttenlocher, Marina Vasilyeva, Elina Cymerman, and Susan Levine, "Language Input and Child Syntax," *Cognitive Psychology* 45, no. 3 (2002): 337–374.
11. American Academy of Pediatrics, *Media Guidelines for Parents*, 2005.
12. Kaiser Family Foundation, *Zero to Six*, 2003.

Acknowledgments

From Paige:

[my fellow moms]

First, thanks to the women who shared their parenting insights and personal experiences with me during the writing process—dozens in formal interviews and many more in casual conversations at the park, mom-and-baby activities, and everything in between. (As a new parent, I absorbed a good part of my research through osmosis. Fortunately, new moms love to chat, so I had plenty of material.) Many of your honest admissions, great stories, and "Am I the only one feeling this way?" concerns morphed into anecdotes and advice in this book. Hopefully, the result helps us feel more connected and supported in our new roles.

[the experts]

I sincerely appreciate the input I received from experts in a variety of fields—from work/life policy to infant sleep patterns, from child care logistics to early cognitive development, from personal finances to parental leave. To all who generously agreed to interviews and shared their knowledge, thank you again.

And especially to Dr. Allison Nied, my great friend and collaborator—it's been quite an adventure. Thanks so much for your words of wisdom and honest feedback every step of the way.

[the publishing professionals]

I wrote this manuscript, with Dr. Nied's input, as a sort of literary leap of faith, and I am grateful to the women who ultimately believed in it. My agent Alison Fargis has been a passionate advocate, impeccable professional, and so darn nice. I can't imagine a more gracious colleague or effective ally. Working with my editor Marnie Cochran has been an absolute pleasure. I am continually impressed by her high-energy enthusiasm, creative ideas, and collaborative approach. And Erica Lawrence has managed the copyediting and production process with infinite patience and attention to detail. I didn't know what to expect from the world of publishing, and this process has been more positive and fun than I could have hoped. (Also, thanks to Amanda Beeler, whose kind reference proved invaluable.)

[my friends and family]

You guys know I love you, and you know who you are. My mom deserves special mention for going way above and beyond the call of duty with her incredibly generous baby-sitting assistance, willingness to help, and overall faith in her daughter's wacky plan to write a book. And my dad may be the one person on the planet who's more excited than me about seeing this in print. Finally, to my husband Charlie, my son Bailey, and my daughter Avery—this book is for you.

From Dr. Nied:

I would like to thank Paige for inviting me to collaborate on *The Working Gal's Guide to Babyville*. She continues to inspire me with her sense of humor and fabulous parenting style. And I'm so pleased to be a contributor to this book, which I sincerely believe will be a fantastic resource for many new moms.

Thanks to my husband Stewart and my son Spencer for understanding the hours of writing, research, phone calls, and e-mails that went into this project. And, more importantly, thank you for your unwavering love and support. I'm grateful to my parents, Carol and Thomas, who have always encouraged me to be all that I could be. Thanks to them, I pursued a career that not only is fulfilling but also allows me the flexibility to raise a family of my own. Finally, I would like to honor the memory of my dear friend Audrey. She was a mother for only a short time, but she would have been the superstar of Babyville.

Index